WARPED FACTORS

A Neurotic's Guide to the Universe

Walter Koenig

TAYLOR PUBLISHING
Dallas, Texas

Also by Walter Koenig

NONFICTION
Chekov's Enterprise
FICTION
Buck Alice and the Actor Robot

Published by

Taylor Publishing Company
1550 West Mockingbird Lane
Dallas, Texas 75235
www.taylorpub.com

Library of Congress Cataloging-in-Publication Data

Koenig, Walter.
    Warped factors : a neurotic's guide to the universe / Walter Koenig.
      p.   cm.
    Filmography: p. 307
    Includes bibliographical references and index.
    ISBN 0-87833-991-4
    1. Koenig, Walter. 2. Television actors and actresses—United
States—Biography. 3. Star trek (Television program) I. Title.
PN2287.K684A3   1998
791.45'028'092—dc21
[B]   98–10795
                                        CIP

Printed in the United States of America

10 9 8 7 6 5 4 3 2 1

This book has been printed on acid-free recycled paper.

for
Norman Koenig
(June 1, 1930–January 31, 1994)

Contents

Photo inserts follow page 148.

Acknowledgments

I wish to thank David Gillery, who read each page of this book as I wrote it, declaring that every sentence was superb—knowing, very wisely, what it was my fragile ego needed to hear. I'd also like to thank Janna Parker, who read along with him and confirmed all of his grand lies.

Doug Conway is a friend and occasional business associate. Without his faith in this project and his determination it would never have seen print. That simple.

Like everyone else who has written an autobiography I owe a debt of gratitude to Richard Arnold.

Holly McGuire is the senior editor at Taylor Publishing. As of this writing we have not met but were it not for her enthusiasm *Warped Factors* would have been relegated to the proverbial trunk.

Lauren Koenig is my niece, my brother's daughter. Her devotion to her father during his period of infirmity has done much to restore my childhood's faith and invest this tome with whatever sense of hope that is found between its pages.

To everyone I worked with on *Star Trek* and to those with whom I have been working on *Babylon 5,* my gratitude for so enriching my life.

A special thanks to J. Michael Straczynski. Where do I begin? I'll let the words already written in this book speak for me.

Finally, the most special thanks of all to my wife Judy, my son Andrew, and my daughter Danielle for hanging in there through all the bad stuff. Without their love and inspiration I'd be selling pencils on Main Street.

Foreword: What Goes Around. . .

The Norbreck Castle Hotel, Blackpool. The United Kingdom. Monday, July 14, 1997. 6:00 p.m. A room filled with 3,500 British science fiction fans, on their feet, applauding, shouting, standing on chairs. The phrase "awe-inspiring"—too often overused elsewhere, trivializing that which is neither awesome nor inspiring—comes to mind and lodges firmly in the cerebral cortex which recognizes it as understatement but can't come up with anything more apt. The ovation goes on, and on, and not to put too fine a point on it . . . *on.*

Walter is there, in the midst of it, having just come offstage, sitting with his wife Judy as the wall-to-wall ovation continues in the vast hall beside us. He shakes his head. "It's like going back in time," he says. "I've seen this before, once, with Star Trek; I never thought I'd see it again."

"Then we now have an explanation for what's going on in the other room," I reply. "*Star Trek, Babylon 5*—what's the common denominator? *Walter Koenig.* So you're the one responsible for all this."

He laughed. But I'm still not sure it's all that funny. Something about sympathetic magic, about synchronicity and serendipity and resonance and the good guys coming out on top once in a while; something about having the good fortune to be in the same lottery pool with someone who deserves to have something good happen to him when he finally wins ten million dollars. For Walter, what went around has well and duly come around.

I've been trying to remember how I met Walter, and I'll be damned if there is any one particular incident that I can point to. It's one of those situations where two people casually pass through one another's orbit, with in-common friends, places, occupations, and interests. Walter's an actor and writer. I'm a writer and most recently, producer. Walter loves theater. I love theater. Walter loves comics. I love comics. For a while, Walter taught acting at the Sherwood Oaks

Experimental College in Hollywood, and as near as I can recall, that is where I actually first *saw* him up-close, at an open house, though I didn't go up and speak to him. We would both show up at parties at Dangerous Visions Bookstore, and when I was primary story editor on *The Twilight Zone* version 2.5, Walter came in to pitch on that series.

So Walter was sorta *there,* and I was sorta *here,* and we knew each other well enough to nod, say hello, and exchange a pleasant word or two at parties or bookstore signings. But it was on March 3, 1988 that we first spent any time really talking. That date coincides with Walter's first appearance on my incarnation of *Hour 25,* a talk show airing Friday nights from 10 p.m. to midnight on KPFK-FM Los Angeles.

You spend two hours on the air with someone, without commercial interruptions, you learn a lot about the person.

Prior to that evening, I'd known Walter mainly for his work on the original *Star Trek* television series and the various film incarnations that followed. Mind you, I had always enjoyed the work, but hadn't really given it much *thought* until that night, when I sat opposite the man in a cramped radio booth with our words going outbound toward Proxima Centauri at roughly the speed of starlight.

During that first long midnight discussion, I learned that there was far, far more to Walter Koenig. I saw a skilled performer whose abilities had rarely been given the opportunity to reveal themselves full measure. I saw someone who was funny, wry, introspective, self-effacing, and thoughtful. Also fiercely loyal to his friends, something we have in common. Our roots are both Eastern European, so we also share a genetic predisposition toward believing that we are all one tornado shy of having a house fall on us.

Bottom-line translation: I thought he was a nifty guy.

That was his first appearance on *Hour 25* while I was host.

It was not his last.

I invited him back frequently over the following five years, and when I'd written an episode of *Twilight Zone* too hot for the studio to handle, it was Walter and Judy whom I asked to perform it live on KPFK. That reader's theater performance of "Say Hello, Mister Quigley," later published in several major anthologies, was one of the high-water marks of my tenure on *Hour 25,* and audio tapes of that evening continue to make the rounds at many SF conventions.

One of the things that makes me the *most* crazy is to see talent that, for one reason or another, is not given sufficient freedom to find its own level. I'm a big believer in what the ancient Greeks believed was the definition of happiness: "The exercise of vital powers, along lines of excellence, in a life affording them scope." Emphasis on the last clause: *in a life affording them scope*. For a singer, you have to have the song, and the venue in which to sing it. A writer needs an actor, and an actor needs a role.

Walter has done a great deal to help other people find some small measure of happiness. Some of it is in here. Some of it you don't know, will never know. Because Walter is very private about these things, some of the greater charities of his character will never be reported. That is unfortunate. But it did lead me to one conclusion: that I would one day give him a gift in return for what he had done for so many others, a role with a range that would allow him to fly, to strut, to show what he was capable of doing . . . a role affording him scope.

When my series *Babylon 5* was finally green-lighted after five years of trying to convince someone to give us $21 million per year to produce it, one of the first calls I made was to Walter. Having lately seen his terrific performance in *The Boys in Autumn*, I had crafted a role that I hoped would challenge him in a similar fashion, a role that would from time to time recur. I sent him the script, he loved it, and agreed to do it.

Then came the heart attack. I won't dwell here, since Walter tells the story more eloquently that I could in this space, and you should really hear that from him, not me. Suffice to say we had to recast . . . but only the role was recast, not the intention. I resolved to create something else for Walter, something even better.

Bester—the Psi Cop you love to hate—is my gift to Walter. Because I like Walter a great deal, and in return he has elevated the character to nearly mythic scale, instantly becoming one of *Babylon 5*'s most popular and complex characters.

And this book is Walter's gift to the fans of his work in *Star Trek* and *Babylon 5* and elsewhere. Because he likes his fans a great deal, and respects them, and wants to *talk to you*. Not to preach, not to vent, not to polemicize or pound or settle scores, just to *talk to you*. Sitting like old friends beside the fire, saying "Remember when . . . ?" You can look all you want, but you will find this book refreshingly absent of agendas, political or personal. At a time when the declaration "someday I'll write my biography" has gone from promise to perceived threat, this is a book of kindness and wonder, with extremely funny stories (the introduction alone is worth the price of admission) counterbalanced by the thoughtful, the insightful, the moving, and the dramatic.

Here you will find the Walter Koenig I met over a hot microphone at KPFK–Los Angeles. Here you will see the man behind the performance that helped create not just one, but *two* television phenomena. Here you will find proof that lightning really *does* strike twice in the same place . . . if the lightning rod is of sufficiently worthy metal.

J. MICHAEL STRACZYNSKI
August 4, 1997
Sherman Oaks, California

Short Subject

WE WERE SHOOTING THE TELEVISION EPISODE "THE GAMESTERS of Triskelion." It was October of 1967. Nichelle Nichols was in one cell, I was in another, and Bill Shatner was in a third. We each had our "pain collars" on and were writhing in agony. The close-up was on Bill. He had an arm extended through the bars begging our off-camera jailers to release us from the inflicted torture. It was a very dramatic turn, full of art and energy. Bill's concentration was total, but when the heavy steel door to the soundstage suddenly opened and four small orphan children walked through it ruining the shot, Bill only smiled. He removed the yoke, stepped out of the cell, and crossed the stage to them. They couldn't have been more than five years old. Their backs arched as they looked up at him in awe. The closest one had a cowlick and a tooth missing up front. The boy next to him was a carrot top with lots of freckles. The third child was a girl with long braids and a frilly blouse. The last of the kids was Little Timmy. His ears stuck out and they weren't very well aligned. The left one was a good inch and a half higher than the right. For some reason he seemed self-conscious about it.

Bill made a beeline for this boy and lifted him high in the air. "Star Trek is about everyone respecting everyone else and all of us treating each other as equals," he said quite seriously to the tyke. The huge bank of lights trained on the set for illumination seemed to dim beside Little Timmy's smile.

Bill whispered to his stand-in and gave him a hearty clap on the back. The man disappeared only to return a minute later with a big bag of cupcakes. There were vanilla and chocolate ones and others with all sorts of tasty toppings. Bill offered them around to each of the affection-starved youngsters. "Please sir, can I have some more?" said Carrot Top, twisting a bit in embarrassment. Bill ruffled the boy's hair and smiled just the way the charming Captain Kirk would have.

They left shortly afterwards. We stood quietly watching them go. Then an extraordinary thing happened. We looked over and there was Bill Shatner, his arms spread wide, beaming at us. Jimmy Doohan caught on first and rushed to his side. He clasped Willie's right hand with his left. Simultaneously, George Takei and Nichelle sprinted to his other side. George had been in training for years for this moment and won by the length of a communicator, forging a link with our redoubtable captain's other hand. I thought I saw a brief pout of disappointment on Nichelle's face but it disappeared quickly. She took George's free hand in hers and pressed it to her cheek to show that all was forgiven. Leonard Nimoy, DeForest Kelley, and I took our cue from the others and soon we had all formed a circle.

"It's times like this," said Bill, "when we get to realize some important things. Whether we are Christian or Jewish or Moslem or Buddhist or Hindu, or believe in any one of the great variety of Native American religions, we are, under the skin, all the same, aren't we? We all stand straight and tall but none of us stands above the others, isn't that so?"

We all turned to him. Billy Shatner was not only our Captain Kirk and the star of our show and the one who made almost all the money, he was also our true spiritual leader. I looked around me at the others. Leonard's cheeks were glistening, and I promise you it wasn't sweat. Nichelle's bosom rose as if she were about to burst into song. George's expression was inscrutable, but he later told me that he had, at that instant, composed a haiku for Bill. DeForest cleared his throat several times as if trying to gain control of himself, but it was undoubtedly Jimmy for whom our leader's words were most transporting. As tightly as his eyes were shut I could see the tears squeezing between the lashes. There was a slight tremble to his lips and the color had drained from his face. Short of sexual intercourse this was the closest thing to ecstasy I had ever been privileged to witness.

One of the grips told me afterwards that we stood in a circle like that for nearly ten minutes. It seemed like less than thirty seconds. A phone rang somewhere, finally, and the seven of us, like the petals of a flower in a strong breeze loosening their hold on the life-giving stem, gently relaxed our fingers and let our hands drop away.

Nichelle, Bill, and I put our pain collars back on and prepared to resume our collective agony for the cameras. I had a moment to speak with Nichelle before we began.

"Were you about to sing a song back there?" I asked.

"How did you know that?" she said, surprised.

"Was it 'He's Got the Whole World in his Hands'?"

She looked at me with a warm smile, the memory of our shared experience with Bill still keen. "Yes," she said, "it was."

None of the above ever happened.

Everything else in this book did.

Preview

WHEN I WAS TEN YEARS OLD I WAS TOLD THE STORY OF HOW MY father, seeking retribution for a perceived injustice, had, at the age of four, dropped his pants, hunkered over a fur-lined, smartly polished army boot his father had acquired in trade and, in keeping with the military ambiance, performed a rear guard movement, bombing the target with unerring accuracy. If you think about it objectively, it was classically ironic, a sort of reverse William Tell story of marksmanship. I regret that I could not see it in that light.

My father's narrative had been motivated honorably: Earlier that day the elastic had snapped in my waistband and I had spent six school hours with one hand clutching at the loosened material, terrified that my pants would fall down. It did not help that my classmates found my predicament an inspiration for tasteless humor which, in turn, engendered a rolling kind of laughter that rocked the halls with the seismic equivalent of a moderately intense earthquake. Through a convoluted reasoning process which I was not capable of grasping, Dad had somehow concluded that in *his* "dropped pants" account we would find a common ground that would end my humiliation, dispel my gloom, and, most importantly, put a smile on my face.

What he couldn't understand was that my despair only grew as his story unfolded. My psyche had already suffered a damaging blow; now

I was struck by an even more devastating realization. I didn't find it funny that this little boy had relieved himself in his father's boot. I found it impressive. More, I was awed by it. It had been an act of vengeance that bespoke a formative personality that would one day have to be reckoned with. Here I was shedding tears over a minor embarrassment and my old man, at the tender age of four, had taken a shit in his father's footwear. In a depressed state to begin with, I quickly concluded that I would never be the man—or the child—my father had been.

The anecdotal charm of Daddy's discharge notwithstanding, there is a far more significant reason for including it at the top of this history. Not only does it address the element of intimidation my father's presence—even in story form—played in my life, but it illuminates a self-image that on sunny days lacked a certain muscle tone and which, when the skies threatened, was downright heavy in flaccid tissue and love handles.

All this by way of saying that I limped through childhood, adolescence, and early adulthood without a clue as to how my life would turn out. I breached my third decade with no serious dreams. I believed I would find some success as an actor, but also that maybe in ten or fifteen years I'd look for the fire exit. The successes were always wedged between a greater number of disappointments, and I didn't want to be there when my already charred ego did an auto-da-fe. It was nothing I ever articulated to myself but certainly it was there, the possibility anyway, lurking in my unconscious.

I detail all of this in the hope of providing some insight. The man writing this biography was not preordained for celebrity. That *Star Trek* happened, that I got caught up in it, that I've drifted in its wake for twenty-nine years is as much a surprise to me as it would have been to Miss Form, my fifth grade teacher at P.S. 98 whose daily salutation began with the words "yah doity skunk, yah!" The fact is, I'm pretty much like everybody else out there (well, maybe just an itty-bitty more neurotic), so I really think it's a kick in the ass that I'm actually getting paid to put this all down on paper.

The ground rules, then, are very simple: Don't look for signs of early genius or the Hand Of God in any of this. It simply isn't there. I guess what it's really all about is this: despite a plethora of evidence to the contrary and a strong disinclination to walk a mile in my grandfather's shoes, once in awhile, maybe once in a lifetime, if you are lucky, you step in it anyway.

✻

The Planet Earth was formed 4.5 billion years ago. For the first quarter of its life it was a ball of liquid. 400 million years later it developed a rock crust that alternately melted and hardened with time. When it was a still-young two billion years old oceans and atmosphere developed and continental shelves shaped themselves. At that point the geological nature of the world was pretty much as it is today.

When I think about it, I see definite similarities here to my own evolution. I, too, started out as gas and dust and went through various early transformations which, just like the Earth, locked the "me" I was to become pretty much in place at a relatively tender age. In fact, it was in my seventh year that character and personality formed irreversibly and destined me to a psychological orbit pretty much as predictable as this planet's spin around the sun every three hundred and sixty-five days.

Yeah, I know, the analogy sounds a trifle pretentious, but then show me an actor who *doesn't* mean the whole world to himself.

ONE

"Child's Play"

From the age of four and until the time I was twenty-one my family maintained the same apartment at 119 Payson Avenue on the northern tip of Manhattan in the Inwood section of the city. The Second World War came and went, zoot suits and pork pie hats followed a similar course, the Iron Curtain dropped, Senator McCarthy cast a dark shadow, crooners and balladeers made room for the rhythms of rock and roll, the Yankees finally lost, James Dean died, and we *never* paid more than sixty-seven fifty a month in rent.

Mr. and Mrs. Garfinkel were our landlords, and I was taught to believe they were the unholy spawn of a jackal and a water moccasin. The only way the rent could be raised was by upgrading the apartment and my father, like a general in the trenches, withstood every assault by the Garfinkels to beautify our little domicile. As a result, our bathtub, our toilet, and our refrigerator—nay, our *icebox*—were quirkish to the point of achieving anthropomorphic status. We were convinced they existed only to serve themselves and had a functioning consciousness dedicated to undermining our mental health. The bathtub plumbing frequently failed to shut off, resulting in an overflow that caused seepage into the apartment below. The toilet would, upon a full moon, regurgitate the preceding day's oblation. Milk and eggs freshly deposited in our antiquated cooling device spoiled before they could ever be sampled.

In seventeen years the walls were never painted, and I can remember spending countless hours bed-ridden with measles and chickenpox staring at the ceiling and conjuring images from the designs created by the blistered paint.

Our apartment building was next to an overgrown vacant lot home only to cockroaches and mice, who frequently grew melancholy for the laughter of little children and came visiting. When my father complained and demanded their eradication the Garfinkels countered that extermination came under the general heading of beautification and that the rent would have to be raised to accommodate the slaughter.

My father was a proud man not easily intimidated, as I've already indicated, and so while other kids in the apartment house lived unencumbered by pests with only their toys underfoot we became sanctuary to all the persecuted and diseased vermin the neighborhood had to offer. In an attempt to keep noble the image I had of Dad, I tried very hard to think of our apartment as America itself welcoming to its shores the sick and the destitute yearning to be free. I also consoled myself with the reminder that our rent remained steady at sixty-seven fifty.

Of course there was also a bright side to this incipient plague. My brother Norm and I would ball up a pair of dark-colored socks, crouch below our mother's field of vision, and roll them across the kitchen floor as she was preparing dinner. We tried to time it to the precise moment she was holding a sharp utensil of some sort. Seen from the corner of her eye, the ersatz rodent invariably elicited from Mom a Russian expletive fraught with acrimony and spoken at impressive volume and inspired a standing broad jump whose elevation defied the laws of physics. At the same time, she fired off the current weapon of choice, a fork or knife, with an accuracy that more often than not caused a mortal wound to our argyles.

It was the absolute inevitability of her reaction—scream, leap, attack—that we found so hilarious, and it was her infinite capacity to forgive that allowed us to repeat this act of sadism again and again. Such is a mother's love.

Four things happened in my seventh year that have, for the rest of my life, shaped the way I think and behave: The "other shoe" syndrome found everlasting life in my cerebral cortex, my true sexual identity was revealed to me (although I was later to question it), I developed a paranoid fear of authority, and I was, for the first time, exposed to the pernicious lure of the theater.

There was war in Europe and the South Pacific. The Nazis and the "Japs" were really bad guys. Butter, sugar, and meat were rationed, and bubble gum ceased to exist altogether. The block warden's whistle cued our pulled blinds, our doused lights, and the prayer that it was just another drill, and the four-letter word that wasn't—the phrase "concentration camp"—found voice only in our whispers.

All the same, it was Monday on a September morn in the Indian summer of 1943. The air was fresh and sweet, the trees had started to take on autumn hues, and I was happy with anticipation for the beginning of a new school year.

Mom had walked the four blocks with me to P.S. 52, the school I had been attending since kindergarten. Like all New York public schools it was four-story brick with wire fence accoutrement enclosing a cracked and pitted but still charming cement playground.

However, the facade at P.S. 52 was a little cleaner. You could actually see the grout between the bricks, and there were tall shrubs surrounding the structure on three sides that gave it a less-forbidding appearance than most such institutions. This would be my third year here. Kindergarten and first grade had been uneventful, and I had no reason to believe second grade would be different. Such is the innocence of children.

And so it was with a light heart that I climbed the steps to my new classroom, my hand warmly clasped in Mom's. It was with a progressively heavier heart that I trudged farther and farther down the hall, my now numbing limb dispassionately clutched in my mother's. Posted on each door was the teacher's name (all the teachers were women) and underneath it the section of second grade she taught.

We passed 2A-1, 2A-2, 2A-3 . . . As the numbers went up my spirits came down. Even at that tender age I knew that the numbers indicated the level of performance expected of the students in each class section in inverse ratio. The lower the class number a student was assigned, the greater the expectation. We passed 2A-4, 2A-5, 2A- 6 . . . and still hadn't found my teacher's name. Dread consumed me. I was no longer in the escort of my Yiddisha Momela with a heart the size of a New York borough. It was the Guardian Fiend of the Inferno, with a steel claw that crushed the fingers and ripped through the tendons of my once-proud extremity and was dragging me toward a fate I had before believed incomprehensible. But then there it was:

MISS FARRELL

2A-7

Students in 2A-1 were destined to skip a grade and someday become Eagle Scouts. Those in 2A-2 and 2A-3 had their multiplication tables down cold and already had experienced some insight into long division. 2A-4 through 2A-6 pupils had mastered the rudiments of cursive handwriting, could carry a tune, and were generally the most popular kids in the grade. Girls were equally represented with boys in the first six sections.

2A-7, 2A-8, and 2A-9 were not so much sections as they were pens and stalls. Admission here was by being dropped through a trap door and poked at with a long stick. Among these students, tongue lapping of nasal mucous and farting on cue were art forms, and, in keeping with Darwin's theory of survival, an early death was a foregone conclusion. Eighty percent of these children were male. They ate mustard sandwiches for lunch, could remember the names of only three people outside their immediate family, and hadn't conquered the intricacies of saluting the flag.

Imagine my mortification when I realized I had been dumped among these miscreants. Imagine how I pleaded with the mother of all mother-betrayers to release my hand, to let me go home, to start over in Uruguay. Imagine, if you will, the life-shaping moment as the classroom door swung open at the precise instant I screamed out: "I DON'T WANT TO BE IN THIS SISSY CLASS!!"

Now imagine the former district attorney of Gotham City—who, after suffering an explosion which permanently disfigured him and his psyche, changed from Harvey Dent to Two-Face and became an arch foe of Batman—and you begin to get a picture of the woman staring out at me from inside the classroom.

This was Miss Farrell. Through either a stroke or a stroke of nature the left side of her face was twisted into a permanent grin that exposed not only the sharp, tearing canine tooth on that side of her head but the three grinding molars as well. Quite frankly, she was frightening to look at when she was merely hibernating. When she became angry the degree of terror rose exponentially. On such occasions, the drawn-back lips would twitch at an ever-accelerating pace and seem to bounce on her face like some alien creature attempting to leap into her ear. (Years later when I was doing *StarTrek II* I recalled that image and was able to scream with authenticity at the human-controlled antics of an otherwise inert Ceti Eel prop.)

In her defense it must be said that, viewed only from her right side, Miss Farrell did not appear threatening at all. That is, of course, unless you harbor an irrational fear of the recently expired. Everything to starboard was limp and languishing like the sagging sails of a ghost ship fated to endlessly drift in stagnant waters. (I was always more afraid of predatory carnivores like the werewolf than I was of zombies and, consequently, pined for those moments when she flashed her "Flying Dutchman" side at me.)

In any case, it was this beast master who was staring at me when I screamed in dismay at being sentenced to the second grade compound known as 2A-7. "I DON'T WANT TO BE IN THIS SISSY CLASS!" I had shouted, and never once in the two hundred or so days I spent in her classroom did she ever let me forget I had uttered those words. And here lies the explanation for the "other shoe" syndrome. Every time I gave an incorrect answer, which was as frequently as every day since she asked me questions that even the students in 2A-1 couldn't answer, Miss Farrell would list to port and declaim for all to hear, "And *you* didn't want to be in this sissy class!" Perhaps in time I would have become inured to this daily humiliation had it not been for two things: One, my schoolmates responded to this invective with such consistently spontaneous delight that one would have thought they were each time hearing it for the first time (it is only in retrospect that I have come to realize that as porous as their memories were, it probably *was*, each time, a new experience for them), and two, the chill that rattled my bones at the expression of malignant triumph that invariably played berserkly across half of Miss Farrell's face became a frost that wouldn't thaw in my very marrow.

And so each day I sat stiffly in my seat, my hands tightly clasped waiting for the inevitable denouncement: "and *you* didn't want to be in this sissy class!" My only hope was that it would come early so that it could be gotten over with. I even considered purposely saying something stupid to invoke the diatribe and so be done with it. "The bat you swing is b-a-t. The bat that flies is b-a-t-t because it has two wings." In the end I never had the nerve. It was bad enough that she was going to pound me. I couldn't also put the cudgel in her hands. And so I waited, and as she became more and more aware of my apprehension, I waited longer. We'd go home for lunch. We'd come back. Two o'clock would roll around. When would the other shoe drop? Two-thirty. My shoulders would creep up to align with my temples. My head would all but disappear. Two-forty-five. "Walter Koenig, add six plus four plus five plus one and multiply the sum by two. Quick! Quick! Quick!" So frozen would I become that I couldn't even attach a meaning to the sounds she was making. She could have been speaking English, but then again it might have been a long-lost Bulgarian dialect. It was a paralyzing hysterical reaction that would plague me again in the years to come. "AND YOU DIDN'T WANT TO BE IN THIS *SISSY* CLASS!!"

I heard this so often, it became so much a part of my mental set, that to this day I am conditioned to believe that no matter how placidly things are going somewhere overhead there is a very heavy shoe with very sharp spikes waiting to crash down between my ears.

Just when it appeared that the school year would be interminable and that I would never survive it, a ray of sunshine by way of Czechoslovakia dispelled the gloom, if only briefly. Suzi arrived in January. She was an emigre who had escaped the horror in Europe only to find herself set down amongst the wild life of 2A-7. It was only her unfamiliarity with English that caused her to be placed with our feral horde, and I will fight to the death anyone who disputes this contention. Suzi was beautiful. She had long hair, which she pulled back to expose an immaculate forehead, gray eyes, and a tiny nose that pointed skyward. The first time she smiled at me and her nose crinkled and her cheeks dimpled and rose, causing her eyes to partially shut, and she sing-songed the words "I-liking-you," I knew I was hopelessly in love. The fact that the words "I-liking-you" were the only English she knew and was a dispensation she bestowed on every boy in the class was an infinitesimal flaw I was willing to overlook.

However, it was Valentine's Day, February 1944, that stands out as the day my sexual identity was forever after carved in testosterone. (As I said, I had cause to suspect otherwise later on.) Miss Farrell had decided that we should all give each other handmade cards to celebrate the holiday. It was so unlike her that I realize now she knew something I didn't.

I had decided to create only one card, but on that I worked painstakingly. I spared no Crayola and made rainbows on the front that were exquisite combinations of purples and blacks and greens and pinks. I cut hearts out of shopping bags and pasted them everywhere. I composed a poem that cleverly demonstrated the girl of my dream's mastery of English:

It is true, I-liking-you.

Such was my love that I put ethics aside and had my brother, who was six years older and of an artistic bent, draw a picture of a plump Cupid shooting an arrow at a handsome boy and girl for the inside of the card, and then I took credit for it.

All this I put in an envelope with Suzi's name on it and dropped into a big basket with the other cards prepared by the children. Except that almost none of the others had gone to the trouble of making cards. Only a neat stack of store-bought Valentine greetings shared occupancy with mine.

As it turned out Suzi's mother had bought these at Suzi's request. For every boy in the class. All twenty-three of them. Except there were twenty-*four* male gender students in 2A-7.

Yeah.

And so it came to pass that I realized I was a flaming heterosexual, as in carrying-a-torch-and-going-down-in-flames-for-the-unrequited-love-of-a-female-person-and-still-coming-back-for-more flaming heterosexual.

But 1943 and 1944 weren't all good.

I remember coming home from school one day and climbing the hill toward home in a most apprehensive state. On most occasions Payson Avenue was a welcome sight. It was a one-way, partially cobblestoned street whose eastern perimeter was apartment houses and whose western border was Inwood Park. The park was a two-mile-deep woods with Indian caves, grassy knolls, and steep roads. An interesting feature is that the Hudson River and the Harlem River merge behind it making it, in effect, a peninsula.

At this point in my childhood the other neighborhood kids and I mainly used these inspiring environs to throw dirt bombs at each other. Later, we would go there to recreate Johnny Weissmuller's and Douglas Fairbanks Jr.'s best scenes from the Tarzan and Sinbad movies. And as we approached adolescence and matured still further we used it to explore for Indian bones, gather chestnuts to hollow pipe bowls from, and to harvest those burrs which produced the itching powder we desperately needed to toss down each other's backs.

However, on this particular day in my seventh year I wasn't contemplating joyous frivolity. A police car had passed me at high speed going up the hill. My immediate concerns were either that my mother had been hit by a car while shopping, the police had come to arrest my brother for some ingenious but delinquent act, or that my father's strong political beliefs had provoked an official investigation. Miss Farrell had succeeded even beyond her own twisted expectations. My by-now reflex reaction was that something dreadful involving me had happened or was about to.

As I came closer I saw that the police car was not parked at my apartment house but at the one to the north on the other side of the empty lot. I admit to overwhelming relief. On this day, at least, no one of my blood would suffer the three "D"s: Decapitation, the Dungeon, or Deportation.

It was eerie. A parked police car was not a familiar sight on Payson Avenue, and yet no crowd had gathered. It was three-thirty on a weekday afternoon and there was a barren, desolated feeling to the neighborhood. The benches across the street that rimmed the park and faced the apartment houses were empty. Normally there would be young women reading and middle-aged women knitting and older women with kerchiefs humming and oldest men with canes thumping on insects that crawled by.

It was just one of those things, the empty benches. It had probably happened before and I had not noticed. But as the minutes passed and I found myself rooted to the entrance of the building waiting . . . waiting in what felt like a suffocating hush . . . I began to wish that I was not standing there alone. What I really wished was that I could just turn away, go home and ignore the hypnotic pull of impending disaster. Failing that, I kept looking for a crowd to surround me and help absorb the shock of whatever it was that was going to happen. No one came. Then it happened. The double doors to the apartment house flew open and two uniformed cops burst through, dragging between them a very tall woman whose face was grotesquely smeared in cold cream and whose housecoat was heavily soiled. Unwinding hair curlers dangled and bounced about her head like a Coney Island ride whose gears had stripped. She kept twisting her body trying to pull away from the officers and screaming words that were unintelligible. As terrifying as all this was, the most incomprehensible element was that she was *handcuffed*. People in movies and comic books were handcuffed. Real criminals, I supposed, got handcuffed. People who lived next door and were the mothers of children did not get handcuffed. This more than anything signified to me guilt and punishment.

The woman was strong and beefy in her early thirties. The cops were smaller. She yanked one of them off his feet and then they both lost their balance. She crashed to the ground and, unable to cushion the blow, smacked the pavement face first. When she raised her head I was lined up in her sight. Blood and cold cream swirled on her face like a barber's pole and she looked at me with what had to be unmitigated condemnation. *You little son-of-a-bitch. Why don't you stop this, why do you let them do this to me?* It's what I read in her eyes and for a long time, couldn't dislodge from my consciousness.

They finally rammed her into the patrol car and drove away. I never learned why she had been arrested or what happened to her after that. The fact is, I was afraid to know and never asked. What if the infraction was something minor, something I didn't even know was a crime, something anyone could do by accident, some mistake that even *my* mother could make?

The thought that policemen could come to your street in real life and haul you away was very scary. Like every child I understood in the abstract that I existed only through the mercy of grown-ups, but until this occasion I did not comprehend how oppressively impotent I truly was.

Very quickly I was learning that authority figures who could change your destiny, those who carried guns and wore uniforms, were to be avoided at all costs.

As testament to the pervasive anxiety that this incident precipitated, I found that the only way I could cope with the endlessly repeating image of the woman being dragged off was by making her the perpetrator of the most ghoulish acts imaginable. If she was a fiend and, therefore, unlike anyone in my family or, for that matter, anyone I knew, then what happened to her could not happen to me or the people I cared about.

And so it was that while other children lulled themselves to sleep with fantasies about comic book hero adventures, I found solace and ultimately a restless slumber in sanguinary images of the cold cream lady gouging the eyes from her own mother, axing her underfed children, and quartering the whimpering dog.

★

Among the organizations my father belonged to was the American Labor Party. It was a New York State political party that started in the

late thirties and was an amalgam of individuals and philosophies that
ranged from left of Democrat to those espousing passionate communist
beliefs. My father espoused passionate communist beliefs.

The Progressive Party later evolved from the A.L.P. and named
Henry Wallace, who had served as vice-president under Franklin
Roosevelt from 1941 to 1945, as their third-party nominee for president in 1948. Wallace had been secretary of commerce in 1945 and
1946 but had been asked to resign by President Truman because of his
outspoken opposition to the U.S. "get tough" policy toward Russia.
My father was devoutly committed to Wallace and helped organize his
presidential campaign in New York.

The point is, my father was very involved in politics at the time
and went to lots of meetings in storefront shops set up by one political
entity or another. And to these meetings he frequently dragged his
seven-year-old son. I think he believed that while I sat on the floor
drawing pictures of harridans in clown white disemboweling their off-
spring I would by osmosis learn about the exploitation of the masses.

I provide this background so that you can share with me the total
disinterest I experienced when I was told I would be accompanying my
family in spending my summer vacation at Camp Arrowhead, the
American Labor Party *adult* retreat for the chess-playing, essay-writing,
pipe-smoking intellectuals that the party nourished so conscientiously.

Not only would it be incredibly boring but I just knew that these
people in their wisdom and in their deep respect for all things living
would treat me not as a child still short of his eighth birthday but as a
miniature grown-up. This, of course, meant that I would be asked, in
deadly seriousness, while tobacco fumes invaded my trachea, what I felt
about our foreign policy, the labor movement, and racial inequality.

None among them would decry my lack of knowledge as Miss
Farrell had done, but there would be those little patronizing nods and
smiles which I knew too well from the meetings I had attended. These
were the gestures that eloquently spoke to the conclusion that not only
wasn't I a prodigy but that I had recently arrived from some second
grade class with a high 2A number. Did I need this? I mean, after ten
months in Miss Farrell's ego annihilating vivarium did I need to go
through it again on my summer vacation?

Yes and no.

TWO

"An Actor's Revenge"

CAMP ARROWHEAD AS IT TURNED OUT WAS NOT ALTOGETHER A BAD summer vacation. For one thing, I discovered apple cider. I had never before tasted this ambrosia and I immediately became addicted. There was a machine in the recreation room that dispensed it without charge and I found myself unable to resist temptation, drinking cup after cup in a manner that was disproportionate to my body size and to my numerical representation among the camp population. I rationalized my gluttony by interpreting the communist manifesto motto— "Everyone according to his need"—to include fruit juice dependency.

It is true that there were no boys my age at Camp Arrowhead, but there were two girls a year or two older than I. I can only assume that their parents believed in freedoms that extended beyond those proposed by Karl Marx, for the girls seemed to spend their whole day, every day, performing cartwheels on the front lawn in front of the main building without any clothes on. It was about this time that I became an avid birdwatcher and set up my post near that same main building. I don't think I fooled any of the adults, but the two girls appeared totally oblivious to my voyeurism. Of course I was still not yet eight years old, and I had no idea what to do about these marvelous new feelings. I got as far as thinking that it would be nifty if the three of us could go swimming without bathing suits in the camp waterhole, but beyond that I was stymied. The fact is, I wasn't even sure why I thought it would be nifty.

I was too young to play softball or volleyball with the adults, but I did acquire some skill at Ping-Pong. By the end of camp I was good enough to beat all the women and compete with most of the men. I may not have been conversant with the dictatorship of the proletariat, but I had a pretty mean backhand.

I lay down this litany of under-achievement not to argue the merits of self-effacing narration but to set the stage (so to speak) for what happened next. Apple juice, naked girls, and Ping-Pong were all well and good, but they did not a happy camper make. Between the trials of 2A-7 and my sense of intellectual displacement at Camp Arrowhead I was suffering from "badly battered ego syndrome" and ripe for any event that would restore some self-esteem.

And then they decided to do a play.

Actually, it was a musical—a satire—about the atom bomb. Good old conservative Camp Arrowhead.

> Shoot that atom at me madam—
> let us both cooperate.
> Let us double without trouble
> the means with which to propagate.

My mother was part of a chorus that sang in the show. She really had a good time. Everybody did. How do I remember these lyrics after so many years? Because I was in the show, too, and I had the best time of all.

It is quite true that bad childhood experiences can create a blueprint for later behavior, but it is also true that things remembered of a joyful nature can have a motivating pull just as powerful and enduring.

It was someone's inspired idea to cast me as the professor who explains how the atomic bomb is put together. The speech they gave me exceeded my reading skills, so I learned the words by having them repeated to me. I was put in a tweed coat many sizes too large, adorned in huge owlish glasses, and required to carry a lit pipe.

I stepped out of the wings, puffed on the pipe, cleared my throat, and addressed the assembled with the following soliloquy:

"The Hans Strassman Experiment with Uranium 235 indicates that neutrons were also used during the fission process and that the trigger to set off atomic breakdown consisted of a bit of Uranium and a pinch of U-235.

"Pour these ingredients into a wooden bowl. Stir vigorously. Place in oven and bake violently. After a temperature of 250 electron volts per split uranium atom, garnish with radioactive energy. Simple, isn't it?"

Was I adorable? Yes. Did I bring the house down? Absolutely. Standing ovation, the whole bit. I was loved, I was admired, I was talented! It was like one of those cartoons where the beleaguered victim is squashed flat and then the air is pumped back into him. Even better: *had I not been crucified and was I not now risen?*

Okay, okay, maybe I'm getting a little carried away. But it was the first time I had ever acted and suddenly I felt born to the trade. I cannot remember any event prior to this experience which made me feel so convincingly that I was a genuine person with an identity uniquely my own. Is it any wonder that fifty-two years later I still know those lines fluently? And is it any wonder that fifty-two years later I'm still acting before audiences, still in mortal combat with self-doubt, still trying to re-create "Hans Strassman" and the blissful state of love, acceptance, and respect that was the prize for my forty-five-second performance?

THREE

"The History of the World, Part One"

NAHUM KOENIGSBERG WAS FROM A SMALL VILLAGE NEAR VILNIUS, Lithuania. He was a watch repairman, possibly even a maker of watches, a stern, sober man who, from all accounts, was skillful at his craft. He married Goldie in 1888 and the couple agreed to visit America on their honeymoon. They had not been here long when they decided to emigrate permanently. They settled in Boston and had a daughter two years later.

Goldie became homesick, however, and in 1892 they returned to Lithuania. The following year Isadore Koenigsberg was born.

In 1898, weary of Czarist oppression, Lenin and other Marxists founded the Russian Social Democratic Party. It was the same year that little Izzy took a dump in Daddy's seven-leaguers. It may well have been that at four years and five months my father's act was a sympathetic protest against a monarchical autocratic society and a vote for a revolutionary change of command. I wouldn't put it past him.

At the turn of the century about nine percent of all Lithuanians were Russians. The Koenigsbergs were Russians. About eight percent of all Lithuanians were Jews. The Koenigsbergs were Jews. It's not every family that can belong to two different minorities at the same time and be vilified for both. Lithuania had come under the rule of the Russian czar in 1795, and two bloody rebellions in the eighteen hundreds failed to win it independence. Many Lithuanian people saw the Russians among them as the enemy.

On the other hand, the Russian pogroms of the late nineteenth century were a czarist inspiration, with pretty much the same objective as Nazi "race purification" thirty-five years later. Since Lithuania was under czarist control, the persecution of Jews was not limited by territorial borders.

The Koenigsbergs were feeling the heat.

In 1914 Russia entered the First World War and suffered massive casualties at the front and severe food shortages at home. Every country under its influence had to share in the cost, including Lithuania. On top of that, German troops occupied the country from 1914 to 1918. The Lithuanians were even less happy with the Czar and Russians in general than before. Anti-semitism, being a way of life, was just another ingredient in the mix.

The hills were alive with the sound of hate, and in 1915 the Family Koenigsberg, this time with four daughters and a son in tow, took off once more for the promised land of America.

They settled in Chicago, and grandfather Nahum eventually found work in his chosen trade. My father Isadore remained a devoted son and brother to his family, but he also needed to venture forth and make his own life.

During the 1920s he sailed with the merchant marine, taught figure skating, played flute in an orchestra, and ran a nightclub in Chicago. Dad insisted that he opened the nightclub just so he could hire a Russian nobleman, an expatriate associate of the czar, to be his doorman. He loved the irony.

Akim Tamiroff, who would go on to be a very successful Hollywood character actor (he received an Academy Award nomination for Best Supporting Actor in *For Whom the Bell Tolls*), was a drinking buddy and a partner of his in the club. Like my father he had also come from the old country. Many years later when I visited Los Angeles as an eleven-year-old, Dad took me onto my first movie set. George Raft and Akim Tamiroff were starring in a film called *Outpost to Morocco,* and I got to watch a scene from the catwalk above the action. Some action. The pace at which they worked was so slow I had all I could do to keep from nodding off and taking a twenty-foot plunge. Although I remember next to nothing about this Foreign Legion movie, I do recall very distinctly the inspiring words Mr. Tamiroff bestowed on me afterwards. He leaned down close and squeezed my cheek between two fingers. He had eyebrows so bushy they could have, with the proper training, covered his shining dome of a head; a mature potato of a nose; and jowls that made a flapping sound in the breeze. He smiled at me and said, "You look jas lak me ven I vas liddle boy." Something to look forward to.

Sometime in the 1930s Dad landed a job with RCA Victor. He told me about attending a sales meeting in Ft. Wayne, Indiana. It was held in a spacious boardroom around a long conference table surrounded by about fifteen wooden chairs. They were all identical except for the one with the soft blue cushion. Isadore naturally assumed that the gentleman chairing the meeting would be sitting there and chuckled to himself over the bad case of hemorrhoids he must be experiencing. (We've already documented Dad's preoccupation with things of a scatological nature.)

Isadore had not rushed to find a seat but neither had he dawdled and yet, quite suddenly, all the chairs were occupied save the one with the blue cushion. He still believed this one was for the person heading the conference, and immediately began to suspect a conspiracy in the works. My father believed in conspiracies; in fact, he wallowed in them. There were very few Jews working for RCA Victor, and my father was convinced that the game of musical chairs was a conscious plot on the part of all those in attendance. He was a Jew and was, therefore, to be humiliated by having to stand throughout the meeting. Isadore was not a man to take such slights lightly. He balled his fists and stepped forward. "I demand to be seated!" Those in the room looked around in surprise. At least half pointed at the empty padded seat in response. It was only then that he realized that the chairman had already deposited himself in a chair. What the hell was going on? Could he have misjudged his fellow reps? Was he overreacting? Was he seeing a bigot behind every tree when, in fact, it was only the moss on the shady side? And now he was embarrassed. He found himself slinking toward the table feeling very foolish indeed. He had hoped everyone's attention would be drawn elsewhere, but as he approached the chairman rose and pulled the chair out for him. All eyes were focused there. Isadore swore to himself he would never again be quick to judge. He had learned his lesson. The chairman whispered in his ear as Dad settled on the cushion. "We know you Hebrews have tails, son, and we were just trying to be considerate."

❖

My father spoke Polish as well as Russian, Yiddish, and English, and he could get by in German and French. In 1937, about six months after I was born, RCA Victor sent him off to Europe as their representative. My mother, brother, and I went with him. We sailed there on the *Queen Mary,* and less than a year later returned on the *Normandy.* These were the two most celebrated passenger ships of the time.

Our first stop was Warsaw. We stayed there long enough for my brother, who was six and a half, to learn Polish and forget how to read English. We left there two years to the month before Hitler invaded Poland.

We sat in a Berlin train station waiting to make a connection to Paris. Nazi soldiers patrolled the platform. In 1935 Hitler had passed a law taking away all the rights of Jews as German citizens, and the systematic extermination of six million people had begun. Soldiers asked to see our identification papers. The name Koenigsberg had been shortened to Koenig by emigration officials when my father first arrived in the States. Our American citizenship was documented on the passports, but our name was so German-sounding the soldiers wanted to know more about us. My father proceeded to lie to them in German about our Teutonic heritage. They were impressed. Their parting comment was that we should reconsider and stay in Germany. Great things were about to happen in the Fatherland.

Our stay in Paris was cut short by illness—mine. I became sick from the milk that was available, and developed a severe case of colitis. The doctors decreed that I would not live if my diet weren't changed. In the land of Louis Pasteur pasteurized milk was not an option.

Once more we traveled the Atlantic. Again we took up residency in Chicago and, in the process, probably broke a record for the number of dwellings a family of four could inhabit in the shortest amount of time. My father had lost his job with RCA Victor, and we were forced to move every month on the day *before* the rent was due. As you can tell by now, Dad had a thing about paying for lodgings. This went on for two years. During this entire period Isadore dipped into his pockets for rent money a total of five times. We also never unpacked.

In 1939 we moved to New York, to a section of Brooklyn called Seagate, near Coney Island. In 1993 I was back in the area for an autograph session at a local comic book store. On a whim I asked the driver to take me to Seagate. It was and still is a guarded community, and

we had to bribe the guard with signed copies of the comic book stories
I had written. I had lived in Seagate until the summer of 1941, and had
not returned since and yet it was *exactly* as I had remembered it.
Nothing had changed. Very, very spooky, but also very reassuring. Not
all fables are fiction. Brigadoon lives! I drove around in awe, consciously restraining myself from the urge to cram my thumb between
my lips.

My half-sister Vera (my mother's daughter by a previous marriage) had been living with relatives while we were in Europe. She was
spared the apartment-hopping on our return, but she joined us for our
New York sojourn. She was thirteen years older than I and was frequently called upon to babysit. I'll never forgive her for dealing with a
fussy eater by hiding the chicken under mounds of revolting spinach.

By now my father had established a business he called the Latin
American Air Conditioning Company. Perhaps at first he actually did
sell air conditioners to Latin Americans, but in time he became a job-
ber for any product he could buy inexpensively and turn over at a profit. He literally sold everything from eyeglasses to elevators.

Evidently, he did well enough for us to move again. We arrived on
Payson Avenue six months before the United States declared war on
Japan, and three months before I first stepped foot on the enemy terri-
tory of P.S. 52.

Sometime during my tenure at P.S. 52 they restructured the grade
school system in the area. My school now left off after grade three and
resumed with grades seven through nine. If one wished to attend grades
four through six a relocation was in order.

P.S. 98 was about ten blocks to the north but actually pretty
much equidistant from my centrally located address. The brick walls
were dirtier at P.S. 98. The cracks in the playground cement were
wider and deeper. The wire fencing that surrounded the school, however, was more effective. Not only was it high and barbed at the top to
discourage trespassers but it was also rusted. Anyone foolish enough
to try and scale it would undoubtedly suffer open wounds that would
lead to lockjaw.

My wife Judy and I visited New York in 1984 and I decided to
show her the old neighborhood. It certainly had changed, but nothing
had deteriorated so much as the school at which I spent fourth through
sixth grades. If before it had been a gloomy, uninspiring institution of

learning, its present appearance called to mind something out of Lovecraft or Dickens. Soot covered everything. The building was solid black in color. The windows were filthy, and barred on the second floor. It looked like a penitentiary—an abandoned penitentiary, in which the bones of the inmates still remained chained to the dank rat-infested walls. Inmates who, by the way, had all been criminally insane. And not just criminally insane—serial killers, mass murderers of scruffy kittens and scrappy orphans.

It was truly appalling. It seemed inconceivable that the place was still a functioning grade school and that human children still went there to get an education. The words stick in my throat, but I guess I was lucky to go to P.S. 98 when I did back in the fall of 1945.

My stay at P.S. 98 was notable on several counts. The first, undoubtedly, was Mrs. Rothman, with whom I fell in love. The amazing thing was that she knew it and didn't mind. She was my very pretty twenty-six-year-old fourth grade teacher. She found excuses to keep me after school and then took me out for hot chocolate. It was such a far cry from any student-teacher relationship I had known that I couldn't believe it was happening to me. I wore the label "teacher's pet" with pride. And when I say "pet," we're not talking gerbils or white mice here. I mean, you can be fond of rodents but you don't necessarily respect them. Mrs. Rothman was genuinely interested in who I was.

It was a fateful winter's afternoon. The sun was already setting. Mrs. Rothman and I sat hunched over our hot chocolates at the counter of Stein's Candy Store. Behind us were racks of comic books featuring Superman, Joe Palooka, and Nancy and Sluggo. In front of us was a mirror from which our reflections shone. Sitting on the stools, she didn't seem that much taller than I. Our elbows touched, mine through my mackinaw, hers through her winter coat. She looked up into the mirror, saw me staring at her, and smiled. And then she did a most unusual thing. She leaned over and whispered in my ear. I'll never forget her warm breath and the words that spread through my body, leaving behind the most extraordinary feeling of comfort. The sweet hot chocolate I was drinking was an indifferent brew, tasteless and unremembered. The words scattered through my being, then came together and finally nestled in my heart. "You're going to be a very successful person, Walter, just remember that."

I felt exalted, euphoric, and incredibly grateful. At that moment I was determined to prove her right. I wanted to do something exceptional that would make me worthy of her faith. And then I hit on it. I had a secret weapon that nobody knew about. I was a very talented actor, probably better than anyone else in the school, and some of our class were about to be cast in a play to be seen not only by the other students but by parents and teachers as well. I *had* to be in this play. I had to be just as spectacular as I had been as the Professor. This would be my way of paying Mrs. Rothman back for the confidence she had shown in me.

And would you believe it, I did get cast. The play was all about the various goods we had to conserve because of the war. Things like silk and newspapers and rubber. My speech was about the virtues of tin. It was to be the last speech and, therefore, very important. Sort of like the climax to the entire performance. The curtain would drop after my dramatic delivery, then rise, and then each of us in turn would step forward and take our individual bows. The applause for me would be off the scale.

Now check out this scenario. If this isn't the perfect *Wonder Years* TV story it doesn't exist: Boy loves teacher, teacher respects boy, boy proves he is worthy of teacher's respect. Okay, I know what you're thinking. What about that bitter sweet element, that slight touch of irony? Boy is good but not stupendous. There is also a shy girl cast in the play. She's from a broken home, and when she delivers her lines about rationing soap the audience weeps. She ends up the star, receiving a standing ovation. I could buy that. I could live with that. I could live with almost anything but what actually did happen.

The closer we got to production the more important this project seemed to me. We had a special "drama coach" working with us, and so Mrs. Rothman did not see any of the rehearsals. I would have just that one shot to prove to her how good I was.

As the date approached the pressure built. What if I stunk it up? What if my mouth went dry and I squeaked and couldn't be heard? What if I forgot my lines? The more I thought about *that* possibility the more haunted I became by it. I was going to forget my lines and destroy Mrs. Rothman's belief in me. It became a *fait accompli*.

The day arrived. I stood backstage waiting for the curtain to rise and for us all to step forward and form the single line across the apron of the stage. "And last but not least is tin . . ." "And last but not least is tin . . ." I kept repeating it to myself like a rosary. "Hail Mary full of grace . . ." Except, since I had several Catholic friends, I knew the rosary better. "Blessed be the fruit of thy womb . . ." All I could remember about tin was that it was last but not least.

And then I knew clearly, as clearly as I knew that I would never get past the first seven words of the speech, that the other shoe was about to drop. There was no way that I could have the success I had as the Professor in the summer of '43 and not have to pay a penalty for it somewhere down the line. This was it. The winter of my discontent, the winter of '45. The curtain rose, and so did my shoulders. My head sunk into my chest. Each child, one after the other, gave the speech assigned them. We learned about nylon and aluminum foil as well as paper and rubber and soap and silk. Conserve them all, was the earnest plea, was the well-spoken, loudly declaimed, dramatically rendered proclamation of the six little fuckers that preceded me.

There are no surprises to come. I was the proverbial gibbering idiot. "And last but not least is tin . . . . And last but not least is tin. . . ." Over and over again until they finally dropped the curtain and put an end to my agony.

I didn't come to school the next day. I couldn't face Mrs. Rothman. It was not a confrontation I could continue to postpone, however. My parents saw to that.

On the morning following I flopped into my seat, my head down, never once making eye contact with my teacher. The day progressed at a tortuously slow pace. Mrs. Rothman didn't call on me. At first I was relieved, and then I began to feel that I was being purposely ignored. She was so disillusioned that she couldn't bear to speak my name. The misery I was experiencing was every bit as awful as I had anticipated. The woman I loved had given up on me.

The bell rang. I tried to slip from the room under the cover of a crowd. I heard my name called and then I was standing before Mrs. Rothman and the room had emptied and we were alone. She looked at me for a long moment and then smiled. She extended her hand and when I tentatively took it she drew me close to her. She bent down and spoke softly. "You're going to be a very important person, Walter, remember that."

I left in a daze. I could not understand why she still believed in me. It wasn't until years later that I began to put it together. When she whispered in my ear that cold day at Stein's Candy Store she wasn't bearing witness to my potential. She was addressing my insecurity. She didn't know how I was going to turn out. She just wanted me to know that someone understood my fear, my self-doubt, and was sharing my pain. When I failed in the play she repeated the same words. It was not a surprise to her. She had seen me fail before and how each time it had caused me anguish. That day in the classroom, like that day in the candy store, the two of us alone, my hand in hers, she was not foretelling my future, she was restating our friendship.

★

One of the rituals of being a kid in New York in the forties was Halloween. It was written in the Book of Graffiti that "two weeks prior to the sacred day thine closest friends and thine most mortal enemies will mark thy clothing and thy body with pastel chalk and whomp thee over thine head with stockings full of enriched flour." No matter how excessive (contusions and concussions being normal fare) the accompanying gleeful shriek of "HALLOWEEN!" made these acts pardonable. This tradition was so entrenched in our preadolescent culture that had one of our kind been brought up on a homicide charge during this festive period a defense that made the holiday an accessory might well have gotten the penalty reduced.

I, of course, did not shirk my responsibility to this consecrated mission of violence, and I kept my pockets bulging with chalk sticks of various hues. It was only the oft-repeated rebuke that "children were starving in Europe" that kept me from arming myself with stockings of nutritious flour as well.

All of this tagging and bashing, however, was only preamble to the hooliganism of Halloween night itself. That's when we dressed in scary costumes and begged for nickels and dimes from every friendly neighbor on the block but left milk bottles filled with water dyed red and tipped against the doors of those ill-disposed toward our charity. We also soaped car windshields and threw rocks at the windows of apartments where we suspected Nazi spies lurked.

It was our reign of terror. The one night when we got even with the adults who controlled our lives so arbitrarily the rest of the year. It wasn't supposed to work the other way. We weren't the ones who were supposed to get shook up. We weren't the ones who were supposed to go to bed with nightmares. Little Wally Koenig wasn't the one who was supposed to awaken before the dawn and shudder over what had occurred just hours before on the night of October 31, 1945 and worry that it presaged events yet to come.

I had returned home a little after nine o'clock from my unholy campaign against the living and was washing off my undead makeup when there was a loud knocking at the door. *Nobody* knocked on our door—everyone rang the bell. My only thought was that the police had tracked me from the last windshield I had savaged and had come to arrest me. I looked in the mirror, saw my face lathered, and was immediately struck by what I perceived as a resemblance to the cold cream lady the cops had dragged off two years before.

My father was away (again) and my mother had given up all the nickels she intended to on this night. It was up to me to answer the progressively louder and increasingly more insistent pounding on our apartment door.

I hurriedly washed off what was left of my vampire disguise, knowing that it made no difference. The guys in the uniforms with the guns would immediately know I was the vandal and haul me down to headquarters in cuffs.

Had I taps on my shoes I would have made Bojangles proud, so furiously were my legs vibrating when I opened the door. It wasn't the police at all. It was some boy a little taller than me but dressed in high heels, an old black dress with huge balloons stuffed in the top, and a curly blonde fright wig. I did not know him but I wouldn't have recognized him in any case so garishly applied was the lipstick, eyebrow pencil, and powder he had used. The generous assessment would be that he was seized by convulsions at the precise moment he had begun painting his face. The less-favorable interpretation would put him right up there with "Baby Jane" on the dementia graph. I was truly startled by his appearance, and the wild grin he had carved into his features had me edging the door closed.

"Who are you supposed to be?" I asked meekly.

"You doity skunk yah, you doity skunk yah!" he shouted back, poking at me with his finger.

I had no adequate reply to this and remained standing rather stupidly in the doorway.

"I'm Miss Form, you jerk! I teach fifth grade at P.S. 98!"

He then underhanded some candy corn at me, which I later discovered was not the hostile act I assumed it to be, and ran off cackling to himself.

I went to bed that night hoping that there was no such creature as Miss Form teaching at P.S. 98, and if there was that this boy had not been her student, for if he had she must surely have turned him into the maniac I had just met and if he had and she did then I hoped it wasn't fifth grade she taught because that was the grade I was going into the next year and I knew with deadly certainty that I couldn't survive in her class and if she did and I had to then I hoped the school would burn down before then and I would be spared.

It didn't and I wasn't.

In addition to an aversion for uniformed authority I also harbor a deeply entrenched sensitivity toward women who give orders. I'm of an introspective nature, and still find it wholly enigmatic that I do consistently react so reflexively and with so much anger to females who exercise power with me. My mother's relationship with my father was submissive in nature and she was evenhanded in the way she treated us, so I know that antipathetic feelings I have toward domineering women did not originate with her.

Believe it or not, it was only when I had reviewed what I had written about Miss Farrell and began plotting my comments about Miss Form did I realize that it was these two ladies in my life who were chiefly responsible for this aspect of my multifaceted neuroses.

And speaking of neuroses, when I sit back at this late date and try to puzzle together what I thought then was Miss Form's bizarre and bewildering behavior swings, I conclude now that we were being taught by a certifiable manic-depressive captive to strong paranoiac influences.

Miss Form was an intimidating woman. Her hair looked like something between Medusa's coif and the plant debris left behind when the ocean tide rolls back out. She had a prominent jaw, the shoulders of a linebacker, and hands the size of garbage truck scoops. To be caught in her painful clutches meant that you were headed for the dumpster, at least figuratively. The boy who costumed himself in her image on Halloween was probably more accurate than he realized. She really did look like a man in drag.

"Yah doity skunk yah" was an appellation bestowed on each of the male students many times during the school year. On the one hand, it was like a family name that bound us closer together. There was Morty Yah-Doity-Skunk-Yah and Eugene Yah-Doity-Skunk-Yah and Stephen Yah-Doity-Skunk-Yah and Walter Yah-Doity-Skunk-Yah. There was some collective comfort to be had from our mutual denigration. On the other hand, at the first sign of engorged neck veins and a hyperthyroid bulging of her eyeballs we scattered like mice in all directions. This was the warning that she was entering the state of "ecstatic malignity" from which all "Yah doity skunk yah"s emanated. In her defense it must be acknowledged that her choice of victim was not arbitrary. The one seized was always one of those closest to her when her hinges slipped. The idea was to duck and run. The student slowest afoot on any particular day would be grabbed by the collar, dragged to the front of the room, and shaken with such extreme vigor that his head would bounce between his shoulder blades and chest to the accompanying up-tempo rhythms of a Gene Krupa. The lyrics, of course, were always the same.

Knowing that I wasn't being singled out was helpful, but even so, my anxiety level never dropped below semi-hysterical due to the unpredictability of the attack. *When was it going to be my turn again?*

Compouning my feelings of instability was Miss Form's penchant for throwing parties on the day following the patented student abuse. The teacher would bring out her portable phonograph and play for us all the songs from *Finian's Rainbow* while passing around candy bars, cookies, and soda pop. (The kid who had come to my door on Halloween had this obviously in mind when he tossed the candy corn at me.)

As often as we were yelled at and as reliable as were the parties that followed, is it any wonder that I learned all the lyrics from all the songs of that 1947 Broadway musical during the course of the school year?

Miss Form's party time came with a marked change in her personality. To be sure, her congeniality was a tad unctuous, but when she started playing her thirty-three-and-a-thirds and began feeling those "Londonderry breezes," a wistfulness overwhelmed her. It was as if she had been transformed, if not into a little girl again, at least into a non-hostile eleven-year-old-boy. At such times she could have been a mate of mine. All the more reason to feel tossed overboard and keelhauled when two days later the ship's log recorded that I was still and forever a "doity skunk."

Having no clear sense of what any one day might bring, from chocolate chips to choke holds, I responded like any true-blue red-blooded American boy. I developed a stammer that prevented me from stringing together as many as four intelligible words at a time. Obviously, I alone among my classmates could claim this patriotic distinction.

There was another maladaptive manifestation as well. My handwriting deteriorated so badly that it could well have served as an unbreakable code to confound the Axis. To put it in another perspective: Picture someone inexperienced on the trampoline with limbs randomly bouncing and tumbling forward and back, landing on his stomach, landing on his neck, dipping over first one edge and then another, and then put a tracer on this helter skelter notion that would provide visual documentation, and you'd get a sense of what my hand-writing had reduced itself to. There was some musing about the possibility I had contracted a disorder of the central nervous system. When that could not be substantiated the first whispers about psychiatric consultation were heard in the land.

In retrospect, am I bitter about the unsettling, negatively charged environment that Miss Form's fifth grade class provided? Not really. When I think back on this woman from the road I have traveled—a lifetime of real and apparent crises and the accompanying emotional upheaval that have dogged each step—I find room in my knapsack for a little compassion. Think of the demons that propelled the rage that caused her to rattle our bones and think of the guilt that followed the rage and compelled her to provide us with candy. And, finally, think of the woman who sat with her records and pretended that her life wasn't as it appeared and that somewhere over Finian's rainbow there was still hope for something better.

And, anyway, when I got to sixth grade there was another play and everything changed again.

FOUR

"The Boy Who Could Fly"

THERE ARE EVENTS IN EVERYONE'S LIFE AS THERE HAVE BEEN IN MINE that have resonance long after the fact. It is the reason why, years later, the glottis still constricts, the pulse still pounds, the vision still blurs, and the underarms still moisten when faced with conflict. The feelings responsible for these physiological processes were forged from child-hood experiences that had a lot to do with failure. In some way, large or small, we did not meet the challenge then, and a measure of self-doubt does forever after reverberate on our psychic tuning fork.

Conversely, not all confrontations end in defeat. There are stand-offs and modest victories and occasionally, maybe once a decade, a glorious triumph. Such an event demands its own amplification, and can be recalled when needed as a ringing endorsement of our ability to succeed.

In the sixth grade I was cast in a costume epic as the king who shouts "off with his head" at every available opportunity. It was the lead role and I have never given a better performance. Although such a fact can be viewed as discouraging, since I performed the part when I was twelve, I choose to see it in terms of a performance I'm *capable* of achieving, even if I have not yet returned to that lofty level in the suc-ceeding forty-eight years. I mean this sincerely; I believe I was brilliant. Never before or since have I experienced such an extraordinary sense of liberation. There wasn't anything I didn't feel I could achieve on the stage. During the dinner scene in our single performance I had one of several inspired moments. I remember picking up the knife, fork, and spoon in front of me, tossing them into the air, and juggling them to rhythms worthy of Keith Moon while simultaneously bellowing "off with his head" and other assorted dialogue. To be sure, I had tried this before with spaldings (pink rubber balls with which every New York kid played stickball) but had never had even the most minimal success. Nevertheless, I was able to keep everything aloft for nearly half a minute. It brought the house down. Parents and students alike were falling over themselves. Even after the fork finally clattered to the floor the laughter and applause persisted. Of course, I'm not suggesting that juggling is the ultimate test of theatrical aptitude. But the presence I had on the stage and the degree of freedom and control that I brought to the role was for me a form of magic. If the part had called for me to soar from the apron and circle the rafters I think I might have accomplished that as well. People talk about power as being money and position, but I'm here to tell you that there is no greater rush, no stronger sense of omnipotence, than standing within a proscenium in front of a full house and knowing that you can do no wrong.

Why did it all go so well? Why was I so blissfully graced on this one occasion? If I knew the secret Olivier and I would probably have been chums and Brando, De Niro, and Duvall would have made pilgrimages to my door bearing frankincense and myrrh. What I do know is that I experienced it in 1948 and having done it once I'm hopeful that I can recapture that feeling some time again, maybe even before the turn of the century.

It was shortly after that that I stopped stuttering.

⚡

It was the early forties. To those on the block still emerging from the dark age of pre-mechanical refrigeration the ice wagon continued to be a staple. The driver, probably in his fifties, was short and Greek with a heavy moustache, a thick chest, and disproportionately large arms. He wore an apron which was always stained and, whether it was summer or winter, a blue knit stocking cap and leather gloves. The tools of his trade were an ice pick and tongs. He'd hack at the ice in the back of the wagon and hoist a chunk to his shoulder. He made his deliveries staircase after staircase, apartment after apartment, until one day he did not return.

It was not, however, as you might suspect. It was not *his* heart that gave out but that of Kazimazakos. That's the name I remember, but it was probably nothing like that at all. She was the nag that pulled his wagon, a spavined old mare with a lifeless tail who drooled and snorted and allowed me to love her unconditionally. I had not yet spent a summer in the country and become familiar with horses. More the wonder then to see an animal this size on a city street right there in front of me! Because it was docile and tolerated my patting I imagined a bond between us. When the iceman went inside I whispered secret words to her and rubbed the soft place under her chin. At night, as I waited for sleep to descend, I would slip into her stall, leap on her back, crash the barriers to freedom, and ride the high wind to the Bronx.

Kazimazakos was not replaced, and there was no successor to the iceman. The last of the neighborhood hold-outs bought Frigidaires and Norges. I never again saw a horse on Payson Avenue. An era had begun to ebb.

But it wasn't dead yet. There were still the coal trucks. They were manned by workers whose races were indistinguishable. Soot lay over them like a shroud. I wanted to hear them talk but they rushed through their labor in angry silence. I think they hated the job they did or, at the very least, those who had been spared their toil. They were so ominously grim and so thick with coal dust that they seemed to have arrived from another planet. I couldn't imagine them with families of their own living in apartments like us. There were some Flash Gordon comic books stowed under my bed. I figured maybe these guys were from Mongo too.

They would come on a late December afternoon and back their heavily laden truck perpendicular to the apartment building. The long-bedded eight-wheeler extended deep into the street and caused the traffic to come to a halt. Up went the tailgate, and the coal tumbled down a portable chute and piled through a basement window into the furnace room. While our homes were warmer for their having been there the winter's air seemed colder in their wake.

Even as our physical needs were being provided for by the ice man and the coal man so was our more aesthetic side being attended to by Kate Smith, *Big Sister, The Romance of Helen Trent,* and *Our Gal Sunday.* There was no cafeteria at P.S. 52, so each of us trudged home from grammar school for the luncheon meal. My mother, a basically lonely woman, I think, had as her most constant companion the radio soap operas. Whose mother didn't back in those early forties? The radio was always on, and if I didn't dawdle and thus miscalculate I arrived in time to endure Kate Smith singing, as she did every day, "God Bless America." (Which was really quite ironic, since my father spent evenings on the sofa fantasizing muscular adventures against capitalism while the Moscow Symphony Orchestra performed "The Internationale" on his 78s. For the uninitiated, that's the revolutionary workers' anthem the Communist Party adopted as its own.)

I remember that *Big Sister* was sponsored by Rinso White, ("The happy little washday song") and that Helen Trent "was dashed against the rocks of despair but fought back bravely, successfully to prove what so many women longed to prove, that romance could begin at thirty-five and beyond," and that Our Gal Sunday "came from the little mining town of Silver Creek, Colorado and tried to find happiness as the wife of the wealthy and titled Englishman, Lord Henry Winthrop."

Simplistic stuff to be sure, but so evocative of the times. It was the time, after all, of the horse-drawn ice wagon and the other-worldly coal truckers. And it was also the time of the rag monger who strolled our avenue pushing a bonnetless baby carriage piled high with worn double-breasted suits and ankle-length dresses. He came during lunchtime as Helen Trent was dragging herself from the reef and wading ashore. "BUY-CASH-CLOTHES!" he bellowed, and occasionally a window would open and a finger would beckon to him. I never felt sorry for him because he was a businessman, an entrepreneur. He had cash in his pocket and was eager to buy your garments or sell you his.

Is there some ironic statement to be made here counterpointing the purple drama of *Our Gal Sunday* and the modest ambition of the merchants of ice, coal, and rags? Not to my way of thinking, because about it all there was a forthrightness, an unabashedness, an unself-consciousness. Life was not necessarily easy and art was sometimes artless but there was no attendant shame or ridicule. The people in my neighborhood would no more deride the struggles of the humble workman than they would the implausible histrionics of their favorite soap operas. Cynicism was not a watchword, ingenuousness was. The forties might have been corny, but then that was their charm.

However, as the end of the decade approached the world changed. The Cold War became a permafrost and the House Committee on Un-American Activities was its knee-jerk reaction.

FIVE

"The Hunt for Red October"

IN 1947 THE COMMITTEE HELD HEARINGS INTO THE INFLUENCE OF communism in the motion picture industry. It became our version of the Spanish Inquisition or Robespierre's Committee on Public Safety or the shadow councils of South American dictatorships. The witch hunt was on, and it was frightening to see the power these individuals wielded. If there were people trying to overthrow the government they were not uncovered in significant numbers, but in the process of determining that many careers were destroyed. Worst of all, it caused us to turn on each other, to give each other up to save our own skins, to betray that most sacred of human ideals—friendship and loyalty. In 1948 the Committee started probing for communists in the State Department, and we responded as we had in Hollywood. We threw down our arms and without a fight surrendered our own. We pointed fingers and named the blameless. The cancer spread. Committees were formed in the Senate and in state legislatures to root out communists in public and private industry. Again we rolled over, we let it happen. Loyalty oaths were sworn in public, but from the testimony given in secret, patriotic Americans lost their jobs, were blacklisted, were branded traitors.

By 1950 the leader of the pack was Senator Joseph Raymond McCarthy. He wielded a sword that indiscriminately sliced through the fabric of American life. No one was safe from his denunciations, and no one in Congress had the courage to challenge him. He rode a wave of fear and society's decaying moral character. Eventually he would accuse the Eisenhower administration and the U.S. Army of treason. He succeeded as long as he did, I believe, because he operated in an atmosphere of cultural self-contempt. We had lost our sense of fairness, we had lost pride in ourselves, in our ingenuousness. No more was life about the nobility of honest work and love and romance. It was about survival at any cost. The time of the iceman, the coal man, and the rag man was gone. Soap operas were an anachronism. The people in my neighborhood sniggered and scoffed and smiled sardonically. They had grown up and knew now what it was *really* all about, and it sure the hell wasn't about character and integrity. Like an ancient and decrepit grandfather who had outlived his time, we buried the age of innocence.

❖

In the summer of 1946 my father had his first heart attack. No surgery was performed. The prescribed rehabilitation called for bed rest and quiet. My brother and I were shipped off to a dude ranch, where I learned to ride a horse. It was a cow pony and a gelding and his name was Atomic. Nevertheless, I called him Kazimazakos and referred to him as "her" and "she." I wouldn't be dissuaded. Actually, I was pretty obnoxious about it. The cowboys threw up their hands and kicked the tumbleweeds and the ranch hands fanned their cowlicks and nodded sagely. Those it didn't piss off figured I was one of them "sissyboys" with a stash of lace underwear at the bottom of his suitcase.

The fact was, I was in a state of constant anxiety. I was separated from my father and was receiving only sporadic accounts of his recovery, and I wasn't sure if I could believe those. I was in turmoil and feeling very insecure. As I perceive it now, I was probably looking for something to hang my ten-gallon psyche on, something that would return some stability to my life. The camaraderie I had fabricated with the iceman's horse and our midnight flights to freedom were among the most reassuring fantasies I had yet conceived. I guess in a way I was regressing to an earlier time, one in which I could still be the little kid for whom life was just generally sweeter and whose experience with death was no more threatening than the oven in the witch's gingerbread house. Fantasy has always been part of my modus operandi. If I could not have escaped into daydreams at treacherously stressful moments in my life I probably would not have survived the panic that fought to consume me.

The damnedest thing was that in addition to this psychological processing I developed a most bizarre and embarrassing tick. I'm sure it could have been an inspirational source for people with Tourette's Syndrome. It began innocently enough with my horseback riding. Being astride a horse for an hour on a hot summer day resulted in considerable perspiration and caused one's underwear *(boy's* boxer shorts, by the way) to stick in one's rear end. I could manage an occasional clandestine pluck to liberate cotton from flesh, but that stopped being satisfactory when contact with the horse ceased being an initiating requisite. I began to imagine that my boxers had achieved some kind of prankish life form state and on their own, were riding up between the cheeks of my behind. The discomfort became constant, and the remedy I had previously employed no longer seemed appropriate. An occasional "pluck" might be tolerable, but obsessively grabbing at one's ass seemed low on the scale of socially acceptable behavior. Instead, I developed this extraordinary hitch in my gait in which my right leg would shoot up and out to the side. The theory was that this would shake loose the capricious garment from the seat of sequestration and provide me the relief I urgently sought. Of course, for someone so totally whacked out as I was this was only a temporary solution. Five or six more steps down the road and then, again, up the crevice the cursed cloth would creep. My brother told me that at such moments I resembled nothing so much as a cocker spaniel conscientiously marking the trees on its route.

So there I'd be walking with one of the wranglers, he with his bowed legs and clanging spurs, blithely spitting tobacco juice, and me with my tilting buttock, skyward kicks, and inane conversation desperately designed to distract from the mad dance I was compelled to perform.

I wish I could tell you that this aberrational behavior ended when we returned from the dude ranch. In fact, it went on for another year. Relief finally came in the fifth grade when I took up stuttering as a replacement neurosis. I am proud to say that I was symptom-free after that for nearly a decade, or until I discovered another part of my anatomy with remarkable autonomous properties and a capacity for inventive movement heretofore undocumented. It was the English stage director hired in my summer stock season of 1956 who first gave it a clinical appellation when he one day came looking for me. "You hoo," he shouted to the other actors, "has anyone seen that *bunny nose* fellow?"

☾

It was decided that I would not go back to P.S. 52 for seventh grade but attend, instead, a private school in Riverdale, New York called Fieldston. This school went from seventh grade through high school and it was there I was to spend the next six years. At the same time, my parents offered to provide me with some psychiatric consultation. These two moves—placing me in a learning atmosphere where the teachers were enlightened and the classes were small, and setting me up with a therapist who might keep me symptom-free—were supposed to be complementary actions. Each was supposed to assist the other in shoring up my psychological health. In actuality, Fieldston was such a stressful learning environment that the good doctor had all he could do to salvage what little self-esteem and emotional stability I was clinging to at the time I enrolled there.

The program was dedicated to academic excellence, and those who couldn't keep up were relegated to "special" classes. Not only was I assigned Penmanship for the Pinheaded but Spelling for the Slack Brained and Math for the Vacant Minded. To downplay competition between students letter grades were not assigned at Fieldston, but it was the acme of ivory tower naiveté to assume you could commit people to "special" classes and not have them branded by their peers with a scarlet "S" for "Stupid."

With a few notable exceptions Fieldston remained a stress-filled environment throughout my tenure there. Undoubtedly, though, the most appalling of my experiences was self-inflicted, and occurred in the spring as our first school year was winding down.

If I had developed a reputation as being slow of wit I had also achieved some notoriety for being the fastest runner in the class. I use the word "notoriety" advisedly. One did not "celebrate" athletic prowess at Fieldston. At best such endeavors were endured; at worst they proved the theorem that athleticism and intelligence were inversely related.

It was the day of the big meet on our one-fifth-mile track. Our times in this race would be written down and preserved for years to come. Everyone, including our gym teacher, Clarey, was predicting that I would break the record for seventh graders that had stood since before the Second World War. I found myself in a strange position. Wouldn't triumphing on the track simply confirm my Neanderthal status? Maybe, but the alternative didn't hold even the possibility of conjecture and, therefore, debate was out of the question. It was dead certain that if I failed at the one skill for which I had received at least some recognition the effect on me would be catastrophic.

There were fifty-five of us at the start line, and when the gun sounded I immediately broke to the front. No one tried to match my stride. By the time I was halfway around the oval I was twenty-five yards ahead of my closest challengers. By the time I was three-quarters home I had extended the lead to forty yards. I came around the last turn with only Clarey and his stopwatch ahead of me. I could have skipped down the final straightaway and still finished first and shattered the record.

And then suddenly I was seized by a devastating notion. What was the one thing that could happen that would be worse than anything else and the one thing whose inevitability seemed more certain with every step I took? The "other shoe," of course! The other shoe would drop, and somehow I would be passed in the last few yards. I would lose the race and my inadequacy would be confirmed. I couldn't let that happen, so I executed the one turn which I knew would defy the gods, Fate, the other shoe, whatever. No. I didn't reach down, tap into some magical source of energy, and sprint to the tape in record time. What I did was reach down, tap into the place where the darkest thoughts fester, and purposely trip and fall to the ground so I'd have an excuse for not winning.

Then the race was over and there was no picture of a finely conditioned greyhound breaking the ribbon to satisfy the mind's eye. In its place was only a Rorschach inkblot, one of those psychological drawings which if you looked at it closely enough appeared to be a sick puppy writhing in pretend agony on a cinder floor.

Dr. Sorrel was a Freudian psychiatrist, which meant that he hardly ever spoke during our sessions. I generally provided all the voices heard in the room—id, ego, and superego—and he generally murmured to himself and made scratching sounds with a pen. I was, therefore, unsuspecting when I began to regale him with the track debacle a few days later. The doctor's desk was positioned behind the couch with the gray corduroy slipcover on which I lay. A matching gray corduroy patch, to keep me from being distracted, rested over my eyes. I had just recounted the moment of my collapse, both physical and psychological, when I heard a crashing sound behind me. My first reaction was that the good doctor in a state of shock had tumbled to the floor, tipping over his chair in the process. I sat up and spun around. To be sure, his chair had jettisoned and was up against the radiator, but he was not prostrate. In fact, he was rising, rising, rising from behind his desk like the lost city of Atlantis rising out of the sea. The scene had an eerie, slow-motion feel to it which enhanced the sense that he was not simply standing erect but continuing to grow until he loomed over me, enveloped me, swallowed me up. He raised his arm and pointed at me. The gesture was so insulting and accusatory and the expression on his face so condemning I felt my "crime" must rank right up there with eating one's young and having sex with the dead.

I'm sure with time I've given it a film noir patina, because I remember the whole thing now as if it happened in black and white with filtered light and heavy shadows. I conceive Sorrel now as more like a warden than my doctor, and his finger of scorn was not across an empty span but through the bars of a cell. "THAT'S NEUROTIC! DON'T EVER DO THAT AGAIN!" are the exact words he used at the time. "You're through, Mugsy, we're giving you the chair!" is the way it echoes in my head.

I believe there is a secret therapy known among the Freudian fraternity that is not disclosed to the rest of us. My theory is that the non-communicative consultation is a Machiavellian ploy designed to make more effective that one specific moment when the analyst does finally blow and go berserk. I'll tell you this—I think it works, because I never again allowed myself the degree of self-destruction I indulged in that day on the school track. I believe that at the heart of the innermost circle where the coven of thirteen psychiatrists toil and bubble they call this secret therapy "Scaring the Shit Out of the Patient."

★

If I had, until now, oblique misgivings about my father's involvement with communism, they became decidedly more acute the first time I uncrumpled the wadded note paper that had been jammed into our mailbox. "Shit communists get out!" was the cryptic salutation. In the same delivery was a Lone Ranger premium I had been impatiently awaiting. As happens with shocking experiences, an irrational association was woven between the two events. The premium got stuffed into the back of a drawer and my appreciation of the Masked Man dimmed considerably. I think my reaction was by way of self-protection. If I could at some level lay off responsibility for the hate mail on blazing six guns and the *William Tell Overture,* I could distance myself from a reality that was difficult to confront—that someone in my apartment building, probably someone who I frequently passed on the stairs, someone with whom I had possibly exchanged smiles was the person leaving these implicitly threatening missives. The year was 1949, I was thirteen years old, and my psychological deflections notwithstanding, I couldn't avoid a pervasive anxiety that at times immobilized me.

The fact was, there was no one I felt I could trust. Anyone could be the perpetrator. The Irish Catholics on the sixth floor, the German Jews on the third floor, the woman whose dog I walked, the parents of my friend down the hall, the Hungarian family in the next apartment, the New York Giants baseball player, the Czech superintendent who called every kid on the block a "sumnamabitch" anyway and once in a drunken rage threw a monkey wrench at a group of us.

And, of course, the notes kept coming. At first I had a morbid curiosity about them and volunteered each day to collect the mail. That was definitely a mistake. Each time one appeared it was like turning over a school paper and discovering a failing grade. The blood drained from my head, my stomach capsized, I had trouble breathing. I never got used to it. I finally avoided the mail deliveries and all mention of them. In a way that made it worse. With my folks now tightlipped out of respect for my wishes I was free to imagine that not only were they arriving with greater frequency but that the inscribed threats had become increasingly more explicit. "We're going to cut your balls off and stuff them down your throats, you Commie bastards" was sort of along the lines of what I envisioned.

My apprehension took a new form and intensified manifold on a particularly bad Sunday. My father had asked me to go down the street and pick up a copy of *The New York Times*. They were out at Stein's Candy Store so I chose the periodical that I had seen Dad read on countless occasions. I dropped the few pages that comprised the *The Daily Worker*, the official newspaper of the Communist Party, on his bed thinking that my resourcefulness would be lightly applauded. I assumed he would take comfort in reports about workers of the world uniting with nothing to lose but their chains.

In fact, he was instantly apoplectic. He launched himself from the bed and flung the paper from him as if it were a Molotov Cocktail about to explode. "What the hell did you do?" he demanded rhetorically. As I remained frozen with only my legs quivering he repeated the question several times at ever-increasing volume. In short order my panic gained a full head of steam or, more precisely, a head full of unmanageable thoughts that kicked and bucked and made rational thinking beyond me. That I had done something catastrophically stupid in buying the paper was unquestioned, but specifically what that was was beyond the chaotic functioning of my brain.

But then a most chilling thing happened. He abruptly calmed down. There were several moments of dead silence while I continued to stand there, my legs shaking. "Son, I have to ask you something . . ." His voice took on a distinctly different tone. I heard weariness, detachment, and resignation, and I was struck by the feeling that I had never before met *this* voice, *this* man. He looked into my eyes and I knew I was about to hear something that would make the danger under which we lived more real than all the hate mail we had so far received. I felt an urgent need to go to the bathroom but he kept me rooted with the look in his eyes.

His calmness induced my own. My brain slowed down and I began thinking more clearly. I realize now that that was his intention. He wanted to be sure he had my complete attention, and that my answer would be accurately reported. He spoke quietly and slowly and what he said was every bit as bad as I could have imagined. "Do you think you were followed?" he asked.

I had not known until then that my parents' concern extended beyond the anti-Commie ravings of a closet crazy. In fact, my father had learned from a friendly neighbor that the FBI had been making door-to-door inquiries. That would certainly explain how and why we had become the target of our lowlife correspondent.

I suppose they had done well to keep it from me, but learning about it now in such a dramatic way had me more agitated than I might otherwise have been. The concept that the Federal Bureau of Investigation might have agents planted behind store counters, hovering in back alleys, merging with shadows, and tailing me to and from the candy store had me decidedly paranoid. One of my particular fixations was the Good Humor Ice Cream truck driver. He in his spanking-clean white uniform and his little patriotic bells seemed like a perfect candidate to be a disguised investigator for the "American way of life."

I'll never know how serious the FBI's inquiries were and how close we came to being rounded up in the wave of Commie hysteria that had the country by the throat. I do know it was very real and very serious to my folks, and consequently very serious to me.

The pressure was getting to us all, and it wasn't long after that a ritual purging of my family's political and cultural history occurred. On my father's orders, down the incinerator went all the albums of his beloved Russian music. Down as well went the teachings of Karl Marx and Lenin. The works of Howard Fast were not spared nor, for some reason I don't understand, the novels of Jack London.

It was ironic that he put to his own head the very weapons he railed against, censorship and the obviation of cultural identity. I suppose in the most romantic of all worlds he would have stood fast to the end, a martyr to his cause. But not in this world, where he had a family to support, one child in therapy and attending an expensive private school, and another about to go off to college. It would be the greatest hypocrisy for me to condemn his capitulation, and I won't do it. There are many things I can take exception to about good old Dad, but I won't argue his passion and idealism, even knowing they had finite boundaries.

And then one day he disappeared.

He just didn't show up. Not that night or the next or the one after that. It was the early fall of 1949. The days stretched into weeks and the weeks into months. Neither my mother nor I had any idea where my father was. Norm, who knew what had happened but had been sworn to secrecy, never let on. Mom had always been a very emotional person but now she fell into a routine of beating on her chest, pulling at her hair, and chanting to herself. *"Gutt en nu, Gutt en nu, Gutt en nu"* ("My God, my God, my God") was the chorus and the verse. She was in a state of constant hysteria and tiptoeing on the edge of sanity. Watching her fall apart didn't add to my own sense of security.

A little money had been left behind in an envelope, but that was spent in a month's time. My mother started borrowing from her sisters just to supply us with food. After the second thirty days the phone was shut off. It was rather ironic. I was going to the most expensive private school in New York City and we couldn't pay our phone bill. It also seemed like an omen. When a primary means of communication is severed the one you're hoping to contact seems that much farther away, that much more remote. It was about then I decided that Isadore was either in flight from the FBI or dead.

I found comfort in the comedies and dramas that played on the radio. I buried myself in the fantasy of these shows. I was the funny pal of Henry Aldridge, The Great Gildersleeve's bank clerk. I shared trunk space with Charlie McCarthy and Mortimer Snerd. I, too, could "cloud men's minds," and I had my own trenchcoat and unfashionable shoes for my work on *This Is Your FBI* (I imagine for the latter show it was a case of "if you can't beat 'em, join 'em").

As you might guess, *This Is Your FBI* held an additional fascination for me. They had a "Ten Most Wanted" list after each program.
Week after week "Bad Eye" Salutsky was the top criminal at large but
as time passed and there was no word from Dad I became obsessed
with the idea that sooner or later Salutsky would have to share air time
with Izzie "the Commie Rat" Koenig.

Then the nightmares began. The big phonograph-radio console in
the living room had a light the size of a quarter that glowed a fuzz-like
textured bright green when the radio warmed up. That light invaded
my dreams. It followed me like an eye. Like "Bad Eye" Salutsky's bad
eye. It was the Top Ten gangster but it was also the FBI. They were all
rolled into one and they wanted to know where Isadore was hiding.

What they didn't know was that my father had died. He had died
just like the mobsters who met their end on *Bulldog Drummond,* and
The Shadow and *Nick Carter, Master Detective.* I saw it happening in
my dreams night after night. I woke up exhausted and depressed and
couldn't shake the feeling that it had really occurred. I dragged through
the day in a state of mourning, and just as the heaviness would start to
lift it would be night again and the dreams would come once more.

I do believe that the explanation for these nightmares lies beyond
the obvious anxiety that a long absence would induce. I'm convinced
that my subconscious was preparing me for Dad's passing, a death
which I had already assumed was inevitable and close at hand after his
heart attack in 1946. It was the old "other shoe" syndrome again. I
knew it was coming and I had to be ready, I had to be conditioned.
And I was. When he died seven years later I heard the news without
blinking. The psychic surgery I had been performing on myself for
years was a success. I had managed to transform myself into a proper
little android.

The third month was drawing to a close, Christmas bells had
begun to faintly ring, and our second eviction notice was in hand. It
was then that my father returned. I'd like to be able to tell you that life
is black and white and that dad was a drunken bum who had gone on
a ninety-day bender with a barhopping floozy. A righteous anger
toward him for leaving us nearly destitute and emotionally depleted
would have been a cathartic venting for the deep resentment Mom and
I felt. But the old man didn't drink and I was never aware of any sexual indiscretions.

What had really happened was rather extraordinary. My father's
adventure had been a heroic one. I was forced to admire him for his

courage and repress my resentment for his act of abandonment. I did not feel I had a right to my anger and so, myself, applied the poultice to the injury he had caused. What is the old saying? "He who is his own doctor has a fool for a patient." It must be so. Wounds thus treated don't heal.

Some of the background for this story is secondhand. I do know that my father's sister, Jessie, had contracted breast cancer and there was talk at the time of a cure behind the Iron Curtain. My cousin Dan Barton insists that Jessie's husband Joe (our mutual uncle), a militantly leftist Chicago physician, had sent a letter to Joseph Stalin, Marshal of the Soviet Union and supreme dictator, requesting safe passage into Russia for her treatment. Bear in mind that this was 1949 and the Cold War had been fully launched. A letter written by Vyacheslav Molotov was received in return. (Since Molotov was the Soviet Prime Minister and helped create his nation's policy of hostility toward the United States this really seems quite remarkable and is the reason I applied the qualifier to the top of this paragraph.) As the story goes, the Commissar of Foreign Affairs explained in his note that scientific progress in this field had been limited and that when such a remedy was found it would be made available to the world.

The rest I know from my father's lips. He decided that despite any information to the contrary, the cure was real and that he would personally accompany Jessie to Russia and pound on Stalin's door if necessary to acquire the treatment she needed. I find this astonishing, and it was the source of my great admiration for him. This was the man who went bonkers when I brought home *The Daily Worker,* and yet his devotion and loyalty to his sister was stronger than his fear of not one but two superpowers. The Iron Curtain had descended with a deadly clang. Americans were prohibited by their government from traveling in the Soviet Union, and the Russians sure as hell promised a dungeon in Siberia to any U.S. citizen caught within their boundaries.

Not only had Russian medicine not found a cure for cancer but apparently there were large pockets among the satellite countries where penicillin was in short supply. Somehow Isadore had found a source of black market penicillin, and he slipped from country to country through Eastern Europe trading it for forged passports. (No wonder we had no money for Milky Ways and Baby Ruths—Dad was throwing it away on lifesaving drugs.) He got as far as the Russian border and was stopped cold. That was it. *Fini.* He never made it to Moscow and Stalin's door.

That first night home he leaned back against the kitchen stove, told us the story, and cried. I had never seen Dad do that before. His regret was not in having abandoned us without explanation but in his failure to help his sister. We were really not an issue for him. Talk about conflict: I've never been able to forgive his act of desertion. My anger to this day is palpable. On the other hand, how can you not have enormous respect for a man so bravely and selflessly motivated? How do I resolve it? I don't. I will always feel a raging ambivalence toward him. I've come to accept it. Unfortunately, it doesn't make for plaque-free arteries and a settled tummy.

In 1952, my sophomore year in high school, we did Ibsen's *Peer Gynt*. I was chosen for the title role. Once again, theater had come to my rescue but this time in a distinctly different way.

For the first three years at Fieldston I had found myself being inextricably drawn backwards, away from the spotlight, away from the crowd even, towards a distant and isolated background. The next step was to be sucked into the wallpaper and disappear entirely. Then came *Peer Gynt* and once again everything changed.

Within us all, I think, is the secret belief that we have something magical to offer. If we go a lifetime and never fulfill our dreams we curse the darkness, dry up, and turn to parchment while concocting a pacifying balm of "what might have beens" to dab at cracked and yellowing egos. At the age of fifteen I was not unlike most angst-ridden teenagers. After three years of social anonymity and mediocre performance I was convinced my life would play out at some subterranean level of achievement with only gnomes and trolls as companions. Sound melodramatic? Just ask today's friendly local adolescent how he or she views the future.

My classmates knew little about me. I didn't come from the Central Park West-Park Avenue section of Manhattan where many of them lived and where even the chauffeurs had "old money," nor could I call home the suburban towns of Riverdale and Scarsdale, where the money was crisper but just as bankable and where the rest of the Fieldston students resided. I had never been invited for a sleepover, I had never been invited to a party, I had never been invited to join the gang for a Saturday afternoon movie. None of this bothered me because I didn't know it existed. Imagine a mongrel puppy having learned to adapt to its small cage at the animal shelter. What is, is. It doesn't know enough to be unsettled by its circumstances.

Then came the play and I'm suddenly a celebrity. I'm discovered to have a talent that places me apart from the rest. Performers have always held a unique position in society. Even when they were vilified as miscreants and excluded from the public inn they were admired for the sorcery they performed in capturing the attention of their audiences. Wouldn't everyone like to stand in the spotlight and experience the validation that only the applause of the crowd can provide?

The puppy is defleaed, his matted coat brushed out and his toenails clipped. He is seized by the scruff of his neck, unceremoniously yanked from his cage, and thrust before a curious public. What do you know—he can sit up, roll over, and bark on command! Isn't he precious? That's pretty much the way I felt when I learned soon after being cast in the play that there were, indeed, such things as sleepovers, parties, and Saturday outings with the gang. This isn't meant to suggest that I was embittered by the superficiality of my peers. To be sure, I never lost sight of the fact that my newly acquired popularity was directly attributable to my success as an actor. But any port in a storm, and I was resolved to enjoy the attention while it lasted. I was particularly pleased with one observation I recorded at the time. On more than a few occasions I murmured to my freshly minted pals that the class in general was performing their own little play. In taking me to their collective bosom and sponsoring me for any number of social events they were acting out in microcosm the patron roles their parents played in fostering the talents of young artists in their society.

It would be years before I would consciously permit myself to consider a life in the theater. Though I began college as a premed major and graduated with a degree in psychology, wasn't it predetermined that I would pursue a career as an actor? Certainly I had an aptitude for it and a need to express myself in that manner, but even more important, I derived my most significant feelings of self-worth from the approbation I received for my work as a performer. I'm not saying this is healthy. In fact, it's quite neurotic. Self-esteem is supposed to come from one's self, not the opinions of others, but then how many actors would have chosen this field were it not for a sense of inadequacy? In the absence of a taste for alcohol and an interest in drugs, the one narcotic available to fill the void, to make one feel good about oneself, to create that very special "high," is the smell of the greasepaint and, most emphatically, the roar of the crowd. *Peer Gynt* did that for me, and even if I didn't know it at the time it set me on a course that was inviolate and irreversible.

As one might suspect, a concomitant benefit derived from my new status was a heightened interest from the female sector. I was also on the track team, and I learned that there was a loosely structured group of seventh and eighth grade girls who attended the meets to cheer me on. It was my first fan club. Curiously, fifteen years later when I was doing *Star Trek* it was also seventh and eighth grade girls who thought I was "groovy" and were my most ardent fans.

More to the point, however, was the interest shown by a classmate named Jill. She was my first real girlfriend. I remember that I gave her a silver locket, took her to a movie and necked with her on the living-room sofa—once. There are those who would argue that such an event is not a religious experience, and yet it definitely bore a similarity to the miraculous birth of Jesus. I wish I could tell you that the result here too was a state of awe but, in fact, what I was subjected to was a state of shock with far-reaching implications and consequences.

As I recall, Jill was wearing a bra, a blouse, and a sweater and, possibly, a vest, a jacket, and a fur coat. It wouldn't have mattered. My state of arousal was such that she could have been encased in a suit of armour or protected by a wall of lead and I still would have responded the same. I knew from casual observation where on the human anatomy the female bosom should be and so, despite the layers of protective garb, I managed to place my hand in the general area. Obviously there was not much in the way of tactile sensation, but that wasn't really the point—no pun intended. It was the *idea* that I had made contact, no matter how remote, with an actual girl's breast that had me ecstatic. So ecstatic, alas, that, without Jill ever knowing, I totally lost control. With that in mind then, who is to say, that it wasn't a kind of religious ecstasy I had experienced? The King of Kings was a birth managed without the benefit of human interplay, and my orgasm was just as immaculate.

Unfortunately, this opened the floodgates, so to speak, to a whole new set of anxieties. I was immediately convinced that I was physiologically impaired and that I could look forward to a lifetime of premature ejaculation. I would never be able to have sexual congress, I would never be able to satisfy a partner and, of course, I would never be able to have children. I envisioned scenarios where I would be forced to wear protective covering on my hands and have the liaison take place in pitch blackness. Perhaps if I could sneak up on the coital act before my mind alerted my body to what was happening I could effect junction before my hormones betrayed me. When I played out this fantasy in my head I realized that dialogue along the lines of "Honey, do you mind if I wear gloves and a blindfold?" would have to be part of the script. At that point I decided I was fated to lead a life of celibacy. It was a very depressing thought. My relationship with Jill began to deteriorate soon afterwards. We never necked again.

✳

In 1949 Klaus Fuchs, a physicist who had been part of the Manhattan Project at Los Alamos during the development of the atomic bomb, confessed to British authorities that he had been a Russian spy. He named an American, David Greenglass, as a co-conspirator. Greenglass had also been on the New Mexico project, working at the nuclear weapons laboratory in 1944 and 1945. He was arrested in 1950 and incriminated his sister Ethel Rosenberg and her husband Julius Rosenberg as being part of an espionage ring that passed along information about atomic weapons, fuses, and gunfire mechanisms of Russian agents. The husband and wife were tried by a jury in a United States civil court presided over by Judge Irving Kaufman in 1951. They were found guilty, and Judge Kaufman sentenced them to death by electrocution.

During the trial my father was convinced the Rosenbergs would be declared innocent. Because witnesses had given conflicting accounts, especially in regard to Ethel's involvement, and because of questionable behavior on the part of the FBI, prosecutors, and the judge himself, it was my father's opinion, as well as many others, that a guilty verdict could not be brought in.

As has been recently disclosed by the CIA through newly declassified transcripts, there was substantial evidence against Julius Rosenberg. However, this information was not submitted during the trial because the government did not want to compromise the National Security Agency. The evidence against Rosenberg was developed through the agency's ability to break the code the Russians were using, and they didn't want the Soviets to know this.

The case the government presented, its hands tied, was weak. There were many critics who considered it flimsy and circumstantial, and the outcome one that had been railroaded through. This was particularly true in regard to Ethel Rosenberg, whose involvement has still not been proven, even by the information recently uncovered.

Thus my father's reaction was one of outrage when the jury's verdict was rendered. He was incredulous when the judge passed sentence, and in despair when the Supreme Court denied all appeals. Twice President Dwight D. Eisenhower refused pleas for clemency and on June 19, 1953 Ethel and Julius Rosenberg, leaving two small sons behind, were put to death in the electric chair in Sing Sing prison. At that point my father's reaction turned to one of paranoia, and he wasn't alone.

Whether or not they had relatives who had suffered and perished in concentration camps, Jews everywhere felt themselves in compact with those who had met that terrible fate during the years of Nazism. In 1953, a scant eight years after World War II, that identification was still fresh and strong. Now, however, it was not Germany but the United States where Jews were being arrested, charged with treason, subjected to kangaroo courts, and ordered to be killed. To compound the grievance it was a Jewish judge who pronounced the sentence. Do you remember the upper-class Jews of the Fatherland who thought of themselves as Germans first? In so doing they disassociated themselves from their brethren and in the process betrayed them. *"Certainly, Hitler did not mean us!"*

Wasn't Kaufman like that, or worse, wasn't he just a puppet being used to mask an anti-Semitic movement that was about to sweep the country? My God, this was peacetime! When was the last time Americans (Americans with two small children to be orphaned) had been executed for treason when there was no war? Never. But it had happened in Germany in the 1930s under the Nazi campaign for racial purification, and in that case too the victims were of the Jewish faith.

Is it any wonder then that the words whispered in every Jewish community concerned the possibility of relocation camps, of Jews throughout the land being herded into boxcars and resettled in remote desert areas to be forgotten and left to die?

We look back now and scoff at the possibility of such an undertaking, but the precedent had been set with Japanese Americans in 1942 and, as the old saying goes, even paranoids have enemies.

In late June of 1953 my father called us all together and told us that at a moment's notice we should be prepared to run for our lives. Canada would be our destination. He was a man of the world and I was only a teenager. I had no reason not to believe him. I was seized by a sense of fatalism. The next shoe to drop would have my own bloody and dismembered limb attached to it. I waited throughout the summer and throughout the following year for the order to be given, for the federal government to sweep down upon us and drag us away to the accompaniment of railroad crossties clickity-clacking beneath our feet.

In the spring of 1954 I was cast in the lead role of the senior class play, Shaw's *The Devil's Disciple,* and voted co-captain of the high school track team. To the uninitiated lower graders I was presumed to be a big man on campus. In fact, I existed in a state of free-floating anxiety. This, in turn, led to a lot of stress. And that, in turn, probably helped lay the groundwork for the hippity-hop two-step my "bunny" nose would perform two facial-tic summers later.

I graduated June 10, 1954. I was glad to be out of high school. Now I wanted to get as far away from the Big Apple as I could. I still believed, as my father had taught me, that the purge of American Jews was inevitable and that it would begin in New York. You couldn't get much farther away from the skyscrapers than the heartland of America, and no deeper into the heartland than the cornfields of Iowa, and that is where my neurotic's tour of the universe took me next.

SIX

"Children of the Corn"

WHAT CAN YOU SAY ABOUT IOWA THAT HASN'T BEEN SAID A thousand times in song? "I-O-WA-HA HERE I COME, RIGHT BACK WHERE I STARTED FROM" . . . "KE-O-KOK, KE-O-KOK, THAT WONDERFUL TOWN, THAT WONDERFUL TOWN . . ." "I LOVE CEDAR RAPIDS IN THE SPRINGTIME WHEN IT DRIZZLES . . ." See what I mean? If ever a deep sea bass found itself flapjacking on the dunes of the Sahara it was me at Grinnell College, Grinnell, Iowa in the fall of 1954.

Grinnell was a small liberal arts school of nine hundred students. Its origin had Calvinist pretensions, and in the fifties a religious semi-conservative influence was still present.

The sixties and seventies would bring to the college a philosophical metamorphosis. As the Viet Nam war heated up the student body found its social and political voice. There was a committed protest movement. It was vociferous and militant. There were demonstrations. That made the local newspapers. Several women marched naked across the campus. That made *Time* magazine.

By the eighties Grinnell's political profile had plateaued somewhat, but at the same time the school had risen to unprecedented academic prominence. It was listed among the top ten undergraduate liberal arts colleges in the country. To this day it continues to achieve scholastic honors.

We all lived in "houses" at Grinnell which were very much like fraternities without the Latin. We even had Hell Week and Hell Night. I remember telling an upperclassman on Hell Night that I couldn't swallow raw eggs because it gave me asthma and if I started coughing it might unleash a dormant lung disease that could be highly contagious. (Well, I did say that the student body's intellectual apogee didn't occur until the eighties.)

I enrolled at Grinnell with the plan to focus on a premedical curriculum. My brother Norm was then in his third year of medical school on his way to becoming a topflight surgeon. We harbored the romantic notion that after the requisite postgraduate schooling I'd specialize in psychiatry and we would eventually open offices together. "You fix 'em, me unfixate 'em," something like that.

Why I thought that I would do better in college physical science courses than I had in high school is probably attributable to the hole in the ozone layer. I can only assume that my brain was being bombarded by massive quantities of ultraviolet rays.

Dr. Hans Wynberg taught both chemistry classes I took. I sensed that he liked me and so I immediately developed an incredible respect for him. The problem was that I was a woeful student. Within the state of Iowa I discovered the state of high anxiety. It existed just across the border into his classroom. The toll for entry on at least one occasion was an attack of hysterical blindness.

On this particularly fretful day I entered the room and discovered test questions written on the blackboard. My chair was toward the back and as I squinted to make out the words and formulas a most extraordinary phenomenon occurred. Some of the letters began doing a time step. Symbols which just moments before had appeared severe and sedentary were now "on toe," pirouetting across the slate. At first I thought I was hallucinating, but then I realized I was probably just losing my sight. I suddenly couldn't tell letters from numbers. It was as if a great wind had entered through the window and blown all the chalk scratches into little piles across the blackboard. It was totally indecipherable. I was told later what happened next. Evidently, I dropped to the floor and, so as not to obstruct my classmates' view, wiggled myself on elbows and knees to the front of the room like a marine cradling a rifle while avoiding overhead gunfire. I was still in a crouch position with my nose pressed to the blackboard when the giggles began. It was about then I once again became conscious of my surroundings. The good professor, an Austrian with a pronounced accent, accompanied me back to my seat. "You just zit here und relax. Everyzing vill be alright." How I yearned for him to yell at me. His pity was mortifying.

On a day a year later, while taking the second chemistry course, he called me into his office. My work in this class was significantly more inept than it had been in the previous one, and it was reflected in the shambling state of my emotions. "Valter, I zink you should leaf shcool. You are not yet ready for colletch." I was devastated. He was giving up on me! But the worst was yet to come: "You should join ze army. They vill giff you discipline, help you grow up, make a man out of you." Never was advice given more conscientiously but to poorer effect. If my psyche had been running on near-empty before, his counsel left me now trying to function on vapor trails. The army, for Christ sakes! Uniforms, cops, women being dragged out of apartment buildings!

Then there was the halfback on the football team who punched me in the jaw during a pickup game of basketball. His name was Sanders. I wish I could tell you that he was much bigger than me. He wasn't. But he was definitely tougher. We had gone up for a rebound on successive plays and each time I had given him a little hip. He retaliated with a sucker punch. I took one swing at him, missed, threw the ball at him, missed, called him a name, and walked away. *Walked away.* WALKED AWAY!

We gathered in front of the men's dining room that evening waiting for it to open. Sanders was there with his back to me. I had only to tap him on the shoulder and when he turned around put a fist in his mouth. I kept telling myself to do it. I didn't. There are events that stay with you forever. If they don't actually shape your life, they haunt it. I have told this story on a few occasions, probably as a catharsis, because it won't go away. Women raise their eyebrows: "What's the big deal?" Men know better.

In my first year at Grinnell I was cast as Orin in the Freshman Showcase production of *Mourning Becomes Electra* by Eugene O'Neill. The head of the theater department attended the dress rehearsal. When we finished he raced down the aisle and beckoned me to the apron. He had not seen me perform before. I crouched down and he just stared into my eyes. He was quite speechless. He shook his head slowly and whispered "wonderful" or some other adjective equally ennobling. He also murmured something about not wearing bright-colored socks on stage and then disappeared.

The good thing was that he was the highest authority figure yet to compliment my work. The bad thing was that all the restrained but profoundly felt emotion with which I vested the role was tapped not so much from my warehouse of psychic disorder but from emotional disarray directly attributable to feelings of insecurity about playing the part. The distinction is that once I became more comfortable performing the role I lost the neurotic edge that made it interesting. I did not have the technique or experience to draw from the more constant well of turbulent emotion that lived within me. I was okay as Orin but I never heard from the head of the theater department again.

I did ask the guys in my dorm to come see the show. None of them showed up. That which had brought me admiration among the sleek and sophisticated of the metropolis was obviously less than diverting to the future farmers of America.

The summer before and the summer after my freshman year at Grinnell I worked as a counselor at the University Settlement House camp located outside of Beacon, New York. University Settlement House, on the lower east side in New York City, was a place for kids to go after school. They had all the activities there that one would associate with an organization trying to enrich the lives of their charges while also keeping them off the street.

The upstate camp was more of the same. It catered to underprivileged children who could not otherwise afford two weeks in the country. Folk music was one of the staples of the camp program, no doubt due to the presence of legendary folk singer Pete Seeger. His father-in-law was in charge of the sprawling grounds of the camp and Pete owned a home (and still does) in Beacon. When each new batch of kids would arrive for their two weeks he would come over, guitar and banjo strapped to his shoulder, and sing songs with them around the campfire. Being a loner was more than just a neurotic disposition with me, it felt more like an act of God. But when Pete Seeger threw his head back and sang about "John Henry" and "Joe Hill" and "The Talking Atomic Blues" and we joined in I felt like I was part of something, like I belonged. Long before Scotty ever beamed us up I felt transported. Pete Seeger has remained the one genuine hero in my life. He sings about brotherhood, he sings about peace, he sings about the dignity of all living creatures and everything he sings about he lives. He is the quintessential man for all seasons. Would there were more like him. That the House Un-American Activities Committee came down on him, that the

Weavers, the group he performed with, was blacklisted, and that he was branded an "undesirable"—is one of the travesties of our time. For shame America.

Although I went through two years at Grinnell without having a single date, I did have identical physical relationships with two different girls during those two summers. In neither case was the relationship platonic, but neither did I lose my virginity. I didn't know what their prior experience had been but I wasn't about to push the issue. I was still deeply concerned about "immaculate ejaculation."

However, I do remember one early morn of particularly passionate groping. This might have been the one time I'd have chanced humiliation and foregone restraint, so enslaved was I by raging hormones. My conflict was monumental. Then, from the field beyond, I heard a chilling howl. We knew that a pack of wild marauding canines were slaughtering the camp sheep. My cabin was close to where they were penned. I was suddenly being offered a choice. I could either stay in the warmth of my lover's arms and attempt to consummate our relationship at last or I could race out into the breaking dawn and get chewed to death by dogs. I'm no fool!

Clad only in my underpants and armed with a broom I burst from the cabin, leapt the fence where the sheep were herded, and confronted the slavering pack. Hearing the tumult, campers and counselors alike tumbled from their beds and rushed to witness the heroic battle. However, almost before they got there the dogs scattered, leaving me alone with the sheep. I had saved them! Certainly I had a right to some well-deserved applause. I was not prepared for laughter. Apparently, my previous state of arousal had not abated. I had managed to protect the woolly bleaters while still very much "at attention." It definitely spoke to a lack of character on the crowd's part that they made a different interpretation. As far as they were concerned what I was trying to do with the sheep didn't look like rescue work.

⭐

Aside from doing the play I can't remember too much about my first year at Grinnell that I'd like to put in a scrapbook. On top of everything else I wanted to kill my first roommate. He had toy cars that he would roll over his bedsheets at two in the morning with the lights on. This was accompanied by various loud noises, along the lines of "toot-toot," "beep-beep," and "CRAAAASH." The angrier I got the more delight he took. The pièce de résistance was a little ambulance that he had half-tucked under his pillow. (He wanted me to know it was there, so he didn't conceal it entirely.) At the appropriate moment after he had caused an untold number of traffic accidents, he brought out the ambulance. The wailing siren noise which he supplied and which I'm sure was one of the few sounds he could make while simultaneously scratching his nose was loud enough to awaken all those he had just rendered comatose. It was then I would leap out of bed, my fists balled, and threaten to kill him. He would then turn out the lights and promptly fall asleep. This became a routine. He'd crash some cars, I'd leap from my bed, he'd sleep like a baby, and I'd be up half the night unable to calm the pounding in my temples.

My second roommate was a sophomore and definitely Mr. All-American Perfect. He was tall, handsome, bright, and socially adept. He was at the head of all his classes no matter what the subject and was adored by the ladies. He has gone on to become a successful doctor with a national reputation. I never met his wife but his daughter introduced herself to me at a Christmas party given by a former agent of mine a few years ago. It goes without saying that she was stunningly beautiful. His name was Jim Wolf. That's his real name; I feel compelled to disclose it now on behalf of all of us who have gone through life laughing bitter ironic tears at God's mismanagement of human gifts.

For all of you out there who feel genetically short-changed, take comfort in the following expose of Dr. Wolf. Jim Wolf spoke in his sleep—but like no one you have ever heard. The rest of us normal people, not afflicted by his egregious defect, never sounded like the unholy mix of Elmer Fudd and Alvin the Chipmunk. Inexplicably, the deep resonant tones of his conscious voice were transformed into a cartoon squeak that only someone with a dysfunctional larynx could emulate. It brought me great comfort to hear his bizarre nocturnal rambling. God existed, and he was just.

If it wasn't bad enough that I roomed with Jim Wolf in my freshman year, I made an unnerving discovery in my sophomore season that confirmed a persistent problem with self-image I had long suspected. (It shouldn't come as a surprise to the reader at this point.) I was shaving in the dormitory bathroom of South Yonkers Hall, where I lived. The mirror ran the length of the wall to accommodate the folks who might line up at the half dozen or so sinks. It was also quite wide, so if you stepped back a few feet you could get a reflection of most of your torso.

On this particular morning I was alone when Ken came in to comb his hair. Ken was kind of moody and quiet and we didn't exchange greetings. He was laboring to get his pompadour just right with a lot of stroking and patting. I stepped back from the sink while drying my face. As I pulled the towel away I noticed we were side by side staring into the mirror. When I tell you that this was all that happened you could well surmise that my life at Grinnell wasn't exactly rich in incident. Well, that too. In this case, however, what was going on in my head was far more significant than could be read from the external event. I knew immediately that the image of the short hairy guy in the mirror was me, but who was this other being? As incredible as it may sound, I had no memory, not in my twenty years of life, of ever before standing next to someone in front of a mirror who was half a foot taller than me. My first impression was an indelible one. We were of different species, and the one I belonged to was not too high on the food chain. "Just from comparing yourselves in the mirror?" you ask. Yup!

It wasn't long after that I could begin imagining the hump growing and the bells tolling and the texture of coarse rope roughening my palms. In case you doubt that such an unfortunate self-perception could inhabit one's mind, three years later I met a student named Paul at drama school who confided that he too felt like he was Quasimodo. The difference was that he was tall with chiseled good looks. If he was the storied hunchback of Notre Dame, who was I? Semi-Quasimodo?

Years later, I ran into Ken at an autograph session in Nashville, Tennessee in the winter of 1996. It speaks to the present state of my mental health that all I saw was a man with a warm smile and white hair.

In late May of 1956, two weeks before school let out, my father came to visit. We sat on his hotel bed talking about my future. Two very unusual and portentous things occurred. He fell asleep in the middle of a sentence *he* was speaking. I found that very strange. How tired he must be! Stranger still was the text of his incomplete thought. "Whether you decide on acting as an avocation or a vocation . . ." He awoke forgetting where he had left off and we went on to other things. I could have reminded him but I didn't want to spoil the moment. Maybe if he started over again he would say it differently and the impact would be lost. "*Whether you decide on acting as an avocation or a vocation . . .*" Those words came back to me again and again over the years, and each time brought me fresh resolve. No one had ever before expressed the possibility that I could actually become a professional actor. That it was my father who said it first was enormously significant. This was the man who had invested his greatest hopes in my brother's career. Who had said to me from earliest childhood, from the time I was three or four, to "be a man" each time I had collapsed in tears. And now this same man a moment before he drifted off gave voice to the idea that my becoming a performer was not a wholly preposterous concept.

I came back the next day to see him off at the train station. We went through a ritual that we had practiced before. He moved down the platform and I moved in the opposite direction. As if on cue we turned simultaneously and waved. We continued walking and then did it again. One last time as he prepared to board. I stood watching as the train moved out and remembered how he had fallen asleep so abruptly in his hotel room. I wondered as I did so often in the years following the 1946 heart attack whether this could be the last time I'd ever see him.

On June 11, 1956 Isadore Koenig complained to his wife of indigestion. He was dead of coronary occlusion before the ambulance arrived. It was less than three weeks after we had waved goodbye at the train station.

The funeral was held in Chicago, in the same cemetery where his mother and sister Jessie were buried. My mother and brother were there with me. As the casket was being lowered a rabbi droned on platitudinously about a man he had never met. Better Dad had been delivered to a pauper's grave than to be dispatched in such hypocrisy. I was enormously offended, but my brother, standing beside me, had begun to shake. Norm had always stood up to my father, matching temper for temper, and I feared that he might now be seized by remorse and guilt. I pictured him leaping on top of the descending coffin. I'd seen the fury of my brother's anger, but I had never seen him break down. I wasn't sure I could handle that, so I screamed out at the rabbi, *"You don't know what the hell you're talking about, you never knew my father!"* Norman was genuinely shocked by my behavior and tried to calm me. In the process, his shaking stopped. My plan to divert him had evidently worked. Or so I believed. Later he confided that he was shaking because he thought *I* was about to jump down into the grave with dad's body. I guess a disposition toward the theatrical runs in our family.

For the week preceding and following the funeral the three of us hunkered down in Norm's Chicago apartment. We hadn't been thrown together in such tight quarters and for such an extended period of time since my brother first went off to college eight years before. I wish I could tell you that we shared our grief and found a deeper love for each other. Actually, my mother and brother fought constantly. It was a battle zone with no hope for a ceasefire. They awoke in anger, my mother complaining about impending impoverishment and my brother retaliating with curses that painted her as being venal and mercenary. I do believe they were both struggling with the demons that are the final revenge of the dead.

My mother, Sarah Strauss Koenig, lived thirty years with a man she didn't love, and now he had abandoned her. It was as if he had done it purposely. There were no liquid assets, and she was terrified that we would all starve. Hysteria ruled her life, but it was acrimony that kept her heart pumping. If she hadn't been able to hate my father for the lost years and the destitute state in which he had left us she might have surrendered to her fear and joined him.

My parents had always fought, always. Back in 1936 when Sarah discovered that she was again pregnant she took a flyer off the highboy in their Chicago apartment hoping to miscarry. She didn't want to bring another child into the world when she was convinced that she and my dad wouldn't stay together. When it didn't work she tried again. She kept telling herself that she only wanted to see if she could touch the ceiling. The second time she crashed to the floor she twisted her ankle. Sarah took it as a sign that that child, me, was meant to be born, and she remained earthbound thereafter. I only learned this from her when I was nearing forty. Curiously, I never doubted my mother's love.

The older my father got the angrier he became. Where was the Daddy who told me Russian fairy tales about Mishka the Mouse and Meeska the Bear back in 1939 when I was three? Where was the man who spoke so passionately about the labor movement and brotherhood and the equality of the races back in 1946 when I was ten? Where was he in 1956 when I was turning twenty? He was dead, long dead. A life of disenchantment, of disillusionment had taken its toll. Communism wasn't working but neither had capitalism. He had lost a lot of money on buildings he had invested in. He had become cynical and irascible and intolerant. He intimidated my mother and probably felt contempt for her. He intimidated me and then demanded I "be a man." But he couldn't intimidate my brother.

Norman stood toe to toe with Isadore again and again. On the one hand, Dad undoubtedly respected my brother for his courage but on the other, the challenge he presented was a crushing blow. In a world that would not bend to his will, neither philosophically, politically, or economically, he had still to contend with a son he could not control. My brother knew this, knew that his defiance further damaged Father's spirit. He also knew that, no matter the consequences, his own survival depended on holding his ground.

And so Norm spent those days with my mother and I at war with the guilt he felt. So angry was he, so conflicted, that he lashed out at her and she lashed out at him and the battle was engaged and fought with a fury reserved only for those whose wounds leak the same blood.

And where was I through all of this? On the sidelines trying to make some sense out of what I was feeling. Or, more accurately, what I wasn't feeling. Surely I should feel something about the man who had placed me in the middle between him and his wife and between him and his oldest son.

My mother, again and again in a torrent of tears, had told me that if it wasn't for me they would have gotten divorced long ago. My father, again and again in a storm of anger, had told me that if it wasn't for me they would have gotten divorced long ago. My father had told me time after time that he was washing his hands of my brother. My brother had told me time after time that he hated my father and wished he would leave and never come back.

Because I never learned how to just walk away from it my role was always to defend my mother, mediate for my brother, and carry the burden of our family discord. What did I feel about all this now? I felt nothing. Where was my own anger, my resentment for forever being the one that it all got dumped on? Shouldn't I be hating my father for that? I felt nothing. What about the tears? Where was that devastating emptiness that had played out in my head from the time of his first heart attack in 1946? What about the fear of loss which had threatened to consume me in 1949 when he disappeared for three months? Shouldn't I at least be experiencing those things? I felt nothing.

I kept waiting for it to hit. It never did. At the time it was very confusing. Was I so shallow a person? Did I not have emotions that ran deeply? Yes, he was tough, impatient, and intimidating, but this was the same man who had sent me to a private school and to a psychiatrist when he couldn't afford it so that I might be a happier person. I knew that he loved me in his own peculiar way, and may even have had some modest sense of pride in my acting talent. So if there wasn't anger and resentment where, at least, was my sadness, my remorse, some small articulation of any kind of feeling to mark this family tragedy?

It was only years later that I understood. It was like the stage actor who had played the same part too long; words had lost their meaning and emotions were irretrievable. I had begun preparing myself for this moment in 1946, when Dad's health became a constant conscious anxiety and his death a self-perpetuating nightmare terror. But now it had all worked out. The timing, that is. He was dead and there was nothing left to feel. The other shoe had finally dropped as I always knew it would—right on my head, but I was forewarned and numbed to the impact. The ten-year-old child had made it possible for the young adult of twenty to escape the pain.

After we buried Dad my brother, having just completed medical school, took off for Los Angeles to begin his internship at a veterans hospital. My mother went back to New York and the arduous task of selling off my father's estate. I traveled to New England to be an apprentice in summer stock.

"You hoo, has anyone seen the bunny nose fellow?" Freud would be the first to tell you that you don't obliterate emotion, you just repress it, and that sooner or later it's going to manifest itself in some other form. In addition to my luggage I brought with me to the Dorset Playhouse in Vermont a brand new tic. It wasn't a thing of beauty, but it was all my own. I had developed a nose twitch. It wasn't a cute little *Bewitched* crinkle. Under stress my snifter leapt about my face, twisting and turning as if trying to wrench itself from its mooring. You think I'm exaggerating? My one attempt at necking with a girl that summer ended disastrously because of it. Believe it or not, her nickname was "Wally." We were sitting in the company truck one evening in a secluded area and I was leaning over to kiss her. She suddenly pushed back and flattened herself against the passenger door. My first reaction was that she had looked over my shoulder and seen the three-fingered maniac who stalks the woods with a meat ax or the slime-dripping alien from another planet with the hypno raygun. I mean, wasn't that the reason those passionate scenes of teenagers in parked cars always ended abruptly in the movies? Maybe, but not this time. She had caught a glimpse of my dancing proboscis just before our lips contacted. At first it startled her, and then it made her giggle. By the time we returned to our quarters her laughter was in full throat.

The roles that I played that summer were minuscule. Perhaps they befitted an apprentice, but still it was not what I had been led to believe would happen. On the other hand, maybe I should have been grateful for the anonymity. The one part I did have of any size was in the play

Susan and God. For this performance I was rewarded with my first professional review: "Walter Koenig in the role of Hutchinson Stubbs left much to be desired."

I had decided before the end of my sophomore year that I wasn't going to return to Grinnell, and now with my father gone and my brother ensconced in Los Angeles I began looking westward. During the summer I applied for a transfer to UCLA and was accepted. UCLA is a state school, and in 1956 the tuition for out-of-state students was one hundred and fifty dollars a semester.

My mother was left behind in New York to turn elevators, a hundred gross of sunglasses, and two office buildings into cash. We all thought she'd be joining us in a couple of months. It took a lot longer than that. For fifteen months, this lifelong sheltered woman, emotionally abused housewife, and doting mother became a tigress.

She entered the battlefield against Dad's enemies and, on far more treacherous ground, took on his "friends." My father believed that no one he knew was "any damned good." After the siege my mother was inclined to agree. Everyone Isadore had business dealings with at the time of his death tried to take advantage of the widow. There were people who had borrowed money from my father and not repaid him. There were those who had received goods and had outstanding bills. There was rent due on the offices in his buildings. There were bankers who wanted to foreclose on his loans. None of these people were ever in for her calls. So she'd rise at five in the morning and travel by subway back and forth across the five boroughs banging on doors, pleading, threatening, cajoling, demanding an audience. They all ended up stealing from her, but it could have been worse. When she was done we were no longer facing destitution. It was an extraordinary act of heroism for a woman whose business skills had heretofore been limited to finding the bargains at the supermarket. I know she took some satisfaction in seeing it through, but I also know she never forgave us for letting her go it alone.

SEVEN

"California Split"

I ARRIVED AT MY LIVING QUARTERS IN LOS ANGELES AT 4:30 IN THE afternoon on September 11, 1956. The date has significance and will be explained shortly. Since the settlement of my father's business holdings was well over a year away I moved in with my brother to save money. His internship was at the Sawtelle Veterans Hospital in Westwood. Interns then as now were paid next to nothing, and the hospital compensated by providing living arrangements for the unmarried men among them. I stayed in my brother's room for about a month and then, when another room became vacant, I moved in there.

The building was a single-story bungalow with about twenty rooms facing each other on opposite sides of a long corridor. There was also a kitchen stocked by the facility with breakfast food, and my brother provided me with a fake pass so that I could have free dinners with the interns at the sister institution up the street. This was the Brentwood Hospital for the Insane. It was an altogether charming experience to go over there by myself as I frequently did and come face to face with someone who had just come from electroshock treatments and/or had recently gouged out the passage between his nostrils.

UCLA was considerably different from Grinnell. It had a huge sprawling campus with more than twenty thousand students. If one so chose it was possible to manage a college career at UCLA in total anonymity. I definitely took advantage of the opportunity. In the two years I was there I made one lasting student friendship. Larry was married and already had the first of five kids. On an occasional weekend I'd go to his place in Inglewood and play tennis with him on a local public court. Once in awhile I'd even stay over. It speaks to a rather cloistered existence in general that he was the first African-American I had ever known. I'm pleased to say that we still maintain contact.

I met Larry in one of the many psychology courses I had signed up for. I had changed my major from premed to psychology with welcome results. My grades improved dramatically, and on that score my stay at the university was considerably more relaxed than it had been at Grinnell.

There were still banshees in the belfry, however. Lack of confidence continued to be a problem. As it had been at Grinnell, I could not bring myself to face rejection from the opposite sex and so I never dated. Worse than even that was my inability to shake the one-punch episode I had had with Sanders, the Grinnell football player. It gnawed at my synapses, causing defects in the neurological chain. I became studiously indifferent to grooming. I shaved infrequently, let my hair grow unfashionably long (we're talking mid-1950s here) and wore clothes that I had owned since my freshman year in high school. I particularly remember one pair of very baggy gold-colored pants badly faded with unraveled cuffs. Sadly, the object in all of this was to incite ridicule. It was a classic case of passive-aggressive behavior. I kept waiting for people to make fun of my appearance so I could challenge them to a fight. If I could just hit one guy I could get back at Sanders, I could restore some sense of dignity, I could be the man my father had always admonished me to be. Fortunately, no one ever took me up on it.

Insight does not necessarily bring maturity. The Grinnell incident is like a malaria that goes into dormancy only to erupt anew every few years. My latest attack was in the eighties, when I went around grabbing by their shirt fronts people who talked in movie theaters.

In the spring of 1957 I signed up for the class that ultimately set me on the road my life has taken. I had had one acting course at Grinnell and received a "C" grade. My instructor's complaint was that I had never engaged with other class members and performed only monologues. I couldn't very well tell him that I was too insecure to ask other students to partner with me. But now at UCLA I decided to try again. My curriculum was heavy in social sciences, and I decided I could use a little diversion. Acting 101 was taught by Ralph Freud and Arthur B. Friedman. My final project was the lead character of the Young Man in the one-act play *Hello Out There* by William Saroyan. Professor Friedman directed it. I remember working myself into a near-panic before the performance and asking him If I could have a prompter backstage since I was sure I'd forget my lines. He told me he'd give me a failing grade if he had to provide one. Strangely, that had a beneficent effect on me. It was like a vote of confidence. He wasn't going to accept the limitations I had placed on myself.

Although I didn't take any other theater courses, I hung around the department auditioning for various student television and film projects. I got to know Professor Friedman better. I met his wife and children. The kids were two, four, six, and eight at the time. Forty years later they are forty-two, forty-four, forty-six, and forty-eight. We have maintained a life long friendship.

In the spring of 1958, as graduation approached, I voiced my concerns to him about the wisdom of pursuing a masters degree in psychology. By then psychology had become the field I disliked least. It was not a hearty recommendation for a career. Arthur was the West Coast representative of the New York-based Neighborhood Playhouse, School of the Theatre. He offered to write them on my behalf, enthusiastically endorsing my talent. He felt I could have some success in the film industry. I hesitated. Rock Hudson sort of personified for me what a movie actor is supposed to look like, and he sure as hell didn't have a hump on *his* back. "What do you have to lose?" Arthur asked. I hesitated some more, and then the words my father had spoken to me on his last trip to Grinnell echoed in my head.

Considerably before that decision had to be made there were other concerns to deal with. Despite an impoverished social life things were running smoothly on other fronts. Or so I thought. It was early April 1957. I had been living rent-free at the Interns Quarters for nearly eight months through the generosity of the Veterans Administration. As you will recall, breakfast and dinner were also being supplied by the federal government by virtue of the communal kitchen we shared and the sumptuous repast provided by the Brentwood Hospital for the Really, Really Nuts.

There had been one uncomfortable moment at Brentwood, but I did not think at the time that it would have repercussions. My brother had been taking delight in introducing me as a visiting brain surgeon from Vienna to senior colleagues who would sit down to dinner with us. He would explain that I was a prodigy who had won the highest honors Austria could bestow including the cherished Cronkite Medal. The word *cronkite* is Yiddish for "sickness." He was really stretching the envelope a little there, but it took me just one ill-advised moment to absolutely shred it.

The escape hatch he always left me was that although I was conversant in several tongues I had not yet conquered English. I did a lot of broad smiling and vigorous nodding exactly as I had seen Japanese visitors do in the movies when they didn't want their hosts to know that they weren't following the conversation. I don't know how prodigal I looked at such times but the pantomime seemed reasonably effective. Until I got cocky.

On this occasion the hospital supervisor joined our dinner party. Norman went through his usual spiel but this time I wouldn't be content with moronic head-bobbing. There were at least six of us at the table, an ample enough audience to spur me toward a more ambitious performance. In halting English, with many doubletalking German utterances of frustration under my breath, I groped majestically for words that approximated those of my native language. It was a beautiful thing to watch—for me. For them it was excruciating. I was turning a five-word sentence into a ten-minute soliloquy. It was like being in a room with someone who has an uncontrollable stutter. There is a desperate impulse to help them out. And so it was here. Everyone jumped in guessing what it was I was trying to say. They shouted out words as if it were a game of charades. I kept smiling sadly and shaking my head. My brother thought it was hilarious, but for the doctors present it was frustration mounting toward exasperation, mounting toward the urge to kill. I choose to think of it as the ultimate revenge for someone who sucked at science courses and could never have gotten into medical school.

Because I was eating my dinner meals at the hospital on a phony pass we couldn't admit to the supervisor that it was all a gag. As the Bard once said in a prescient moment (probably with this very situation in mind), "The evil that men do lives after them." Not more than a week later I was again eating dinner at the hospital. I was alone this time when the hospital supervisor, this time with knitted brow and a look of concern, sat down next to me. It had been a kick before, faking being a foreigner. I had been performing, and my brother was a very appreciative audience. But now I felt ridiculous. It was just this guy and me and, one on one, I had no idea how I was supposed to escape detection. I actually thought about throwing up. At least it would give me an excuse to get the hell out of there. But lo, he whipped out a pocket-sized English-German dictionary and started flipping pages. He wanted to communicate with me, he wanted to make me feel welcome! His sincerity was so heartfelt that I felt hopelessly guilt-ridden. It was as if he was offering me home-baked cookies and I had just come from murdering his children.

He kept finding words in German to say to me. Words which I assumed were meant to be greetings. All I could think to do was repeat them back with an occasional "yah, yah," "zer gut!," "ach du leber," and anything else I could remember from World War II movies. When the German words he recited got longer and I began butchering them I knew the jig was up. He didn't say anything. Just put the book away and stared at me. I made a point of checking my watch, pointing to it and then with several frantic little bows departing. I knew I had been found out and that I wouldn't be eating dinner at the hospital anymore, but I did think that was the end of it.

In fact, I still felt my luck was holding after a peculiar encounter with a couple of cops. My brother had appropriated my father's old Lincoln and driven it cross country to Los Angeles. It rattled some but we managed to get around in it. I had been studying all day for a test and was still in my unshaved, disreputably attired mode when I was hit by a craving for something sweet to eat. Norm was working across the street from the Interns Quarters and didn't need the car. I climbed in and drove it a couple of blocks to a drugstore. When I re-emerged two police officers were standing on the sidewalk, their patrol car blocking the Lincoln. I had evidently committed three infractions: I had parked in the red, I was driving with expired license plates, and I had no driver's license of my own. On top of that, disheveled as I was and with my mouth full of candy bar, I probably looked as if I was coming off a drug high. And on top of that, when they asked me to open the glove compartment a three-pound steel-gray Marine jacknife fell out. It was a war memento given to my father which my brother had rescued and brought along from New York. I had known it was there, I had just forgotten about it. "What do you do, pry off hubcaps with this?" one of them asked. I cannot account for their next reaction unless it had to do with a justifiable sense of revulsion. I couldn't speak, but my legs were shaking with an intensity that would shame a jackhammer while, appropriately, the food was flying from my mouth and scattering with the blast force of exploding cement. I won't say they actually took cover but they did let me go. I mean they just let me go! No cuffs, no ticket, no nothing.

I returned to the Interns Quarters and started up the steps, feeling that every misgiving I ever had about my life was totally unfounded. For one thing, I wasn't seven years old and this wasn't Payson Avenue, Toto. The guys in the police uniforms didn't drag me away as they had that woman. *They had let me go!* The world was not as I had perceived it, and I was just too cool to be believed!

I was about to enter the building when a green car that I recognized as a security vehicle pulled up below me. These cars were used to patrol the Veteran Administration grounds and protect them from shaggy-haired interlopers. The driver came quickly out of the car and demanded to know what I was doing there. He also wore a uniform, a green one, and had a sidearm strapped to his waist. Having just backed down two of Los Angeles' finest in a tense standoff reminiscent of the O.K. Corral, I was not about to let this guy intimidate me. "I'M A DOCTOR, FOR GOD'S SAKE, AND I'M IN A HURRY!" I even permitted myself an attitude of bombastic impatience. Hell, I had only to spit up food to get real police officers scurrying, so surely a demonstration of authority as forceful as this would thoroughly cow this cop wannabe.

"May I see your identification, doctor?" I came back down the steps madly trying to think of a rejoinder that would assuage his suspicions. I was not totally without wit, after all. And hadn't I already been served once this day by my street savvy-deeply ingrained-outlaw streak? Certainly there was some verbal maneuver I could nimbly apply to rescue me from this situation.

"I didn't say I was a doctor. I said I was a doctor's brother." This was truly the most preposterous thing I could have uttered, and I said it unblinkingly, as if by staring at him I could erase from his mind my previous statement. He didn't blink either, and then I realized what he was thinking. He thought I was an escapee from the Brentwood Home for the Badly Disconnected. I showed him what identification I had and explained who my brother was and he finally let me go. As with the hospital supervisor I was enormously embarrassed by being caught in a lie but, again, I thought that the damage to my credibility was localized and there would be no subsequent fallout.

To set the stage for what happened next I must tell you a little about the living arrangements at the Interns Quarters. There weren't any female interns living there, but that isn't to say there weren't any females. They could have filmed a steamy soap opera there, maybe

Young Doctors in Heat. It seemed like the only beings not engaged in sex around the clock was the vampire bat which had found a home in the rafters and me. Such moaning, such groaning, such bumping in the night—and late afternoon—and in the morning with coffee and bagels.

I think the walls were made out of poorly laminated cardboard, because every sound filtered through. I could hear heavy breathing three doors down and the squeal of bedsprings at the opposite end of the building. The worst thing of all was that many of these women were absolutely gorgeous. A young doctor, even a poor-just-starting-out young doctor who is not incredibly attractive, has an advantage with young ladies looking for a secure future. At least so I am led to believe.

In any case, the sexual cacophony put me in a state of constant agitation. It was self-inflicted torture to wander up and down the hall during such episodes, but I couldn't stop myself. It got so that I could time when the quintessential ecstatic moment would occur behind each door. And so I scheduled my little strolls to return to Door Four in ten minutes and Door Six in twelve and Door Three in five. Was my behavior perverted? Maybe, if you accept a loose definition. Was it perverse? Absolutely. When I finally returned to my room it was just to increase the size of the welt on the back of my head where I banged it against the wall.

The Ides of March had passed without incident, but I still had to face the showers of April. In this case it was the equivalent of an uprooting storm and began with thunderous pounding on my door one morning. The sound awakened me, and I staggered from bed totally disoriented. I thought I might still be at Grinnell since, aside from my brother, I never had people visit at my L.A. digs. It must have been a classic case of denial because even after turning the handle and revealing the three giants standing on the threshold my focus went to the bloodsucking bat flying up and down the hall behind them. Why wasn't it asleep, I wondered, surely the dawn had broken? Perhaps it was in distress, a faulty sonar system, I worried, never before caring whether it lived or died. Maybe . . .

"Walter Marvin Koenig?" There was no way I could continue to avoid the reality of the hulking forms blocking my doorway. Of the three men the tallest was six-foot-six. The shortest was also six-foot-six. I knew immediately (God forgive me) there was trouble afoot.

Two of them wore those green security uniforms I mentioned before and the third, and I'll swear to this, was in a trenchcoat and brown shoes. He never spoke, but he was the one who stepped forward, reached into his pocket, and produced identification. If I had a moment to think about it I would have known what was written there without looking. As it was I was not surprised by what I now read. I hate to bore you with this "shoe dropping" stuff again but wasn't it inevitable, a fait accompli, what comes around goes around? I should never have substituted *The Daily Worker* for *The New York Times* on that fateful day in 1949 and brought it home to my father. The words "Federal Bureau of Investigation" leapt out at me and attached themselves to my eyeballs with grappling hooks.

I was told I would have to come with them. That was the last of the conversation we would have. They wouldn't leave while I dressed, fearing, I supposed, that some "evil empire" buddies of mine from Russia were waiting outside ready to blow a hole through the window-less, laminated cardboard walls and help me escape.

And so we drove in silence out of the grounds and for a stretch of fifteen minutes or so through an area with which I was unfamiliar. I sat in the back between the FBI guy and one of the security cops. I kept asking what I had done, but between the one guy counting the telephone poles through the side window and the other fixating on the driver's right ear neither ever answered me.

We arrived at a nondescript brick building and climbed the stairs to a second floor office with the words "Chief of Detectives" stenciled on the frosted glass pane in the wood-framed door. The FBI guy escorted me inside. The two security cops were posted outside guarding the entrance. They looked uncomfortable. It isn't easy being green.

The middle-aged man in the drab suit sitting in the chair didn't rise, didn't smooth his tie, didn't look at me. He seemed intent on an imaginary fissure in the distressed pine of his desktop. His long thumbnail traced a path that arced slightly before doubling back to the departure point. Even after the interrogation began he kept repeating the action. I found myself staring at the motion because he seemed so totally absorbed by it. Was this a sly method of putting me off my guard? Was he cunningly trying to hypnotize me? It was a good thing *The Manchurian Candidate* had not yet been made. My imagination, in unrestrained free fall by now, would surely have found a place for all the film's sinister convolutions in the scenario it was writing.

"How long have you been living at your present residence, Mr. Koenig?"

"A couple of weeks," I said confidently, knowing better than to make my final offer on the first round of negotiations.

"Is that so?"

"Well . . . actually, a little longer than that." God, this guy was tough. His browbeating was getting to me.

"How much longer than that was that?"

What could I do in the face of such penetrating questions? I tried one last time to lie my way out. "Well, I started coming around after the first of the year. Mostly because it was quiet and because I could study for exams for my classes at UCLA where I'm doing very well. My brother is a doctor here, you know. But I didn't actually begin living here until . . ."

He stopped tracing. He reached for a folder and opened it up.

"According to our information you moved into the Interns Quarters at 4:30 in the afternoon on September eleventh, 1956."

"Use your words," we admonish children who resort to hitting. But what if there are no words? What if a desert-dry pallet has caused the words to shrivel and powder like the Oklahoma crops in the wake of the drought and dust storms of *The Grapes of Wrath?*

I couldn't believe it. They had a dossier on me! The FBI guy standing against the wall shifted his feet. There was no other sound in the room. If it had been left to me the place might well have been converted to a monastery with a sacred vow of silence. I couldn't imagine how I'd ever find the wherewithal to speak again. As it turned out I had only begun to be stunned.

"Mr. Koenig, we have reason to believe you have been procuring women for the interns."

So much for the insidious, subversive influence of the Red Menace in our household. For that offense I had never been accosted by the Federal Bureau of Investigation. But for being the mastermind behind a prostitution ring I was now getting the third degree. Wally "the Pimp" Koenig! When I could finally utter a sound what brilliant retort had I to this defamation? What Clarence Darrowesque rebuttal could I now call upon?

"Aw geez, I don't even have a girlfriend." Sad to say, that is exactly what I said. It was truly me at my most pathetic. The FBI guy in the corner coughed. The Chief of Detectives began staring intently at his desk again. This time his hands were quiet but his face was twitching. He was definitely trying to keep from laughing. They, of course, let me go. I was too ridiculous to be taken seriously as a felon.

Whoever had turned me in—the hospital supervisor, the federal officer who had demanded my identification, or some deep-throat stoolie among the interns with a deep-throat girlfriend who didn't like me listening at his door—I will never know.

I was told to write a letter addressed to the Chief of Detectives detailing my occupancy at the housing facility and to pack up and leave the next day. The letter was written and sent immediately but for whatever capricious element of personality I possess I decided to test the waters one more time. I stayed on at the Interns Quarters until June, two months later. There were no more visits from the authorities, but I did, nonetheless, stop roaming the halls.

I returned from summer vacation and moved in with a "rat psychologist" graduate student whose name I found on a bulletin board at UCLA. "Rat Psychology" was the unflattering moniker applied to those who delighted in running starving rodents through labyrinthine mazes in the hope that their angst-ridden brains would learn behind which door the food pellet lay.

Maury was born to the cloth. In fact, there were times when I wondered whether he was not including me in his experiments. Without a doubt he had the most hideous physical habit to which I had ever been witness. We would both be studying in the living room and he would not yet have underlined the first page in his text when his hand would reach to his nose and he would begin twisting it. What's the big deal, you ask? Turn the other nose, you say. After all, didn't I also have a tic involving my snifter? Yes, but I didn't twist and twist and twist until it popped and made a cracking sound like the leg of a table snapping—and then do it again. This would go on for hours. Pop, snap, crack! Pop, snap, crack! (It never reminded me of a breakfast cereal.) He wouldn't look up, but I was half convinced he was drawing graphs in the margin of his book measuring the relationship between the intensity of his nose noises and the collapse of my nervous system. You might describe this as rampant paranoia on my part, but then you didn't know Maury. I would finally scream at him as I did the Grinnell roommate who played with his toy cars on the bedsheets. Without a word and with only the briefest of shrugs he would retire to the bedroom to resume his studying. And he would close the door. And I could still hear his nose cracking!

As I have described ad nauseam, I didn't have a single date at either of the two colleges I attended. Understandably, I spent a lot of time reading. This was generally a pleasant distraction until I picked up a novel titled *The Well of Loneliness* by Radclyffe Hall. The book was about female homosexuality and had made quite a stir. I chose it out of curiosity and almost immediately became morbidly engrossed.

In the 1950s the teaching of psychology courses was not permitted in most high schools. In fact, even on the college level such classes were off limits to freshmen. The thinking was that young people, being unsophisticated and untrained and very impressionable, might identify with the aberrational cases that came out of textbooks. I think this ruling had been made with me in mind. To this day when I read about some fruitcake discovered rotating a billiard ball in his behind while caressing a patent-leather shoe or found burning tana leaves in religious devotion to his own small intestine I think, my God, with just a little more stress in my life that could be me!

Little wonder then that a young man who had been so long deprived of the company of the opposite sex, and had come to feel more and more alienated because of it, would find kinship with others who also felt isolated from mainstream society. Unfortunately, the people I was reading about were all gay, and, even though it was female homosexuality, it became my frame of reference. They were lonely, misunderstood, and unhappy, and so was I. From there it was one very petite step to questioning my own sexual preferences.

You have to understand that in the 1950s the majority of men in this country who were not homosexual were homophobic. It was the old-as-time-itself axiom that that which is not understood is to be feared. And that truism's logical extension becomes that which is to be feared is to be hated. And so you have "faggots" and "queers" and, on the broader plain, "kikes," "niggers," "gooks," "spics," et al.

Now, I always considered myself a liberal who took a balanced view of people who were different than I. I did not make generalizations regarding ethnicity, race, or religion. But the fact remains that after reading two-thirds of *The Well of Loneliness* I was incredibly depressed and fearful. We did not know as convincingly then as we do now about sexual predisposition. The sense was that homosexuality was not genetically imprinted like blue eyes or, for that matter, heterosexuality, but environmentally induced. This meant, figuratively speaking, that you couldn't necessarily stay in the same room with a gay person without possibly "catching" it. I don't think any rational person thought homosexuality possessed the features of an airborne virus, but since Bruce had it and he wasn't born with it maybe I could get it too. Of course, this thinking worked overtime when you already had ruptured capillaries in your psyche leaking self-confidence over your penny loafers. Under such circumstances sexual identity becomes one more thing to be unsure of.

And so, after getting two-thirds of the way through the book and deciding that everything in it related to me and was, therefore, extremely threatening, I became obsessed with getting rid of it. The word "obsessed" in this context is not extravagant. It was a mark of my ignorance and neuroses that I felt contaminated by the existence of this book in my room. My fears bordered on superstition, and playing into them, I decided on a ritual burial. It wasn't a very complicated ritual. I waited for night to descend and for Maury to go to sleep. I had the book in a box my mother had sent me that I sealed with scotch tape at every seam. When I was assured that Maury was gamboling among his mazes I crept down to one of the communal trashcans posted at the sidewalk for the morning's garbage pickup. Then, leaning fully half my body inside, I buried the offending tome as deeply as I could under three feet of pork fat, eye of newt, and rotting melon.

I'm not totally whacko. I was completely aware that my behavior was compulsive and consequently ridiculous and, in fact, the messy deed done I was even able to laugh at it. But then he who laughs at midnight does not necessarily laugh last. When I arrived home the next day the still-sealed box was sitting in the middle of my bed. Five years later I saw the *Twilight Zone* episode about "Talking Tina," the malevolent doll who returns from being stashed in the garbage to kill Telly Savalas. I watched it with an eerie feeling of déjà vu. Were these two events not incredibly similar? I was hit by a flash of insight. Think about it. That sense of command, that no-nonsense demeanor, that physical aggressiveness. Yes, I do believe it.—"Talking Tina" was definitely butch.

I chalk it up to rat-maze madness that Maury chose to put the stinking package precisely where I tuck the bedcovers under my chin. It had been propped against the door when he arrived home earlier. We finally decided that the sanitation guy, seeing a sealed box with my name and address on it, assumed it had been tossed by mistake and tried to return it to me.

Any fear I had that the book's reappearance was an omen concerning the course of my future sexuality was dismissed out of hand. Hogwash! All the same, this time I burned the bloody thing page by page.

One of the great disadvantages of being poor in Los Angeles is not having a car. Since I was no longer living at the Interns Quarters and, therefore, seeing far less of my brother, the Lincoln was not available to me. Buses were the only affordable means of public transportation and they did not always run on time. Since I now had part-time jobs—washing test tubes and beakers in the chem lab and bellhopping at the Beverly Comstock Hotel—my hours were irregular. I sometimes had to make the trip home late at night. On many such occasions I exercised my thumb. I discovered quickly enough that an altruistic bent may not be the motivation behind someone offering a ride. Rather than detail a considerable number of quirky encounters I will offer up only two. In each case there was the potential for jeopardy and, characteristically, I misjudged in which one the real threat lay.

It was a dark and stormy night. (What else?) I was drenched, cold, and marooned on a deserted street corner. My only comfort was a bag of onion bagels. A sallow moon hung in the sky drained and lifeless. There was something ominous about it. Weren't back-alley executions performed in the shadows provided by such bleak illumination? A beat-up Pontiac with one headlight and a dragging tailpipe careened to a halt next to me. The rain was heavy, the moon limp and pale. It was neither a poetic inspiration nor a source of light. I couldn't see inside the car. Nothing stirred. Puddles like poodles lapped at my ankles. The rear door slowly swung open. There were four black guys inside. Two in the front and . . . well, you can guess the rest. They wore similar windbreakers. The lettering read "Death Merchants" or "Killers at Large" or "St. Augustine's Baptist Church," something like that. My eyes had gone out of focus so it was hard to tell.

No one spoke. One of the guys in the back got out so I could sit in the middle. He wasn't happy about getting soaked. I had a moment to decide. If I made a run for it they probably wouldn't chase me in the rain. On the other hand, I tried not to judge people by the scowls of hate on their faces and I didn't want to be judged as just another "whitey" with predetermined prejudices. I got in. We drove in absolute silence. It dawned on me after about five minutes that no one had asked where I lived. It was then I remembered the bagels.

My brother had come home one night when he was sixteen and regaled us with a story about a World War II veteran who had just held him up with a German Luger. The man was down on his luck and desperate. Norm gently offered him the bag of sesame seed rolls he was carrying. The poor guy, ashamed of his behavior and grateful for my brother's sympathetic gesture, broke down and cried. He left without accepting Norm's generosity.

"Anyone want a bagel?" I ventured. No one spoke. I now knew the silence of the last mile, of dead men walking. Wally "the Shmuck" Koenig was going to his execution. The lettering on the jackets was definitely "Merchants of Death." And then the driver's hand reached behind him. The bag was passed front to back clockwise. There was still one left when it was returned to me. We sat there munching quietly for some minutes. I was overjoyed. "The Sharing of the Bagels"! It could be a ceremony that brought the races together. I was thinking about breaking into "Hava Nagela" and coaxing them to join in. I saw my street coming up and without foreboding pointed it out.

They left me off in front of my apartment house. Only after the door closed did I realize that not one word had passed their lips. Now that I look back at it I'm pretty sure the lettering on their jackets said "Four-H Club".

The other hitchhiking experience began benignly. The guy who gave me a lift was probably only a few years older than myself. I was going through a very lonely patch and found myself responsive to his animated conversation. He explained to me that he was a stage hypnotist and performed at a lot of the university fraternity houses. Before long I learned that his assistant had quit and he needed someone to take his place. I told him that I was quite sure that I myself couldn't be hypnotized, so I wouldn't be a good candidate. It was about 9:30 at night when we pulled up in front of my place. I was about to get out when he suggested that he try to put me under, just for grins. You have to understand that it was too early to go to bed and the other prospect, Maury and his nose, could only be deemed a penance. So, what the hell, I leaned back against the seat and closed my eyes. He started telling me that I was getting sleepy etc., etc., etc., and, of course, nothing was happening. I should have said something then but I was figuring it might be a kick to see how far I could take this without him catching on.

"There is a magic carpet in your room and it will take you anywhere you want to go. Climb on the magic carpet."

"Yes . . ." It was all I could do to resist adding "master."

"The carpet is taking you over oceans to foreign lands. Do you feel the wind in your hair?"

"Good . . . wind . . . good." I know, I know, but I don't think the dialogue of a hypnotized person is supposed to be scintillating. I was going here for standard Frankenstein monster repartee.

"Now you're over India and before you is the Taj Mahal . . ."

And then I realized he was leaning toward me with his hand

around my shoulder. This is, of course, when I should have definitely stopped the game, but now I was becoming embarrassed. I didn't want him to think I was making fun of him. This was his livelihood, after all.

"You can see inside and there is a beautiful naked woman lying on the floor waiting for you . . ."

And now he was pulling me toward him and I was in total panic. Why didn't I just forearm him in the chest or at least say "Up yours" and bolt from the car? Ask some virginal girl whose first date turns out to be a masher. I had simply never been in a situation like this before, and without experience the number of responses I could call to mind was extremely limited.

"UUUUUNNNNNGGGGGHHHH!" was what I finally settled for. I think I was picturing the Frankenstein monster awaking and discovering that he's strapped to a table. UUUUUNNNNNGGGGGHHHH!" I moaned once more, stalling and madly trying to think of a way out of this with no parties injured.

"What . . . what's the matter?" He didn't let go, but he was definitely giving pause. I tried for chest-heaving strangled breaths. I wanted him to be as scared shitless as I was.

"My God . . . are you . . . are you . . . ?"

He couldn't finish, but I could. What a closing act I'd make. For just when I needed it most, there it was; the perfect bon mot, the perfect parry and thrust. What a lightning quick mind had I!

"I WANT TO RETURN TO THE UNITED STATES OF AMERICA!" I screamed in a desperately lunatic fashion. My eyes were still closed and I was clawing the air. He immediately opened the driver's door poised for flight. I went back to my, by now, old reliable Frankenstein routine. "Take—me—back."

And so help me that's what he did. "You are leaving India, flying back across the ocean . . ."—I let the breeze waft through my hair once more.—". . . and when you wake up you won't remember any of this." I stumbled out of the car and in a simulated stagger found my way up the stairs to my apartment.

Maury's nose was like the sweet sound of cooing doves.

It was another time. My brother had invited me to a party. At the last minute I had begged off. I couldn't face the social interaction. I was very good at feeling miserable, and as I trudged toward Westwood to eat dinner alone on this Saturday night I was definitely in championship form. It wasn't exactly "The Rubaiyat of Omar Khayyam," but what came to me all at once, almost without permission, almost involuntarily in the course of a one-block walk, was a poem. I never wrote it down or changed a word, and it's always been there for me to call up. And I do call it up occasionally just to remember how bad things had been and to be grateful for whatever progress I've made in the forty years since.

> *Blessings on thee little man:*
> *body bent, torso twisted.*
> *Nature's joke, all misshapen*
> *by the world, alas, forsaken.*
> *If you die before you wake,*
> *pray the Lord your carcass take,*
> *or the earth it will defile,*
> *and worms will say*
> *you ain't our style.*

EIGHT

"New York Stories"

I RECEIVED MY ACCEPTANCE TO THE NEIGHBORHOOD PLAYHOUSE ON April 16, 1958. Once I got past the nylon tights, the ballet slippers, and the dance belt I was required to purchase, I was overjoyed.

My mother had finally arrived in Los Angeles. With money she had squeezed out of my father's businesses we bought a house for her. I stayed there during the summer while working at a day camp as a driver and a counselor. By now I had a driver's license, but I had never operated a bus before. On the first day I managed to wedge it between two trees, effectively sealing the exit door. The children had to be evacuated through a window. The tree had to be felled so that the bus could be liberated. The damage to the vehicle was considerable. They didn't fire me. Things were definitely looking up.

I arrived in New York in early September. I traveled east with another aspiring young actor named Fred Miller, who I met at UCLA. I had lived in Manhattan from the early forties until I went to college. I thought I'd feel comfortable there, but it wasn't to be. A place can totally change without so much as a tree uprooted or a manhole cover replaced. It's all in the perspective. I had previously lived in New York as a child and adolescent. I was used to my basic needs being taken care of: food, shelter, and clothing. Now I had to forage for myself. I had five hundred dollars in my pocket and, after a few days, a rat-infested apartment on the West Side that I shared with Fred. It was scary but it was also exciting.

Fred had signed up for drama classes with one of those teacher-gurus whose own acting career had fallen short; consequently, he spent a lot of time getting his students to worship him. It was exactly like psychiatric transference, where the patient begins to perceive the doctor as father, mother, brother, sister, lover, whatever. Ethical analysts discourage this kind of attachment. A lot of these acting coaches revel in it. We used to talk about "professional students." The twenty-year-olds who became thirty-year-olds who became forty-year-olds who were still taking classes from the same people, or those to whom they had passed the scepter. These instructors were always "brilliant" and "near genius," particularly if they bullied the student on nine of his class performances and offered measured approval on the tenth. It is part of an insidiously unstated system that programs the impressionable and vulnerable student to think of himself as a bad child who must earn the respect of the parent. He lives for the day he receives praise, no matter how faint, and is conditioned to accept it as a bestowal made upon him by an omniscient power. The more the student idealizes the giver the more significant the gift, and the more worthy he feels for having been gifted. No wonder so many of these folks remain professional students never looking for work, never having to face the disinterest of a merciless industry. Far better to have some attention paid, even if it's frequently abusive in the shelter of your acting class, than to live in the streets of rejection and anonymity.

I went with Fred to his orientation meeting. The building was old and musty-smelling. We passed through a narrow doorway. A naked light bulb hung from a ceiling chain. A hand-printed sign with an arrow pointing up was our guide. Our objective was the dimly illuminated second floor landing above us. I know I gulped. I was dog paddling in a sea of depression that was rising past my armpits. Jesus. Was this the kind of place where *I* was going to spend the next two years of *my* life? I was thinking Maxim Gorky's *The Lower Depths*. Fred was obviously reading my thoughts. With a sly smile and a better sense of altitude he said, *The Dark at the Top of the Stairs.*

From there Fred went with me to see the Neighborhood Playhouse. It was located on 54th Street between First and Second Avenue on the East Side. I saw immediately that my concerns were unfounded. The facade looked like it had been recently sandblasted and the interior of the four-story building was immaculate. The basement level held the lockers and showers. The auditorium and its wide and deep stage occupied the first floor. The upper levels had long dance rooms with barre and mirrors that extended the length of the wall. Fencing was taught there as well. There were also rooms for acting classes, and speech classes. Voice classes were held in the auditorium. It was an embarrassment of riches, and I did feel embarrassed. It was as though I had taken my shoeless friend from his shanty on the other side of the tracks and invited him to my parents' mansion.

There was about the place a sturdiness, a sense of stability, and it rubbed off on the students. Eventually, we would have to join the war and try to earn a living, but when that day came it wouldn't be to engage the enemy as peasants with sticks for weapons. We were from the House of Neighborhood, and its coat of arms marked us as a cut above. The battle would be no less severe but we would come prepared. Fred's reaction of diffident appreciation was similar to my own. I think he said something like "Fuuuuuuuuck!"

There were just over a hundred students in our incoming class in September 1958. A natural attrition process reduced the class size to about seventy by the time the school year was over. Some of these students were not invited back for the second year of this two-year curriculum or for their own reasons they chose not to return.

Among the initiates who stood beside me in ballet slippers and tights on that fateful first day feeling just as ridiculous as I did were three young men who would go on to become movie stars. James Caan of *The Godfather, Funny Lady, Misery,* and probably three dozen others. Dabney Coleman of *Nine To Five, War Games,* and *Cloak and Dagger* and the star of at least three television series. And Christopher Lloyd, who was the mad scientist in the *Back to the Future* films, the Klingon, Captain Kruge, in *Star Trek III,* as well as Reverend Jim in TV's *Taxi* among his many other credits.

On the distaff side were three student actors who would also star in motion pictures and/or on the New York stage. Jessica Walter will always be remembered *for Play Misty For Me, The Group,* and *The Flamingo Kid* among other film roles. Brenda Vaccaro starred in the films *Midnight Cowboy, I Love My Wife, Zorro, The Gay Blade* and on the New York stage, and Elizabeth Ashley starred in *The Carpetbaggers, Ship of Fools, Marriage of a Young Stockbroker* in film and won acclaim as Maggie in a Broadway revival of *Cat on a Hot Tin Roof.*

You might ask, did anyone then sense who among us might achieve glory in the years to follow? Maybe not, but we all knew who the best actor was; it was Shirley Dalziel. Who? Well, right there is the great inequity of our biz. Shirley was an actress of depth and persuasion who brought a fine sense of reality to the characters she played. Her work was admired by teachers and students alike. But Shirley wasn't a classical ingenue. She did not fit into a mold. She was a character actress who was too young to do the parts for which she was suited. She would have to wait her time. How do you tell a talented young person full of passion and ambition that she might not find work for another fifteen or twenty years? It's got to be crushing. I don't know what's happened to Ms. Dalziel. I do know I haven't seen her name on any marquees, and if there was a place there for our other triumphant classmates then there should have been room for Shirley, too.

Although we probably didn't understand it at the time we were, by way of her example, witness in microcosm to the facts of show business life. Success is capricious. Luck is a huge component, as is who you know and how you look. Resolve is a factor, a disproportionate sense of your own worth in the face of unmanageable odds against you helps, and, yes, talent plays a part in there somewhere. Only the last ingredient defines an artist, and yet without all the others you wake up one morning to a strange face in the mirror and remember dimly that you once had a dream and wonder where all the promise has gone.

That first year at the Neighborhood Playhouse was the only time in my life that I loved going to school. This despite the fact that I was the only one among our number who absolutely couldn't carry a tune and that our modern dance teacher, Martha Graham, the great dancer and choreographer, said that I looked like an aging rabbinical student as I pranced across the floor. I think it was the shoulders. I could never get them to drop below my sideburns.

I had some minor successes in the acting classes. No more than the other students, but at least there I felt the playing field was level. I do remember that we did, as an exercise on the big stage, Clifford Odet's *Golden Boy*. We did it without makeup or costume and I played Papa Bonaparte, the title character's aging father. I remember being congratulated for my performance by other students and being told that Oleta Carns, on the school's administrative staff, had left the room in tears because I had so reminded her of her deceased parent. I was twenty-two at the time and felt flattered that I was believable as a much older man.

David Pressman, who was then the head of the Drama

Department, began his critique afterward by regaling us with the work of Morris Carnovsky in the same role on the Broadway stage. Mr. Carnovsky was by any standard a terrific performer but he was also a professional actor many years my senior when he played the part. By comparison and implication Mr. Pressman had found my work wanting. How curious, I thought, that he would take such a tack. Not so curious, I discovered, as events were to unfold a year later.

I learned many things at the Playhouse about theatrical presence and technique and truthful acting through the practice of doing. There is no shortcut for experiencing the process again and again in a classroom environment. In this atmosphere one frequently learns best by his mistakes, and when the teachers are supportive then failure is part of growth. Richard Edelman and, most importantly, Mordecai Lawner were the two drama instructors I remember best in this regard. I wish I could recall which of the two said to me the one thing which, more than any other, provided the key to my development as an actor. It was something along these lines: "We each have a 'personal comment' that we express through performance. It is as much a clue to our personality as anything we do and unless it is understood and controlled it will always color the work and guide it in a particular direction. If you permit it, it will limit your self-exploration and, therefore, the range of your acting. In your case, Walter, it is self-pity."

Now of course I absolutely hated hearing that, and I don't much like repeating it even at this late date. The thing is, though, the comment was so dead-on I couldn't even begin to mount a defense. (Just flip back a few pages and read the poem I composed if you need convincing.) It was totally humiliating to be seen in such a light but because I also recognized it immediately as an insightful statement of unimpeachable truth there was, as well, a sense of relief. The most hackneyed of cliches feels like the most appropriate way to describe the experience: I felt at once that a door was opening. When acting is only used cathartically as a means of expressing one's own angst, then no matter how heartfelt and sensitive the work it very quickly becomes predictable and dull—not only to the audience but also to one's self. How many times can you play the "dark Russian soul" beating interminably at his own breast? But with the guidance of my instructor, I was seeing that there was more than one way to approach a role.

This all occurred while doing a classroom scene from *Golden Boy*. This time I was playing the son, Joe Bonaparte, the violin-playing boxer with the weak eyes. When I started rehearsing my m.o. was to make the weak eyes the foundation for the character. I instinctively related to Joe's flaw, not to the qualities that drove him to be a fighter. Now I was being coaxed to perceive him differently. This was actually a spunky guy with a pretty good sense of himself. The more I explored the character the more exciting it became because I discovered that, in fact, those qualities did exist in me, too. To be sure, fear of censure prevented me from presenting myself that way to the world. It was that old (here we go again) dropped-shoe syndrome. As soon as Walter "Henny Penny" Koenig felt too good about himself the sky would fall. But now I was learning that the stage was a free pass. It was a license to examine and give life to every aspect of personality, from the lightest and silliest to the darkest and most disturbing. People have expressed surprise that I could convincingly go from the cocky Chekov of *Star Trek* to the menacing Bester of *Babylon 5*. I don't mean to sound self-aggrandizing, because I'm sure there are thousands of competent actors whose versatility is greater than the public imagines. It's just that I truly believe that my growth as an actor began on that fateful day when I stopped thinking about Joe Bonaparte's eyes and started concentrating on his fists.

The five hundred dollars I came east with was being rapidly depleted, and a couple of months into my first year at the Playhouse I went looking for a job. I ran into an old Ethics teacher of mine from Fieldston High School, the renowned Algernon Black, and he recommended that I seek employment in a hospital. He made a cryptic statement about it being an important life experience and despite the fact that we really didn't know each other I took his advice. (It turned out to be very accurate.) What the hell, hadn't I eaten dinner in a hospital? How much harder could working in one be? By osmosis alone I should be able to function satisfactorily.

I applied at Mt. Sinai Hospital in Manhattan for the position of orderly and was accepted immediately. No doubt it had to do with my ability to lie eloquently about my past history at this kind of job (it was all I could do not to include that I was also a Viennese brain surgeon), and the fact that very few other people would accept ninety-seven cents an hour to wipe the behinds of very old men.

My first night was a baptism of fire or, in this case, a baptism by ice. I was escorted by the head orderly to my first patient. He was a kid of about sixteen who was, in fact, packed head to foot in crushed ice. I suppose this is acceptable therapy to reduce fever but it struck me at the moment as a treatment held over from medieval times. I expected to find leeches plastered to his veins as well. My first thought was, "My

God, what inner sanctum of Druid rites had I stumbled into?" The youngster was on his back comatose with IVs and tubes patched into what seemed like every conceivable vein and orifice. His parents stood at the foot of the bed mute and rigid.

"Take his temperature," said the head orderly.

I found it strange that he would so rudely address the patient's parents and looked to them for a righteous sense of umbrage.

"Take his temperature, I said!"

The parents were looking back at me with an expression more akin to confoundment. It was then it dawned on me that the taker-of-the-temperature-by-lifting-up-the-testicles-and-inserting-the-object-into-the-anus was supposed to be me. I had never placed a thermometer in my own rectum before and here I was being ordered to stick a piece of glass up the frozen ass of a teenager whose nuts were blocking the view. Needless to say, I didn't handle anything terribly well. But worse to come was what happened when I was finally ordered to remove it. By now my hands were shaking so badly I looked like I might be a candidate for an adjoining bed. The parents, with a rapidly mounting concern, became, if possible, stiffer and quieter. Lead is more flexible, deep space noisier. I could tell they had misgivings about me, which didn't add to my own sense of confidence. I reached between the tangle of intravenous lines and started to withdraw the thermometer. I no sooner retrieved it, however, then my arm went into spasm. It flew up past my ear and did a mad little dance around my head and shoulders. I guess I was trying to avoid the tubes and IV lines but instead was only managing to wrap myself more tightly in them. It was just a matter of seconds before half of them tore loose of their moorings in the youngster's body. At precisely that moment, of course, the teenager who hadn't spoken a word in six days screamed in agony. I am put in mind of the wailing of ensnared wolves who would rather chew off a foot than bear the pain of a metal trap. Naturally, I screamed when the boy screamed and his parents, not knowing whether to rejoice at this return to consciousness or share their child's suffering, screamed loudest of all. This, in turn, had a curious snowball effect. Once begun, no one could seem to stop screaming. We each took turns and then started over again.

It finally ended when my superior pushed me out of the room, shoved a chart in my hand, and ordered me to record the patient's temperature. He then rushed back in to restore order. Unfortunately, I was not quite out of the woods. Recording the temperature required being able to read the thermometer. Somehow I had managed to dodge this skill in my first twenty-two years of life. I kept turning it around and around but I couldn't find the damn mercury. I finally decided on a high fever, one approximating that which had been reported by the previous shift. Better to err on the side of caution, I reasoned.

The next day I went to see my brother, who had by then gotten married and was back in New York performing his medical residency at a Veterans Hospital in the Bronx. He explained all the subtleties and nuances of thermometer reading to me in that age before electronically controlled digital readouts.

I settled into a routine of going to school for eight hours and then rushing over to the hospital for the 4 p.m.-to-midnight shift before going home to bed. Sometimes when I did the late shift from midnight to eight in the morning I retired for the night in a chair in the visitor's lounge.

It was on one such occasion that Murphy wrote a new definition to his infamous law.

It was the middle of winter, actually close to Christmas, lending a chilly irony to the whole proceedings, when I started my late-night shift. Winter meant pneumonia, which also meant that you could time your pulse by the regularity with which the oldest patients were expiring. I was awakened for the third time on my fourth call to haul a body down to the morgue. Each time I had had to deal with a nervewracking sort of Russian Roulette game of "organ, organ, try-not-to-open-the-morgue-drawer-with-the-autopsied-organs" when piling the newest resident into these cold storage lockers. I was working in tandem with another orderly who was scared even more shitless than I was of seeing an exposed heart that might still be beating, or a severed head with fluttering eyelids, if we guessed wrong as to which were the empty drawers. We had been flipping a coin each time to see who would take the first peek, and each time he lost he invariably ended up opening one of the occupied lockers. To this point I had lucked out, but I knew the odds against me were getting shorter.

So I was not in a terribly good mood at four in the morning when I was again charged with transporting a cadaver. Only this time the guy wasn't dead, not exactly anyway. The patient's wife was in the room as well as the doctor. The old man, an octogenarian, was in the throes of "death breathing," violent shuddering breaths that came every fifteen or twenty seconds and tortured his emaciated chest.

"Take his temperature," the doctor ordered.

"What?" I couldn't believe it. I knew monologues that were longer than the dying man's lifespan.

"Take his temperature!"

"There's no point!" Jesus Christ, let the guy die in peace! I was outraged, and in my anger I totally lost sight of the little old Jewish lady wringing her hands in the corner. She had probably been this man's wife for the past fifty years, and the absurdity of sticking a thermometer in his expiring flesh was totally lost on her. What was lost on *me* was her pain. All I knew was that I was being told to do something that was without purpose and offensive to me and I was pissed. And just as I knew it would happen I inserted a thermometer into a living body and seconds later withdrew it from a corpse.

"God damn it!" I said aloud, and began the difficult job of lifting the body on to a gurney. The doctor glared but said nothing. I slammed out of there furiously pushing the cadaver. It wasn't until I was halfway down the corridor that I allowed the sound of the weeping woman behind me to filter through. So much for my indignation. Where the hell was my compassion? I think I broke stride momentarily, but I didn't stop. That's what happens when you work in a hospital and are exposed to sorrow and decay on a constant basis. If you're going to survive emotionally you've got to dull down. You harden a bit and shut yourself off from the misery. At least I did. I'm not proud of it.

Naturally, I lost the coin flip this time and, wouldn't you know it, when I opened the vault drawer there was a pile of entrails inside that looked like they might snake out and crawl up my arm.

I got back to sleep at a quarter of five. At ten of five I was summoned again. The patient in Room 425 needed urgent attention. I dragged myself down there thinking I'd never be able to stay awake at school that day.

The guy was turned away from me when I came in and was waving his hand behind him in a shooing motion. I figured he didn't want me there so I began backing through the door. I was dead tired anyway and wasn't about to argue. Before the door could close, however, I heard a gurgling sound coming from the bed, so I stepped back in. He was still waving his hand behind him but it was more intense now. He was definitely upset that I had come back in and he most definitely didn't want me in the room. Or so I thought. Again I started to remove myself and again the gurgling sound started, this time louder. He still had his back to me.

"Is there anything I can do for you?"

"Gurgle . . . gurgle . . . gurgle . . ." (wave . . . wave . . . wave . . .)

"I can't help you if you don't tell me."

"GURGLE . . . GURGLE . . . GURGLE . . ." (WAVE! . . . WAVE! . . . WAVE! . . .)

"Okay, okay, I'm leaving!"

You've seen those medical shows where they apply defibrillating electric paddles to the chests of heart patients and they kind of bounce off the bed straight up in the air? Well, that's what happened now. I don't know what Mr. Levitation's propulsion system was but he was suddenly several inches off the bed and twisting back toward me. That was kind of scary, but the long boney accusatory finger he was pointing was worse. What the hell had I done? He landed, but the finger remained pointing. I still didn't get it. His face was half-buried in the pillow, and he looked up at me with one eye. Through squashed lips he began haltingly to spell a word:

"P-I-S-S."

"You have to go to the bathroom?"

Again his body flew off the bed. I mean, the aerodynamics were spectacular. "AAAARRRRRGGGGGHHHH!"

And now, finally, I realized he wasn't pointing at me.

"P - I - S - S . . . P - I - S - S!"

There was a full urine bottle on a night table in a direct line of fire between us.

"GET . . . RID . . . OF . . . THE . . . P-I-S-S!"

I couldn't believe it. The guy was offended by the sight of his own pee and had decided that an hour before dawn was a good time to have it disposed of. I was really annoyed and not thinking very clearly.

"Jeez, couldn't you do it yourself, Pop?" Right there in that one line I made two egregious errors. The first thing he did was to throw off his blankets and show me that he had no legs. I could tell by the glint in his eye that he expected me to be stricken by the revelation and I was. For one brief moment I saw the triumph well in him, but my shame was not sufficient victory. The most cardinal of my sins had been to call him "pop" because in so doing I had treated him with disdain, belittled his manhood. It would be easy for a man whose legs were recently amputated to draw that conclusion, and I'm sure he did. He now came after me with all the bitterness his terrible circumstances aroused. He struggled to get out of bed. He hung from the sheets and flopped on the floor. A wound opened on his forehead. He began pulling himself on his hands toward me, leaving in his wake a bloody trail. I stood absolutely frozen, waiting for him to reach me and sink his teeth into my calf. Closer . . . closer . . . And then, of course, I blinked and realized he was still in the bed but hurling such invective at me as to make a longshoreman cringe. It went on and on: "You cocksucking bastard, You fucker of dead cats . . ." My horror-movie scenario wasn't that far off. Murder was on his mind, of that I was sure. A convoy of very large nurses came crashing through the door then and dragged me from the room.

I was pointed in the direction of yet another patient whose call light was on. I stumbled toward it half listening for a Code Blue on the public address system. It was not impossible that "Pop's" heart had seized in the wake of our exchange. I swung open the door wondering what errand of mercy I could carry out for this next needful child of God.

The patient was in his forties, about six-foot-two, and appeared to be very skinny under his hospital gown. He was standing beside his bed, leaning over and tapping on a night table lamp with a soup spoon. At first I thought he was seeking a particular pitch and was about to burst into song. But then he looked up at me and smiled with considerable satisfaction. I was feeling much better until he began giggling.

"What's the joke?"

"Sssshhh."

The night's events were starting to take their toll. I was beginning to feel very weary. "Is there something I can do for you?"

"I just wanted you to hear this." He started giggling again.

I leaned against the wall. I was determined to go with the flow this time. "What?"

"My sister. She's such a card."

About then I looked to see if I was wearing a blue-and-white pinafore and had a dormouse for a companion. "Your sister is in the lamp . . . or is the lamp . . . or is the spoon?"

He straightened up to his full height. "For God's sake, man, I'm just talking to her. She's on the other end. We communicate. COMMUNICATE! A lot of relatives don't!"

He was so right. Sooo right! I mean, you just wanted to nominate him for president of the United States or at least head of a network.

I slipped out of the room and headed back toward my chair in the visitors lounge. My last thoughts before tumbling into a very restless sleep totally bypassed the demented spoon wielder. For him there was a category. But my double amputee—he had me tossing and turning. He had opened an incredibly foul mouth without so much as a second's thought, but he couldn't get the word "piss" out from between his teeth. He had to spell it. Why? Why? Why? I pondered it as I slowly drifted into unconsciousness. When that's your last thought of the day there's obviously something missing in your life. I found it shortly thereafter through a sequence of events that did not necessarily foreshadow the absent component. (It will become clear, trust me.)

It began when I received my notice to report for a pre-induction physical examination for service in the Armed Forces. There was no war in which we were then engaged, in that time between Korea and Vietnam, but the draft was still in effect. I know now that it wasn't true, but at the time I was convinced I wouldn't survive boot camp let alone two years in the Army. I wish I could tell you it was a matter of conscience, but since no American soldiers were killing or dying (for that matter) I did not have that noble excuse to fall back on. It wasn't even "uniforms and guns" anymore. I was past that. What I found disturbing was the anonymity in being one of several hundred thousand people who were ordered to dress alike and act alike and think alike. A romantic might say that I couldn't tolerate the suppression of my staunch individualism, but in actuality I felt threatened by what I perceived as an erasure of my identity. In another frame of reference, my need to perform before an audience was not because of a swollen ego but because of a diminished one. Those actors among us who are thought of as immature and/or childlike are those whose self-approval alone will not provide comfort and sustenance. They are driven harder by the need to stand out and be recognized than better-adjusted folk. Think, then, what it would be like for such a person—well, actually, me—to operate in an environment where conformity is the watchword, and the feature which most authentically distinguishes one person from his fellows are the dogtags he wears around his neck.

With that in mind I went to see Dr. Sorrel, the psychiatrist from my teenage years. My intention was for him to write some kind of letter that would excuse me from the draft. The conversation was a long time getting around to that. He kept asking me personal questions the subtext of which could not be ignored: "Do you have roommates? Are they male? Do you have a girlfriend?"

The inference to be drawn, of course, was a question regarding my sexual disposition. "Are you asking me if I'm gay?"

"Yes."

"I thought a submissive father and a dominating mother was the classical Freudian background for the development of homosexuality. My father was the dominating one and my mother submissive."

"Well, that too."

If I had any misgivings about not pursuing psychology as a career, those three words erased any lingering doubt. The whole damn profession was a juggling act in which a lost grip on one bowling pin just meant replacing it with another. If one psychological theory didn't fit, substitute it with a different one. Once again, I was doubting my sexuality.

"GO TO A PARTY AND FIND A GIRLFRIEND!"

Go to the cemetery, Igor, and bring me back some brains! Yeth mathter! (For some reason I always felt Igor lisped.) It was the same kind of solemn statement laced with overwhelming authority that had punctuated his remarks years ago: "THAT'S NEUROTIC DON'T EVER DO THAT AGAIN!"

I left his office with the promise he would send a note to the Army advising them to do an extensive psychological examination before accepting me—and an admonition to find female companionship at once. My social isolation was a consequence of my fear of rejection, but having my sexual orientation questioned by this most eminent of father figures was worse. And so I went to a party that night, met Joan, and began a relationship that put to bed any doubts I still harbored about my sexuality. Thus, the absent component in my life was inserted, so to speak, and I stopped wondering why "Pop" couldn't say the word "piss." (I told you it would all become clear.)

Having a girlfriend after such a long period of celibacy seemed to create an urgency that I could have lived without. It was as if a clock was ticking somewhere demanding that I cram into this relationship all the problems that, I think, are generally parceled out in the course of several male-female trysts and over a greater amount of time. The problem, in this case, was the homicidal ex-boyfriend, Bruno, the butcher. (I must tell you that this is the only time in this book that I will ever use a pseudonym. I do so to protect his sensibilities and because he might still be in the meat-carving trade.)

Joan and her roommate divided up the one bed they possessed. The roommate got the box-spring and Joan the mattress, which she posited on the floor. It was a Saturday morning. I had stayed over and was still in Morpheus's embrace when upon the door there came a rapping. I was dimly aware of Joan leaving our cozy chamber and answering the knock. There was some muffled conversation and then she was back. She started to cry but before I could begin to ask the reason the front door slammed open and heavy footsteps reverberating loudly in my ears pounded their way across the room toward me.

When I was just a tyke my brother took me to a Saturday matinee thriller about an evil man who limped when he walked. I don't know if Achilles limped too but I definitely had my own version of his weak heel. It was the sound of that leg dragging across the floor. The movie scared me badly and Norm took fiendish delight in replicating the noise at one in the morning. Until now that halting, sliding *thump* had been the sound of footsteps that I had found most chilling. Bruno's march toward me, however, forged its own claim to the head of the list.

"Get up! I'm going to kill you!" was the snappy little refrain with which he greeted me. Believe it or not, my first reaction was one of modesty. I was naked under the bedsheets and felt it an inappropriate state in which to greet company. As you might suspect, decorum wasn't his strong suit. He reached down, grabbed me by the neck, lifted me from the mattress and dangled me at arm's length above the floor. Although not tall, Bruno was built like the odoriferous brick house described in pulp literature.

"I'M GOING TO CALL THE COPS!" screamed Joan repeatedly.

"YOU'RE GOING TO DIE, YOU SONOFABITCH!" bellowed Bruno.

I was picturing the headline in the New York *Daily News*: LOVERS TRIANGLE. ACTOR SEASONED AND SCORED BY MEAT MAN!

To this day I don't know how the tables got turned, but somehow I came down from the air and grabbed him from behind. I pinned his arms to his sides and wrapped him in a bear hug. I ask you to envision this keeping in mind that I was naked at the time. Is it any wonder that the headline that now flashed in my head was one adorning the *National Enquirer*: MENAGE A TROIS. JEALOUS BUTCHER DEBONES ACTOR!

Round and round the room we went, me hanging on for dear life and him grunting and straining like Mighty Joe Young trying to break his shackles. Eventually he tired and gave out. We were all sitting on the mattress by then. Feeling betrayed and deeply wounded by my presence, Bruno hung his head. Somehow or other Joan had failed to properly communicate to him the definition of an *ex*-boyfriend, and now she began to assume some responsibility for the emotional havoc that had been wreaked. In the midst of all this angst I was the voice of reason. I even suggested that he accompany her to work and settle their problems in private. And that's exactly what they did.

I remained sitting on the mattress for close to an hour after they left, mainly because my throat was so bruised I had trouble swallowing and because once the adrenaline had stopped pumping and I started realizing how scary the situation had been my legs turned to custard.

C

January 27, 1959, 39 Whitehall Street, New York City was the date and location of my examination for draft eligibility. I worked up a pretty good case of hysteria in advance and fully anticipated giving an aberrational performance before the draft board that would include violent shaking and biting the furniture.

Things don't always work out the way you expect, however. There were hundreds of us and we were commanded to strip to our skin. We were then lined up and marched around from one station to another as soldiers with clothes on, although otherwise functionally impaired, screamed at us for no reason at all. I was struggling against the dehumanizing effect of having my free will as well as my clothes confiscated and ordered about without any regard for a sense of personal dignity.

"KEEP IT MOVING, ASSHOLES, KEEP IT MOVING!"

"For Chrissakes, we're doing it!" I muttered aloud. That was definitely a mistake.

"YOU A WISE GUY, MISTER, YOU A WISE GUY? PUSHUPS, MISTER, I WANT PUSHUPS!"

I was beginning to wonder whether his compulsion to repeat everything twice wasn't attributable to some kind of synaptic malfunction that caused acute short-term memory loss.

"You've got to be—?"

"DROP AND GIVE ME TWENTY! TWENTY!"

It was going to be thirty if I didn't start soon. I began but quickly realized that in my state of undress it had to appear to any casual observer that I was humping the floor. The only way I could deal with the mortification of bouncing my pecker off the cement short of bolting naked into the street was to remove myself mentally from the proceedings. And that's what I did.

By the time I rose to my feet I was in another place. I no longer felt self-conscious about the nudity and the screaming was as meaningless as ridicule to a toaster oven. When I arrived at the interview with the Army psychiatrist I was Zamboli the Zombie.

"What's your name?"

"Walter Koenig."

"WHAT?"

"Huh...?"

"I CAN'T HEAR YOU!"

"Walter Koenig."

The louder he became the quieter I became. On his fourth pass at finding out about me I was whispering and on his fifth attempt I had slid down in the chair so that only my eyes showed above the desk.

"DO YOU WANT TO GO INTO THE ARMY?"

I blinked twice for yes.

It was about then he picked up a pen with red ink and began writing furiously on my records. He clipped the letter from Dr. Sorrel to his notes.

Several weeks later I received notification that I was unfit for military training. Shoot, I could have told them that.

Back at the Neighborhood Playhouse I was getting along reasonably well with the other students. I think Jimmy Caan thought I was a little strange. We went to a movie together once, a tediously rendered costume epic heavy with pseudo-Shakespearean dialogue. "WHAT SAYETH YOU, SQUIRE CAAN? SUCKETH BADLY YON PICTURETH?" shouted I leaping to my feet and declaiming melodramatically in the middle of the film. I thought it was funny but my outburst caught Jimmy by surprise and he jumped in his seat. I think he thought of me as this quiet little guy who probably nibbled on his fingers. He wasn't prepared to hear me raving. I noticed that he edged up against the opposite armrest for the duration of the screening.

I think I secretly liked shaking him up. He had too much going for him. He was a physical guy but also very funny and cocky. I don't know if anyone thought he was going to be our premier movie star, but he definitely had a swagger and although I envied the self-assurance I didn't like being overwhelmed by it. Getting him to jump a little was just that small display of vulnerability that, in my mind, put us on the same playing field . . . at least at the time.

He was also rebellious and confrontational, but I don't think the demons that hounded him later in his career were apparent then. Maybe they were. He wasn't asked back for the second year. It was not for a lack of talent, but because his argumentative nature had driven one of the speech teachers to despair. She threatened to quit if he was permitted to return. Needless to say, his career didn't suffer by virtue of this minor rejection.

I was among the older students, having completed college, but

Dabney Coleman was at least a couple of years older than me. He was strongly opinionated, and his life was well-ordered. Before coming to the Neighborhood Playhouse he had been a tennis instructor and there was a sense of authority about him as if he were used to giving orders. He parlayed that quality and an acerbic sense of humor into a combination that worked very well for him as an actor. In his best roles he played an insufferable character who made you laugh at him nonetheless. The ability to make fun of yourself can be an endearing quality, and Dabney has had a lock on it his entire career. We didn't pal around at the Playhouse but I did see him a few times in Los Angeles when we were both struggling to make it there.

For many years Dabney was the best tennis player in the Hollywood acting community. Early on, probably around 1961, Jimmy Caan and I went to see him play against Arthur Ashe. Ashe, of course, would in time become one of our greatest champions, winning Wimbleton in 1972 among a hundred other titles during his too-brief life. Dabney seemed to be holding his own in what was not a high-stakes effort on either side . . . at least not until the sun started going down. It was about then that Dabney, quite innocently, made the inopportune remark that he was having trouble seeing Arthur in the growing shadows. Arthur, of course, was African-American, and Dabney still carried the hint of a Texas drawl. The inference was unintentional but on this occasion Ashe wasn't buying it. He stared silently and unmovingly at Dabney for about half a minute. The pace of the match picked up considerably after that.

It was like one of those stories where reality and illusion blur. For all the world it looked as if Dabney's racquet was intact and yet how could it have been? Surely there was a gaping hole in the strings because the balls were whizzing past him in all manner of trajectory as he lunged and stumbled around the court like Ray Milland in *The Lost Weekend.*

I started to giggle. If it sounds now like I was having too much fun at his expense, you must understand that I considered myself a very good Ping-pong player, and just days before this match the future Slap Maxwell had slapped the tar out of my game across a Ping-Pong net. Of course I derived too much glee from his embarrassment and my reaction was petty, but I know the temptation for the reader up until now has been to nominate me for sainthood and I wouldn't want to continue the deception. Anyway, Caan thought it was hysterical too.

If Dabney was the oldest of the students Jessica Walter was among the youngest. I believe she had danced at The Latin Quarter or the Copacabana before attending the Playhouse. She had an extroverted personality and a terrific figure. She also had a New York accent as thick as any wiseguy's but even when she misspoke you couldn't help love her: "Waltah, I don' know why youah so shy, I could go fah you . . . if youwa tawler." My hand to God, her very words.

Elizabeth Ashley had a delicate beauty, a husky voice, and a residual Southern drawl that in combination were enormously fetching. She also had a will to succeed that brooked no interference. She definitely was prepared to use her assets to their best advantage. Of all our group I was least surprised by her achievements.

I ran into her a couple of times over the years. The first occasion was in 1964 on the set of *Ship Of Fools* in which she was one of the leads. I was reading for the part of the German chap who pushes Jose Ferrer around in a wheelchair. I came up to her from behind and tapped her on the shoulder expecting a warm hello and a big hug. She turned around and, without so much as blinking, said: "Oh Walter, are you working 'extra' on our picture?" I don't know what that says about her. Perhaps nothing . . . except that maybe even at that early stage in her career she might have benefited from a tinsel-ectomy.

Brenda Vaccaro was a charmer, friendly and warm. She had a sweet face and a gutsy Mother Earth kind of emotional life. If I remember correctly, the consensus was that she had the talent and presence to make it.

Chris Lloyd was my best friend at the Neighborhood Playhouse. He played Theseus in our second-year production *of A Midsummer-Night's Dream,* and I think it was there that he first tried out the halting, confused, topsy-turvy delivery he perfected as Reverend Jim in *Taxi.* I thought it was hilarious, but the director told him to tone it down. Toning it up, of course, brought him tremendous success on the TV series. I'm sure the writers of the show drew on Chris's background when they created his character. Like his television alter ego he usually dressed as if he had spent the night in an alley, but also like Jim he actually came from enormous wealth. You would never know it, of course, he was so unassuming. He invited me up to his family "place" in Connecticut and it turned out to be a mansion on acres of land. I was most impressed that there were elevators in the home, including those that were for the exclusive use of the help. There was also a massive organ with pipes three stories high that was part of the decor.

In my life the most bonding element in any friendship has been a sense of humor. Chris and I made each other laugh . . . a lot. I thought we would be buddies for life. I was mistaken. I hate being mistaken. It makes me feel that my old man's cynicism was justified.

There were many good and gifted people at the Playhouse who are certainly worthy of mention. You will see some of them listed on the school's show programs I have had reprinted here. The reason I don't detail their lives is self-evident: their talent notwithstanding, because of a lower public profile the reader is less likely to identify their names and form a picture of who they are.

I was invited back for the second year and given a partial scholarship, not so much because of aptitude as dedication. I think it was determined that anyone willing to change soiled bedsheets, shave other people's pubic hair, and haul cadavers to and fro in order to afford drama school had to want to be an actor bad enough. Also, we weren't permitted to hold an outside job in the second year, which meant I couldn't have paid the full tuition and still managed to live on the seventy-five dollars a month I had to spend.

Unfortunately, I cannot tell you that the second term was as rewarding as the first. School now was about showcasing, about being seen by agents and casting directors who could help us find work after we graduated. We still had classes to attend and the opportunity to learn was still available, but learning now seemed more like a byproduct of the process than the primary objective. The primary objective was to be cast in a good role in one of the plays that would be presented to the public during the course of the year. Competition became very keen, and I don't think we rooted for each other as enthusiastically as we had the previous term.

No sooner had I gotten over my elation at being asked back then I began to worry about what my future held in store. I fell victim to the "showcase" mentality probably more than most because I had little confidence in my ability to become a working actor once I had graduated. I wanted to be seen and hired on by some theatrical agency or casting director *now,* so that I wouldn't have to hit the bricks cold when school was over.

The first play we did was Arthur Miller's *The Crucible.* I desperately wanted to play the lead, John Proctor. Monday morning came and the cast list was posted on the bulletin board. I had been assigned a much smaller role by the head of the drama department and the director of the production, David Pressman. When I saw it I went bananas.

I identified my emotion at the time as anger, not panic, but in truth, it was probably the latter. The character I was to play, Thomas Putman, was a man in his fifties. It had already been made abundantly clear to me that I was no Morris Carnovsky. What agent then seeing me in this part of a much older man would want to represent me?

I waited outside the school for Pressman to arrive and then stepped in his path. "Mr. Pressman, I deserve better than this!"

"I can't please everyone, sonny!"

That was the extent of our exchange, but as time would prove it had far-reaching consequences.

My first reaction was to quit school. Can you believe that? I literally started walking away. I got about three blocks when Dr. Sorrel's words started echoing in my head.

"That's neurotic . . .

"That's neurotic . . . that's neurotic . . . that's neurotic . . ." I turned around and headed back, determined to be so freaking good in the role of Thomas Putnam that Pressman would forever after regret his decision. Of course, he didn't. John Harl was excellent in the part of Proctor, proving the director had made the correct choice. But that isn't the point here because what happened next, actually a few weeks later, was truly bizarre.

It was probably initiated by a situation that occurred on a day Harl was absent. Pressman asked for a volunteer to read his part and my hand was the first one up. I gave it my all, and a couple of the other students even complimented me afterwards. I did a double take when I caught a glimpse of our director out of the corner of my eye. He was staring at me. His eyes had narrowed and his lips thinned. The expression on his face was very clear to read: "You're showing me up and I don't like it!"

I thought nothing more about it, and rehearsals continued without incident. Jessica Walter played my wife, and we seemed to work well together. It was the day before the performance and we had just finished the dress rehearsal. Pressman said we would take a couple of minutes and then figure out the curtain call. At precisely that moment I was informed I had a phone call downstairs in the men's locker. I was gone perhaps three or four minutes. I returned through the backstage entrance to absolute silence. No one would look at me. I stepped out on to the stage and came face to face with Pressman, who was standing in the house pointing a finger at me.

"Where—have—you—been?"

I could tell he was having a great deal of trouble keeping himself under control.

"I was answering a phone—"

And then he blew up, but like no one I had ever seen before or since. His face went from red to purple and then, I think, to green. He balled his fists and kicked his body around like a child reared in the wild and captured by great white hunters.

"I won't have any more of this childishness!" he screamed, illustrating what he had in mind, I suppose, with a spray of spittle and much foot stamping. "You have been trying to undermine this production from the first day and I'm not going to take it anymore!"

Hey, I had been arrested by the FBI. I had been verbally abused by patients and physically assaulted by the halfback on the football team and my girlfriend's ex-lover, but never before had I felt myself to be the target of such paranoidal ravings. Did I feel unjustly accused and unfairly condemned? You betcha. But I only left the battlefield bleeding, not dead. I found the instrument with which to cauterize the wound. Just think, I told myself, this was a man who had directed on Broadway and was the head of the drama department of the Neighborhood Playhouse, a very prestigious position, and if he was able to succeed as well as he had while susceptible to such grossly infantile behavior then surely I need not abandon all hope for my own future. I took a lot of comfort and not a little pride in the knowledge that there was a place in the world for all God's creatures, even neurotics.

★

Sydney Pollack, the director of *Tootsie, Out of Africa,* and *The Firm* (from a portfolio of many impressive successes), was a very young man when he came back to the Playhouse in our second year to teach classes. He was several years away from directing his first film, but it was already clear that he was gifted and would one day make his mark in the motion picture industry.

We all went to somebody's house for a party one evening and Syd was there. He had been imbibing liberally and was deep in Bacchus's embrace when I approached him. "So tell me Syd, what kind of parts do you think I'd be right for after I get out of school?"

You have a deep and sensitive soul, Walter, and a fantastic sense of comic timing. I can't believe you wouldn't be right for any role that

Jimmy Dean or Harpo Marx might have played. That was the kind of answer I was looking for. That's not what I got.

"You're not commercial! I never got to kiss the girl and you'll never get to kiss the girl. Nobody's going to hire you unless you get a job in some tiny garret theater somewhere and somebody crawls up there by mistake and sees you!"

About now you might be asking yourself how I could ethically put quote marks around things that were said to me thirty, forty, fifty years ago. Who remembers things word for word? I do. I've never been adept at repressing odious exchanges and traumatic events. They're always there in my mind. And if they're not a part of my waking life then they're just around the corner of my consciousness, casting a long shadow to remind me that they won't go away.

Coming on the heels of my experience with David Pressman, Syd's commentary was not a good thing for me to hear. But you know, it could have been worse. Pollack's words had me reeling, but when you live with the syndrome of "the other shoe" you expect things like this to happen; your psyche has installed a sense of fatalism as the last bastion of defense. Therefore, the element of surprise is less deadly and the potential to self-destruct less likely.

I went to school the next day morose but not suicidal. Pollack came up to me and apologized. I don't remember those words as clearly because they were conciliatory not antagonistic. He explained that he had not been totally in control and was sorry about what had been said. He insisted that I not put any stock in our previous conversation. I know he meant it because twice after that, once in New York and once in Los Angeles, unsolicited, he tried to get me work. More on that to come.

By the spring of 1960 I knew I probably wouldn't stay around New York to look for work after graduation. I was convinced I would have a harder time selling myself as an actor there than in Los Angeles. The major obstacle I saw in returning to L.A. was that I had no funds, and I would most definitely need an automobile in Hollywoodland. I spent many a restless night trying to figure a way to acquire the necessary money. Bear in mind that we were not allowed to hold a job during the school year.

An idea began to hatch in my brain. I knew that as long as I kept my own counsel and didn't listen to the voice of reason it would grow more and more plausible. I finally convinced myself that it would work and rang up the oldest friend I had, Peter Magee, whom I had known since we were both seven years old. He was working construction at the time on a building going up on The Avenue of the Americas in midtown Manhattan. I asked him what the chances were of a rivet falling from a high story and hitting the ground. When he told me it was possible I began mapping out a scenario that would establish my place in the lore of street theater and provide me with my first professional acting job.

The first order of business was acquiring an eyewitness. I approached just about every male in my class and was summarily turned down by them all. Dabney's reaction was to stare past me rather grimly and almost imperceptibly shake his head. I think he felt that just being privy to what I intended to do might make him an accessory. Chris Lloyd cracked up at the idea but after hesitating a moment decided to pass too.

I finally found my "partner" among the first-year students. Hugh was a beat poet with a considerable following in Greenwich Village. I seem to recall that a lot of his work had to do with taking down the Establishment. I didn't know him well but he had introduced me to pot—with which I had no success whatsoever—and I figured if anyone was nutty enough to go along with me it was him. I told him I'd give him a hundred dollars from the "take," and he was immediately enthusiastic and very cool about the whole thing. That was good. That I knew nothing of his acting skills wasn't so good.

On the appointed day Peter met with us for lunch and passed me an eight-pound rivet under the table. He had taken it from the site of the skeletal building he was working on. I offered to cut him in on the deal but he demurred. Walking along exposed girders fifty floors above the ground had made him superstitious and he didn't want to test Fate. He then left. We gave him a few minutes to get back to his job. Hugh sat back and smiled broadly. He loved the adventure of it all, or so I thought. As it was I wasn't apprehensive about what I was going to do, but if I had Hugh's placid countenance and aura of calmness it would have been very reassuring.

I posted him at the curb while I went into a corner bar which had been previously staked out. I had a razor blade in my pocket and a newspaper under my arm. I slipped into the bathroom and cut my cheek with the blade. I turned the newspaper so that it protruded from my arm vertically and covered the place on my face where the blood had begun to spurt. The eight-pound rivet was underneath my jacket tucked under my other arm. I came back out into the sunshine confident that nobody would be looking at me. This was New York, after all.

The plan was for Hugh to step off the sidewalk in my wake and follow me into the street. It had already been calculated that a rivet falling from a great height would drop beyond the sidewalk. He would, therefore, be behind me and see it all happen when the drama unfolded.

There's always something that goes wrong in these "best-laid plans," and as I approached Hugh I suddenly saw what it was. I wouldn't have been surprised if the incision in my cheek had stopped bleeding because I'm sure the blood had drained from my face probably depriving the wound of its plasma. Sometime during the few moments I had left him alone Hugh had undergone a transformation the equal of Dr. Jekyll and caterpillars. His eyes were bouncing and his face twitching to rhythms that no biped could emulate on the dance floor. My cool, pot-smoking beat poet co-conspirator was in a state of unmitigated panic. I never got to his side. He kicked off the curb in front of me and was halfway across the traffic as I left the sidewalk. The whole idea was to have him see me get hit by the bolt and be able to testify to it afterwards. I had no intention of aborting the plan, however. I counted five paces into the street and then screamed in agony and fell to the ground releasing the rivet from under my jacket and letting the newspaper drop to the side. Fortunately, the wound was still bubbling. There was enough blood there to feed a young vampire. Unfortunately, Hugh had not heard me or turned back to see the "accident" occur. I had only one recourse. I writhed on the ground and screamed again. I was loud enough this time to drown out all the blaring horns and screeching brakes that were being tortured by drivers trying to avoid hitting me.

Hugh spun around at last. I would have been better off if he hadn't. If he had somehow made it to the opposite curb and kept going, if he had been able to reach the East River and find transport across its breadth and refuge in some safe house in Queens where he could continue to write poetry, garner awards for literature, and live happily ever after.

"SOMEBODY DO SOMETHING, JUST DON'T STAND THERE!"

That was Hugh. The panic had vanished. A big crowd was gathering and he was now in his element. He stood over me with his legs wide, one hand pointing to the sky and the other on his hip. I'm sure he saw himself in hose, a codpiece, and a jaunty Elizabethan cap with a feather. He repeated the words again, exaggerating vowels and consonants alike in a delivery that bore no resemblance to any actor's, living or dead.

"SOOOMMEBODYYY DOOO SOOOOMMMETHIIINNNG, JUUUST DOOON'T STAAANNND THERRRE!"

I lay on the ground cringing. My agony was real. I absolutely wanted to kill him. Instead I pretended to cry hysterically, giving up my last shred of dignity in an effort to deflect attention from the unbelievable posturing that was taking place above me. As I think back on it now I'm convinced that his enthusiasm for the project was not based on the money or the adventure or as a statement of protest against the insidious nature of omnipotent big business. No, he had read that all the world was a stage and simply decided to seize the day. And just in case he never got another chance he was going to give it everything he had and a lot that he didn't to make the occasion as memorable as he possibly could. And who's to say he didn't? I remembered it, and now maybe you will too.

I was carried into a jerry-built office on the building's premises. Hugh followed after me. With minimal coaxing he confessed to not seeing the accident occur and I ended up signing a paper saying that I was hurt but not dead. We were turning out to be not very good crooks. All the same, I had been "injured," and they were not denying responsibility.

The next step was to send me to a hospital for X-rays. I hadn't thought that far ahead, but I did have a brother working in a Veterans Hospital in the Bronx and it didn't take lightning wit to improvise a suggestion. On my recommendation they called Norm and explained that I had been hit in the face with a bolt from a construction job and that I would need to be examined. They hung up before I could speak to him so he had to live with his worst fears until I arrived in a cab.

He had a small army of doctors, nurses, and medical technicians waiting for me when I pulled up. He raced to open the cab door, and I had one very brief moment alone with him before they descended on me with a stretcher, an oxygen mask, and a priest. Okay, not a priest.

"Norm, I faked it."

He didn't even blink. "We'll have to go through with it."

Days later, after it was all over, he did ask me one question. Had I done it for the kicks or the money. I told him it was the money. He was relieved. He didn't want to think of me as this very weird person whose behavior would only get progressively more bizarre. Well, I *think* it was the money.

I contacted a lawyer through a friend of my brother's and a settlement was negotiated. I gave Hugh his hundred dollars and he was ecstatic. "We can do this in Philly and Boston and Chicago . . ."

It wasn't venality that drove him. It was vanity. He just wanted to go on the road with his splendid performance.

I was at a convention in Orlando in 1981. I was approached by a young man who asked me if the "bolt out of the blue" story was true. He was a recent graduate of the Neighborhood Playhouse and the saga of my crime had evidently been passed down from class to class for the last twenty years. In 1994 I had a meeting with Rick Berman, the Star Trek producer, prior to signing on to do the *Generations* movie. He opened the conversation by recounting the same escapade, explaining that a friend of a friend of a friend had told him about it. I'm sure I'm not supposed to feel this way but I must tell you I was flattered. Here I was a living legend. So why hadn't a song had been composed to honor my notorious deed? Something along the lines of the following would be appropriate (to the tune of "The Ballad of Jesse James"):

> Walter Koenig was a lad who played many a part
> That of Germans, Swedes and a Russian
> but the best of them all was when he took
> a fall
> and pretended he had had a concussion

All I want is a respectable advance, and a healthy royalty.

For those of you not previously convinced that my soul was damned to hell but are now, let me tell you that I've already paid the price for my criminal behavior. When I returned to Los Angeles I used the money I was awarded to buy a second-hand English-made automobile called an Anglia. The exportation of this car was the British Empire's final revenge against the Colonies. I spent as much money in the year I owned it keeping it in repair as I did in initially purchasing it. I always had a teapot filled with water on the passenger seat because any elevation greater than a speed bump caused it to suffer acute dehydration. Of course the brakes failed, as did the clutch, and depending on the time of the month the doors wouldn't open.

Back at the Playhouse we were preparing the final shows of the school year. Much to my surprise, David Pressman cast me in a lead role in the *Theatre Revue* written for the occasion. I don't know if he was motivated by pangs of conscience or the fact that I would one day write my autobiography. In that case he should have left well enough alone, but he didn't. I'll explain in a moment. Everyone else in the show sang but me—I already said I couldn't carry a note—but the part, a beatnik producer, was funny and fun to do and I had a good time.

We also did *A Midsummer Night's Dream*, and just to prove that I didn't have to do a starring part to be happy I played Quince, one of the Rustics, and to this day I remember the experience fondly. One of the first-year students that I had dated but wasn't seeing at the time was taking notes for Pressman during rehearsals. She told me later that at one point right after my monologue he had exclaimed out loud, "Damn but he's good!" Was she lying?

Among the photo material in this book are the programs from these two shows. I've included them as homage to my classmates. Just look at the names of the first-year students who worked on the production crew. Leonard Frye went on to star in the films *The Boys in the Band* and *Fiddler on the Roof,* and John Law (later known as John Phillip Law) played leading roles in *Barbarella* and *The Russians are Coming, The Russians are Coming.*

Our final performance was May 13, 1960. The school year was drawing to a close. Pressman convened one last session to critique our work. Frankly, I thought I had proven myself in the two plays we had just finished doing. I was looking forward to his assessment of my ability. When it became my turn he compared me unfavorably to another actor in our group. The other actor was universally regarded as the weakest talent in the class. I guess she *was* lying.

I had been sharing a sublease with John Harl on Eighth Street between avenues B and C. We each paid twenty-four dollars a month rent. Even at that we couldn't afford a phone. The day school let out I was staring at a dirty window trying to come to grips with my life. What the hell was I supposed to do now? I had no acting job and I had no prospects. I didn't think I should stay in New York but I wasn't really sure about a return to L.A., either. That sinking feeling in my chest was on its toes and holding its breath ready to take the plunge. And then there was a knock on the door. It was a telegram from the Shwartz-Luskin Talent Agency: *I had an audition for a movie!* I stared at the paper disbelieving. This kind of thing only happened *in* movies!

Could life really be that simple? Could I just walk out of school and walk onto a motion picture soundstage? Of course not. But what an incredible high at that moment.

I had no idea how this was all happening. I knew I'd be reading for the part of a juvenile delinquent, and I assumed someone had seen me in the theatrical revue in which I played the beatnik producer and had extrapolated from that performance. But the agency was short on information when I got through to it on the phone. I arrived at the casting office early and decided that a walk once around the block would bring me back at the appointed time. I miscalculated. I returned a few minutes late and the director was on his way out. His assistant stopped him and made an introduction.

"Walter Koenig," said Sydney Pollack, "meet John Frankenheimer." I knew Frankenheimer's work from Playhouse 90 and other live television shows, and his reputation was that of a highly skilled artist. He went on to make *Birdman of Alcatraz, The Manchurian Candidate,* and *Seven Days In May* among other impressive credits.

He mumbled something, either "hello" or "goodbye," and walked away. I guess I was too impressed by the occasion itself to catch which. I didn't even care that I wasn't going to audition for him. I was just so freaking pleased that Pollack had thought enough of my ability to put his own ass on the line by bringing me in. On top of that, even though Frankenheimer had left, Syd told me not to worry. There would be a part in this picture for me, he guaranteed it.

The film was called *The Young Savages* and it starred Burt Lancaster and Shelley Winters. The story involved two gangs and was taken from the New York tabloids. The character Syd had in mind for me was called Big Dom. Obviously, he was supposed to be short. He was sort of the bad-influence leader who tells everyone else what to do. (Curiously, four years later I would play just such a role on the *Alfred Hitchcock Presents* television series.)

Pollack told me to call him every couple of days about my start date on the film. This was a period of euphoria for me. I was strutting on air—as every authentic hoodlum should do—in anticipation of the word that would propel me into my acting career.

After ten days of alternately waiting for the sun to rise so I could call him and then waiting for it to set and then rise and then set and then rise once more so I could call him again I received the bad news. The character I was up for was changed from Big Dom to

Pretty Boy, and another actor was cast in the part. There was another change as well. The picture would now be shot in Los Angeles instead of New York.

"We can't pay your airfare but if you make it to L.A. on your own you'll be in the movie, I guarantee it," said my buddy, Syd.

That was all the impetus I needed to change my address. The rest of my Neighborhood Playhouse classmates had by now begun to pound the pavements. They were valiantly going on every casting call out there regardless of whether the play or the commercial or the TV show was actually looking for an Egyptian mummy, a snapping turtle, or a basset hound. That wasn't for me. I was on my way back to Los Angeles to be a movie star! And wouldn't you know it, I now discovered that when I looked at myself in the mirror from that certain angle, with the blinds shut and a flashing strobelight providing the illumination, there wasn't really that much difference between me and Rock Hudson after all. California, here I come!

NINE

"Back to Bataan"

JOAN AND I TALKED VAGUELY ABOUT STAYING TOGETHER EVEN AFTER I decided to return to L.A., but I think we both knew that the distance between us would prove too great an obstacle. I arrived in L.A. and moved in with my mother. That lasted about six months. I figured I should take an acting class to keep my hand in while waiting for a start date on The Young Savages. Somebody recommended an acting teacher named Ben Bard. He had been the coach for the Twentieth Century-Fox contract players but had been deposed by Sandy Meisner, who had been the head of the acting department at The Neighborhood Playhouse before leaving and being replaced by David Pressman. As they say, "six degrees of separation."

I was in his class twenty-five minutes and was already feeling desperate to get out. Mr. Bard had given us a demonstration performing Marc Antony's famous speech from Shakespeare's *Julius Caesar* in stentorian tones that had me nostalgic for my old friend Hugh and with melodramatic gestures that went out with silent movies. He then asked me to try it. He stopped me after two lines because I hadn't raised my right hand and pulled on my earlobe as he had done on "lend me your ears."

The two hours were interminable, and when the class was finally over I bolted for the door. He commanded me to halt. A director he knew was looking for an actor to play the younger brother in a production of N. Richard Nash's *The Rainmaker*. He thought I'd be right for it. Apparently, the character's ears were not a plot point.

I auditioned for the director and he thought I'd be excellent in the part. I was having some misgivings because there was dialogue that described him as a growing boy with a voracious appetite. Earl Holliman played him in the film adaptation. I brought it to his attention and he told me not to worry. He would cast short actors in the other parts to make me look taller. I left there having convinced myself that it was a perfectly reasonable solution. "Oh, what fools we mortals be when first we practice to deceive". . . ourselves.

Things were working out fantastically. I was going to be in a movie *and* a play. I was now combining strutting on air with walking tall on it. As he had in New York, Syd had instructed me to call him at his Los Angeles number every day or two. This had been going on for a couple weeks. "Any day now," he kept reassuring me.

It was a Sunday. The smog had lifted. You could actually see white billowy clouds in the sky and feel a touch of freshness in the air and, of course, the sun was shining. It was good to be alive and be a burgeoning movie star and a promising stage actor. I was about to leave for my first rehearsal of *The Rainmaker*. I had missed Pollack on my last phone attempt and decided I should try him one more time before I left. There is a sound that people make who hold your career in their hands that foreshadows the dire news they are about to impart. It's by way of preparing you, I suppose. I heard it now.

"Uuuuhhh, I can't use you in the picture, Walter. The rules in L.A. are different than they are in New York. They won't let me cast 'extras' here."

Extras! EXTRAS!' I hung up wondering how this misunderstanding could have occurred. I knew that in New York "extras" were treated with more respect. It was acceptable there for actors to take that kind of work without damaging their chance at real roles. In Los Angeles extras are considered movable furniture. This is not so much a comment about their ability as it is the regard in which they are held by the people who do the hiring. There was no way in hell I was ever going to be an extra. So it was a case of adding a mortal insult to a pernicious injury to say I didn't even qualify for that.

I reeled out of the house trying to maintain some emotional balance. My God, I had flown three thousand miles for this shot and now I had been told that there wasn't any shot and that, in fact, none had ever existed. I didn't know it then but what I have learned in the last thirty-six years is that more often than not what an actor's career is about are promises that are lighter than air. I'm not talking about me, I'm talking about actors, the whole lot of us, the ninety-some-thousand members of our guild. Because we are so willing and adept as performers at taking a fantasy and from it creating a reality we lose sight of where reality ends and the fantasy begins in our own lives. We suspend disbelief when we act the way a child does when he uses his fingers for a six-shooter. In the same way, we have childhood's faith in the truth of what we have been told when over and over again we are either misled or encouraged to imagine that there is more there than meets the eye. "Promises, promises, promises," someone once said. Does it sound like I'm whining? I suppose. But then ask any hundred actors you come across if they don't frequently feel "had" by this business and see if you don't get a consensus. That isn't to say I was angry at Pollack. I wasn't. First of all, I was in too much shock to feel much of anything and, then, I did truly believe his intentions were good. He could have turned off on me long before then if that wasn't the case.

I drove the twenty minutes to my first rehearsal of *The Rainmaker* trying to convince myself that the play was a better opportunity anyway. I wasn't succeeding. To my surprise the cast was already sitting around a table reading aloud when I arrived. I checked my watch. I was still ten minutes early. The director intercepted me before I could reach the table and pulled me aside.

"Weren't we supposed to start at twelve?" I asked.

"I meant to call you."

"Well, I'm here now."

"Yeeeaaah." He drew it out as if there was more he wanted to say.

While he was thinking I did a quick count of the number of people at the table with scripts in their hands. There were six males and one female. That also happened to be the complement of characters in the play. I started bobbing and weaving, trying to avoid the knowledge that was staring me in the face. My fingers fanned through the script I was carrying. "What page are we on?"

He hung his head and rounded his shoulders. He presented a picture of great suffering and the caption was: *You just don't know the shit I've been going through.*

What, I was supposed to feel sorry for this fucker? "You're still in the first act, right?" I was doing a rope-a-dope, trying to slide out of the corner in which I was getting pinned.

"Actually, I had to recast your part. Get a taller actor. I can't believe I forgot to call you."

Wham! It was a rabbit punch and it caught me flush in the kidneys. Now he was taking me by the elbow and directing me toward the door. "HOW THE FUCK COULD YOU NOT CALL ME?" I had definitely turned up the volume.

His hand tightened on my arm. Being a victim hadn't worked, so now I was being shown the hard ass. I yanked my arm away, an inadequate gesture by any measure, and left under my own steam.

So there you have it folks. In the space of twenty-five minutes I'd gone from the next Rock Hudson and the next John Barrymore to a twenty-four-year-old with a really shitty car who lived with his mother. If that wasn't a reality check about showbiz then I can't imagine what could be.

I spent the next few days licking my wounds and crying in my beer but then decided that I was past the point of no return and might as well forge ahead as give up the ghost. I also decided that mixing really lame cliches is not a bad thing if you show how smart you are by calling attention to it.

⚡

I joined another acting class and began seeing a girl I met there. She didn't have a car, and she asked me to take her to an interview she had for an independent movie. You've heard of situations like this: The person whose audition it is doesn't get cast but the escort does. They asked me if I was interested in playing one of the leads. The film was called *Strange Loves* and it was comprised of three short stories. At the core of the trilogy was an examination of homosexuality but in such superficial terms that it did little to advance anyone's knowledge of the subject. To the production's credit there was nothing in the script that was in the least exploitative. The onscreen behavior of the characters was circumspect. No one took off their clothes and there wasn't even any same-gender kissing. All the same, I decided not to do it but recommended a friend of mine, John Morates, for the part.

He was given the role but a few days before they were to start shooting he passed away. I had gone to his apartment to see him and was met by a very irritated landlady who was convinced he had skipped out on the rent. She had been told he had died but didn't believed it. I sensed immediately it was true because I was aware he had a congenital heart condition. This was the first time I had experienced the death of a contemporary, and I found myself very troubled by it. I had never met his family and I didn't know how to reach his girlfriend. If there was a funeral service I never heard about it since no one knew how to contact me. I had this need to express my sorrow, to share it with someone who knew him, but we had no friends in common. It felt like I was in a vacuum trying to make a noise and not succeeding. "In space no one can hear you scream," as the promo went. I didn't know the term at the time but what I was looking for was "closure."

Robert Stambler, the producer for *Strange Loves* called me wondering why their leading man hadn't shown up. I explained what had happened and he then asked me if I would reconsider playing the part. I thought about it and said yes. I worked it out in my head that in taking over the role I would be paying tribute to John, that by my playing the character he was supposed to play I could make a statement out loud, that could be heard, about our friendship. I'm sure there is some Buddhist philosophy that could explain this situation more eloquently than I can.

One of the curses of my life is that I hold suspect everybody's motives, my own included. I think we can thank Dad for that. So just to make doubly certain for myself that my intentions were honorable I told Stambler that I would play the part without a salary.

There is an old vaudeville routine in which, when a particular word is said, the person who hears it says, "Slowly I turn," changes character, and starts whacking people over the head. Bud Abbott and Lou Costello revived it for the movies to hilarious effect. My character's name in *Strange Loves* was *Robert*. The producer's son played him at the age of eight, when he is sexually assaulted by a man in the ruins of a huge estate. (It was actually shot on the grounds of what had been the "castle" of the magician Houdini.) At the age of fourteen the boy is again raped, this time by his drunken uncle's girlfriend. Believe it or not, I played him at this tender age by dressing in pajamas that were three sizes too large for me and speaking in a high squeaky voice. I was almost twenty-five at the time. (I guarantee that this performance made nobody forget Mickey Rooney.) I also played Robert at the age of nineteen, when he is once again the object of lust, this time by his fiancée's mother. In each case, the perpetrator of the crime had the curious habit of calling Robert "Roberto." Was this something native to sexually depraved people—adding the "o" to the name Robert? I try not to think about it. Anyway, poor Robert, like the guy in the vaudeville sketch, flips out on this third go-round when he is again called

"Roberto," turns slowly, and strangles his future mother-in-law. The last scene has him being placed in a jail cell with another prisoner who leeringly says, "We're going to be good friends, Robert...o." Can't you just hear the roar of timpani and the clash of cymbals to underscore the irony?

Amazingly enough, this picture got a theatrical release and played on 42nd Street in New York and at the Apollo Arts Movie House on Hollywood Boulevard in L.A. Needless to say, neither location was considered a showcase for films with redeeming value.

The best thing that came out of this experience was a long friendship with Joe D'Agosta, who played the lead role in one of the other segments. Star Trek fans should know his name. He was the casting director on that series and was the person responsible for bringing me in to audition. Long before that, however, he brought me in on another show, and that's a story, quite strange in its own way, which will be detailed down the line.

About six months after returning to Los Angeles I got my first acting job. I immediately moved out of my mother's house and into a bungalow court made up of self-contained little buildings on Serrano Street in east Hollywood. The rent was fifty dollars a month and it came unfurnished. Aside from a Murphy bed and bench chairs and a breakfast table that were cemented to a wall there was no furniture. I managed to live there until I got married in 1965 without ever adding a stick. Material possessions were not an important consideration in my life. My focus was exclusively on trying to jumpstart a career.

I got cast in my first professional job by doing the kind of hustling and self-promotion that I couldn't face in New York. There were two security guards checking cars in at the gate at the ABC studio on Prospect Avenue in Hollywood. I didn't have an appointment so I left my car on a side street and literally climbed over a wall, my stack of eight-by-ten photos and my phony resumes shielded from the rough-surfaced bricks.

I have learned that events which are perceived in advance as being laden with obstacles and, consequently, fraught with anxiety rarely live up to their advance notices. In New York I had envisioned myself obsequiously trying to hand my photos to casting directors and having doors slammed in my face. At ABC I found myself in a narrow corridor with important-sounding names and titles on every door. I had no plan so I decided on inspiration. When that didn't materialize I figured making a fool of myself was the next best alternative. "WEXTRY, WEXTRY!"

I shouted, remembering 1930s movies I had seen about urchin news-boys hawking their wares on street corners. "Read all about it! Read all about it!" I continued as I burst through doors and slammed my picture and bio on desks. I did this without ever hearing a word of rejection. Not quite the remarkable achievement it might sound like. The fact is, I was in and out of each office at such speed that my presence really didn't have a chance to register. That was okay. I was getting the job done and appeasing a conscience that had been at me with accusations of gutlessness.

I had completed my mission in record time and was tiptoeing back up the hall toward the exit when one of the secretaries on whose desk I had left my calling card stepped out and crooked her finger. She had my photo in her hand and kept staring at it as she motioned me to a chair. The picture reminded her of an actor she had a crush on named Corey Allen. He played the bad kid who goes over the cliff in *Rebel Without A Cause* and, as an additional point of reference for Star Trek fans, he directed the pilot episode, "Encounter at Farpoint," of *Star Trek: The Next Generation* twenty-six years later.

She made an appointment for me to see her boss, a casting director named Pam Palifroni, to read for a part on a daytime television series called *Day In Court*. It was a precursor of all those other courtroom shows that have managed to span the last three decades with hardly a change in format. I left there reasonably excited. I also noticed that her conversation was directed almost exclusively to my photograph. To this day I'm not sure that she ever actually looked at me.

I was called back the following week and was cast in my first television role. The character's name was Irving da Dope. I remember little about the part other than he was a dumb New York kid and that I made the people on the set laugh. This led to six other appearances as different characters on the show over the next two years. Of these there is only one worth noting. (It's amazing with what clarity one remembers the truly impressive disasters in one's life.)

I was cast in the role of Jimmy, a delinquent who has to recount how he burgled a house by coming through the skylight and attacking the owner. The script, which had been given me two days before, had an enormous number of lines for my character. I had a fragile hold on them at best when I came to our only rehearsal on the morning of the shoot. There really wasn't much directing to be done since there was hardly any blocking and all the camera angles were by the numbers and set up in advance. To justify his title, what the director could do and did do was to change dialogue around. I can absolutely assure you that this juggling was totally arbitrary and that the script wasn't improved as much as one iota by it. A speech that was on page five was now on page eleven, one on page seven was three pages later, and one on page fifteen had become the opening lines for the show.

I tried to absorb all this but I was now gargling with my own stomach acid. To compound the panic was the knowledge that we were shooting on tape, and at that time you couldn't edit tape. This meant that under no circumstances, no matter how badly the actor might screw up, was he permitted to stop. If he did they'd have to start over again from the beginning. Since the crew was being paid by the hour this meant doubling the budget. A twenty-five-thousand dollar shoot would immediately become a fifty-thousand-dollar shoot.

I knew even before they called "Action!" I wasn't going to get through it, but I was praying that I'd somehow be able to improvise. Just as it is today on these "court" shows, the man playing the judge really was a judge. He sat at a tall desk with the script in front of him. The camera was positioned so the pages wouldn't be in frame, and he was clever about not making it obvious that he was reading his lines. My part demanded a long description—three or four pages worth to begin with—of how I broke into the place, found a gun in a drawer, and, when confronted by the homeowner, almost shot him. I got through the first sentence about coming through the skylight and then went totally blank. "I opened the skylight . . ." ("And last but not least is tin...") "I opened the skylight..." ("And last but not least is tin . . . ") "I opened the skylight . . ." I was on the exact same road to nowhere I had been on in the fourth grade when I had my first blackout as a fledgling performer. I didn't know how lucky I was then when they dropped the curtain on my humiliation. This time I wasn't going to be let off the hook. The judge started prompting me, checking my dialogue in the script laid out before him.

"Isn't it true, Jimmy, that you went to the desk after you came through the skylight?"

"Yes, yes, I went to the desk . . ." *I was going to be able to salvage it after all! Thank god for the judge!* "I went to the desk . . . and . . . I . . . went . . . to . . . the . . . desk . . . "*. . . And I wrote a letter to Santa. Forget it, I still didn't have a clue.*

"Which drawer did you open, Jimmy? (long pause.) Was it the second drawer on the left?"

"Yes! Yes, it was the second drawer on the left and . . . and . . ."

And what? I could have been a ten-ton locomotive on greased rails without brakes pointing down a ninety-degree incline and I still couldn't have gotten up a head of steam. It wasn't coming back to me, not one line. I began shaking my head in despair.

"Don't you shake your head at me, Jimmy!" He was starting to get pissed off like we were really in a courtroom and I wasn't showing him the proper respect. "Do you want to go to jail, Jimmy, is that what you want?" His face was turning red. Veins in his neck were beginning to bulge. This wasn't *Day In Court*, this was Kafka! "I'll ask you again, *do you want to go to jail ? It could be very very bad for you there.*" I didn't know what he was talking about. Jimmy gets probation at the end of the story and here on page one he's practically threatening him with the gas chamber. I couldn't remember a single line but I sure as hell knew that this last bit wasn't in the script. I started to wave my hands to show him I was hopelessly lost and that despite everything we'd have to stop.

He rose from behind the desk and leaned forward on his hands. His arms were trembling. I would have been happy if he had started shouting but his voice came at me in a deadly whisper. I felt like I was facing Jack Palance across a barroom in *Shane*. "Don't you wave your hands at me, mister!"

That was it. I rose from where I was sitting, walked over to the director and yelled "Cut!" I don't know what the executives on the set were thinking but I know the crew wasn't upset. I had just doubled their salaries.

I have no way to explain how I got it right on the next take. I should have been a total basket case by then. As it was, I was sure my career in Hollywood was over, I would never work again. I went to an actors' bar called The Raincheck Room to get drunk but it was so out of character for me I felt ridiculous, and I went home stone sober.

A month later Ms. Palifroni called me in again. This time it was to play my, by now, standard juvenile delinquent on the pilot episode of a new soap opera. The series was called *General Hospital*. It's still on the air and so am I . . . occasionally. What we have here is a happy ending!

✻

It was late 1960. I was told about an acting workshop conducted by a person who had connections in the film industry. I was informed that he invited these people to his sessions and that the actors in the

workshop could make good contacts. I went to a class and was introduced to this important middle-aged man. His name was Peter Dee.
Thus began the most bizarre relationship I have had in the thirty-six
years of my career. I haven't yet gone into much detail about anyone's
psychical nature but it's worth noting a few things about Mr. Dee. He
looked a bit like the actor Van Heflin, but only after somebody had
thrown a switch sending several thousand volts of electricity through
him. His eyes were small but they couldn't be ignored. He never just
looked at you. He looked *into* you, searching your mind as if it were
the Carlsbad Caverns. To him your brain was an enormous network of
underground caves that he was compelled to examine. He'd spin out of
the dead ends, crash past the stalactites and stalagmites, race through
every passage, probe every chamber until he'd found the secret one, the
one in which even the bats wouldn't go, and there in its deepest recess
he would shape from the dimmest insubstantial shadows the embodi-
ment of his most fearful belief—that you were out to get him, you and
everyone else into whose face he had ever looked. Mr. Dee was border-
line psychotic. Is it any wonder that I chose him as my first manager?

Of course, I didn't know this immediately. It took a few months
for the concept to germinate, another couple to bud, and perhaps one
more before it blossomed and I could categorically identify the life
form with whom I had formed a partnership: Audrey II, the carnivo-
rous plant from *Little Shop of Horrors* was like rutabaga compared to
Peter Dee.

He became my manager only after I had attended several of his
workshops and he decided I was his most gifted student. (I admit to this
with a certain degree of embarrassment.) At his insistence we began seeing a lot of each other. He told me that he had been a journalist but, to
use his words, "had been 'eighty-sixed' out of town" for driving his car
through somebody's store window while in a drunken stupor. He
admitted to being an alcoholic but was a member of AA.(Judging from
the difficulties he was still having I gathered it must have been about a
ninety-step program.)

He would tell me about all the people he was lining up for me to
meet and all the deals he was in the process of closing which, if I stuck
with him, would also include me. I was buying it. He was incredibly
dynamic. He had such great confidence and so much determination it
was almost impossible not to believe him. I can see how Sun Yung
Moon and Jim Jones and Charlie Manson developed cult followings.

Just about the time I began to wonder whether he was for real he did arrange for me to have an audition at Warner Bros. They were a hot TV studio, with lightweight successes like *77 Sunset Strip* and *Adventures In Paradise*. These were very commercial shows that were short on content and long on pretty faces and exotic scenery.

Solly Biano was the casting director I was to meet. He reflected well the slick ambiance of the Warner Bros. product. He was meticulously groomed and nattily dressed.

Peter decided that I should do something other than the standard audition piece from *Hatful of Rain* or *Tea and Sympathy*. I wasn't going to be the tough New Yorker like Anthony Franciosa or the sensitive, misunderstood adolescent like John Kerr. No, what he had in mind was Charlie Chaplin. That's right, Charlie Chaplin. If the seventies is closer to your frame of reference think about doing a Chaplinesque audition piece for the glitz and glitter of *Charlie's Angels*. If it's the eighties, envision trying to be cast on *Magnum P.I.* by doing a pantomime of a little guy spinning an imaginary bowler and twirling an imaginary cane while doing a duck walk and flirting with a make-believe eight-foot female devil. *No, no, no, no, no, Walter, you've gone too far! Nobody's going to believe this! You'd have to be craz*— Well, as I said, this was Peter's idea. Of course, that doesn't explain why *I* went along with it. Chalk it up to desperation and flights of fancy and the egomaniacal belief that I could somehow pull it off. Needless to say, I couldn't.

I decided that Mephistophelita was leaning coyly on one hip in the center of the room. This meant that as I circled her first in one direction and then the other I had to occasionally leap in the air to avoid stepping on the five-foot-long tail that she happily wagged and slithered across the floor. I also flounced, winked, sashayed, and spun my eyes, twitched my little pretend moustache, doffed my derby, and jumped up and clicked my heels. If I had been auditioning for a movie about mental disorders I'd have stood a better chance. The madness that inspired the idea for this audition was exceeded only by the lunacy of the person attempting to perform it. Of course, I was totally caught up in what I was doing and wasn't aware of any of this at the time. Only afterward would I remember catching a glimpse of Biano desperately trying to "see" the strumpet I was courting, his effort to make some sense of what I was doing, and his utter failure to do so. At one point his mouth fell open and a thin line of spittle hung between his lips.

I ended by raising my hand above my head and curling my arm as if Beelzebubette had linked hers with mine. I then started toward the door. Just before I exited I looked back over my shoulder, hopped on one leg, gave a little kick with the other, and wiggled my eyebrows. I went through the door and closed it behind me. Still awash in the moment, my first thought was that I might have overdone things a bit by wiggling the eyebrows. I mean, wasn't that a Groucho Marx trademark? I was starting to feel badly about that when, like a spider trolling down a silken thread to weave a trap, another thought dropped into my head and began spinning a web to ensnarl my mind. It succeeded. My brain seized convulsively as I realized what had really been going on: This wasn't about Groucho Marx, this was about the insanity of performing a piece of bizarre esoterica for a guy who wears shades, spats, and black-and-white shoes, and carries a five-inch pearl cigarette holder. I wanted to flee, join a commune in the mountains, put flowers in my hair, and sing "Michael Row The Boat Ashore." Instead I turned the door handle and stepped back into the room.

Solly Biano was more than bewildered. He was stupefied. His limbs hung loosely at his sides. It was as if he had lost all motor control. He might have been a marionette with slack strings. When he finally summoned speech it was in a voice devoid of affect. "I don't get it'" is what he managed. I doubt if the air was any heavier in the hour before prisoners faced the guillotine during the French Revolution. The silence went unabated until at last his mouth began to move again. He was trying to voice some additional thought, perhaps a helpful comment, an enlightening instruction, a precious word of encouragement. Peter and I leaned forward straining to hear something that would resurrect our egos, that would put meaning back in our lives.

"I . . . don't . . . get . . . it," is all he could say. My memory is that we left him like that, staring vacuously and mumbling the same words over and over again.

Peter had a permanently injured hip or leg and when he walked his body lurched to the right. ("The evil man who limped when he walked . . .") This wasn't a problem for me as long as I was to his left. Today, coming out of Warners, I was trapped on his right side between him and the buildings and had only a narrow lane to navigate. We moved rapidly, more a consequence of his mounting anger than any time consideration. He did not speak a word but on every second footfall he'd crash into me and I would end up struggling for balance. I had the distinct feeling that it was more than the properties of inertial thrust that caused these lunges to occur. It felt like we were pack animals and that the alpha beast was showing dominance over the other with aggressive body language.

On the other hand, it probably looked like a surrealistic scene from a Fellini movie: *The street was empty. The two characters had a wide expanse to maneuver in yet they crowded a narrow pathway, continually colliding, the one launching himself against the other while the other staggered to remain upright, and neither of them ever speaking or acknowledging the assault being perpetrated.* All that was missing was the Chaplinesque pantomime, a dwarf, and a calliope.

The silence persisted even after we had reached the car and driven off. Finally, at the first stoplight he twisted in the passenger seat and, winding up his arm, thrust his index finger to within a quarter inch of my nose.

"Don't you ever do that again!"

I could feel his eyes, like pneumatic drills, puncturing the layers of my brain, digging for that deepest cave in which festered the hate he felt sure was harbored there.

"Do what?"

"You purposely screwed that audition up!"

"Why would I do that? I'm the one trying to get work."

"You made a fool out of me!"

''For God's sake, Peter . . . ."

"You didn't do what we rehearsed."

"I did exactly what we rehearsed."

"You fucked it up to embarrass me. You made a fool out of me in front of Solly Biano!"

And so it went for the next fifteen minutes. We pulled into the parking lot of his favorite daytime haunt, Schwab's Drug Store, where Lana Turner was supposedly discovered. He kept taking me there figuring that it might happen for me too. I tried telling him that I didn't wear sweaters but he didn't see the humor.

Telly Savalas of future *Kojak* and *The Dirty Dozen* fame was sitting at the counter. Like Peter Dee, Telly was also Greek. Dee was still fuming and I wanted to distract him. I went up to Savalas with a big smile as if we had met before. He was too much of a gentleman to admit he didn't know me. I then introduced him to Peter and the two began an animated discussion in Greek that appeared satisfying to them both.

The next week Telly showed up at our workshop. Peter conducted a series of improvisations with me as the centerpiece. About a dozen students, in turn, would approach the stage with their own scenarios. I had to figure out who they were and what they wanted and what our relationship was supposed to be and then improvise with them. When we broke for coffee I approached our guest and asked him what he thought of it. I was definitely fishing for a compliment and he dutifully supplied it. Dee caught the end of the conversation but said nothing until the actor left. Then suddenly the arm wound up, the index finger shot out, and I was looking into those malignant eyes once more.

"What do you think you're doing? *I* talk to the guests. *Only* me! You don't *ever* talk to the guests. Got it?" I'm a slow learner, but a picture was starting to take shape. I was thinking it was time to get out. I would have saved myself a lot of stress if I had obeyed that instinct.

But now Peter had a new scheme. He was going to write and produce the story of his life and he wanted me to play him. He said he had been given seed money by Robert Young, the actor who had played the title roles in *Father Knows Best* and *Marcus Welby M.D.* in a long career that also included many starring roles in motion pictures. Peter said that he knew Young from Alcoholics Anonymous and that the benevolent performer had given him five thousand dollars with the promise of matching funds for any cash Peter raised to produce the film. Well, he got the five thousand from somewhere. I guess it was from Robert Young, because he did rent space at a studio directly across from Paramount and I was introduced to that fine actor there.

Dee showed me contracts attesting to the fact that he had hired James Wong Howe, the great cinematographer, and Katrina Paxinou, a famous Greek actress who had won the Academy Award in the Best Supporting category for *For Whom The Bell Tolls* in 1943. She was to play my mother. I was impressed. It might be worth hanging in there after all. I asked to read the script. It wasn't ready yet, I was told.

His next order of business was to interview actresses. Dee had had three wives, and he was looking to find women who closely approximated them physically. He didn't feel that any of the students in the workshop were right for the roles. In each case, since I would be playing him, he wanted me along so he could observe the chemistry. We met several of them at his office at the studio and a couple at his workshop space. He was having trouble making up his mind but became immediately testy if I established rapport with any of these women. I couldn't quite figure out what was going on. He wanted me there to see if we related well to each other but got pissed if we did. I felt there was a jealousy component in all this, but was he jealous of me or of them? Peter was a card-carrying homophobe who constantly spoke in the most violent terms about all the "queers" in Hollywood. I initially thought that he must feel that he and I were in competition for these actresses' attention. Then I began to wonder if it might not be a case of "the lady doth protest too much" that he might have repressed feelings about me and that he would rather die than admit to them.

Whatever was simmering inside him came to a boil on a night we were supposed to meet yet another aspiring young performer at a popular restaurant on Sunset Strip called Cyrano's. They both arrived before I did and their conversation was well underway. I jumped in when I felt it appropriate, and her attention turned to me. We hit it off quite well and when it was time for her to go I offered to walk her to the door. The room was very crowded and dark but I somehow sensed Dee staring at me even as I made my way back toward his table. The smile on his face was something carved from the dead mouth of a corpse. It didn't fool me for a second. My gait slowed as I approached the table but I could only delay the inevitable. His arm went around my shoulders as if we were great buddies and held me in a close grip as he sat me down. The rictus smile was still in place and went as far back as his rear molars. There was a lot of gold showing.

"Cute, huh?" He winked at me and gestured in the direction of the girl who had just left. I began to relax. He was being playful. I had been wrong. But then, still gripping my shoulder, he leaned over and whispered in my ear. "If you ever do that again I'm going to put a bullet in your head."

So this is when I finally got wise and turned in my resignation, right? Wrong. You must understand that everyone with whom Peter Dee surrounded himself was convinced that he was going to make this film. These people were either other actors from his workshop or associates who, in some undefined way, existed on the periphery of the film industry. It was in the bag, a done deal, a fait accompli. The money was pouring in, they told me. The script was nearly done, they assured me.

Remember before what I said about actors having a problem distinguishing fact from fancy? I wish to amend that statement. It's only *partially* the result of a childlike faith in "the promise." It's also the consequence of an engulfing need that something good *will* happen, that some success *will* occur, that it can't always be disappointment on top of rejection ad infinitum, ad nauseam. In the face of an overwhelming body of contradictory evidence, Peter Dee still made everyone feel that he was a winner. He had a charismatic intensity that was overpowering, and he also knew his audience. These were people who had wallowed in the swamplands of mediocrity and were looking for a savior to take them to a greener, higher ground. They didn't just want it, they were desperate for it.

"This is going to be a fantastic movie, Walter, and your part is incredible. It's going to make you a star!" They looked past his eccentricities to the pot of gold, and they kept filling my head with the party line because each recruit they secured strengthened their own conviction. I do believe that the door-to-door proselytizing of ultra-conservative religious sects is a function of the same process.

And all the time I felt like the guy in the story who discovers that the potato in his soup is really an alien with a hundred eyes and can't find anyone to believe him. After awhile you begin to doubt yourself. How can everyone else be wrong and only you right? Everyone else claims to have discovered something pure and clean and sweet, and all you see is a brown lumpy extraterrestrial with three-hundred-and-sixty-degree vision. Maybe they *are* right. I mean, how can everyone else be wrong except me? It was the question I kept asking myself and the one for which I couldn't find an incontestable answer. I was immobilized by indecision and so, despite threats to my life by this guy, I hung in with him yet a little longer.

However, I was finding it harder and harder to go to his Saturday afternoon workshops. I'd wake in the morning with severe stomach cramps, and it would be hours before I could straighten up. I started making excuses for not attending. I created a running story about my sister, who the first time just needed a ride to see her doctor about swollen feet. But then the situation got progressively worse: The feet became symptomatic of diabetes. Infection set in. There was talk of amputation. The possibility of blindness. She had developed severe depression and was on a suicide watch. My behavior was shameless, but I felt like I was fighting for my life.

Dee was getting suspicious. He phoned me wanting to know why she hadn't died yet. I sensed a touch of sarcasm. I was still trying to play both ends against the middle, so I promised to attend one of his all-night story sessions at the studio and then go to a party he would be throwing the next night at a restaurant on Hollywood Boulevard.

Everything I had to know I learned that evening in his office, but it wasn't until the following night that I was finally able to set myself on an irrevocable course. When he'd first showed me his workspace a couple of months before, the only furniture in the room was a desk and a chair. Nothing had changed. This meant that the six or seven people who crowded into the small area had to position themselves on the floor. The picture reminded me of a religious tapestry woven to inspire awe and worship: The holy man on his throne and his flock in genuflection before him. On the other hand, it's a good thing that pictures *don't* talk. In actuality, Peter was holding court, regaling his audience with tales from his past. (I have tried to be judicious in my use of profanity applying, it only when I thought it had some literary value. To quote his narrative here, however, would be overkill. Certainly, it would devalue the use of four-letter words as colorful punctuation for events I have yet to relate.) Everyone laughed obediently at his stories, groping heroically to find humor in what was a series of anecdotes rife with malevolence and directed toward a wide variety of minorities.

As disturbing as this was, my attention was directed elsewhere. On his desk was a large old typewriter. The more I stared at it the bigger it seemed to grow, a huge, looming, silent presence that could not be ignored. And my take was that that's exactly what Peter Dee was trying desperately to do. He had surrounded himself with sycophants and told his rambling hateful stories again and again night after night to keep at bay the demons that haunted him. If he was left alone he might have to actually face the typewriter and write his script. It occurred to me then that he had yet to write the first word. He simply could not deal with the possibility of failure, and with these devoted companions he never had to. Like the folks in the fable, they never saw the paunch and the pale buttocks. They saw only the exquisite raiments of an emperor, and that's the way Dee wanted it.

As I look back on it now I envision the monolith from *2001* coaxing primates to transform sticks into tools. The typewriter was Peter's monolith, but he had turned away from it and scampered back into the trees. I knew at that moment that he would not be heard from again.

The following evening we convened at a restaurant in the eastern end of Hollywood called the Greek Village. Dee had arranged for tables to be placed end to end so that about twenty of us might find seats. Peter sat at the head. The guys whose lips formed a permanent pucker sat to his immediate left and right. I was two-thirds of the way down, hopefully blocked from his view by the guests sitting between us. Dee was again holding court and his stories were typically vulgar. The laughter was loud and out of proportion. I think even our host sensed this. His jokes became angrier, less forgiving, more insulting. It was as if he were mocking his audience, challenging them to find the entertainment value in the most debasing stories he could conjure. If he could have them doubled over in hysterics with tales from the toilet while eating moussaka and olives then these people were his. He owned them. They would never question why the screenplay they were all banking their futures on had yet to make an appearance. And he was succeeding.

At some point he caught my eye. I had been studiously avoiding contact by concentrating on the plate of food in front of me. It was somewhat like that scene from the Hitchcock movie *Strangers on a Train*, where everyone in the crowd is following the flight of the tennis ball as it flies off the racquets of the two players except for the one guy in the stands who stares straight ahead. In my case I was staring straight ahead at my food while chortling heads all around me bobbed about, each vying with the rest to show that they got the joke best. Dee saw that I wasn't joining in. After the briefest pause he lurched from his chair, came around my side of the table, slapped me on the shoulder, and proceeded, in that lunging manner of his, toward the exit. I assumed I was meant to follow.

We were standing on the sidewalk, somewhat in shadow, and he was pointing at a white stretch limousine illuminated by a lamppost.

"Where'd you get that?" I asked.

"They gave it to me."

"They?"

"Mickey Cohn and Jimmy Hoffa. In exchange for writing favorable biographies about them."

Cohn had run afoul of the law for decades and was reputed to be the West Coast's leading mobster. Hoffa, of course, was the Teamster boss who was reviled by the Attorney General and later ended up the target of a gang hit.

One might include Peter Dee's sanity among other things gone missing. The story was such a preposterous concoction that had I not already decided I would sever my association with him after this night, that would have been all the nudge I needed. Still, he had one more surprise up his sleeve, or should I say in his jacket pocket. He reached in and pulled out a gun. He bounced it in his palm importantly, making a display of his expertise.

"Thirty-eight caliber. Splendid piece. Outstanding craftsmanship," he intoned in a scholarly fashion.

I could imagine the pointy hat, the magnifying glass, and the pipe. Christ, I had Sherlock Holmes standing next to me and all this time I thought it was Moriarty!

I turned to leave. He spun at the same time, in reflex I suppose, but he lost his balance and fell into me. The knee or hip had given out and he was in danger of crashing to the ground. I reached for him with both arms and we found ourselves chest to chest. Well, not exactly chest to chest. Wedged in between our bodies was the gun he was holding. It was pointed at my throat. He started to giggle. It reminds me now of the dirty little giggle that snot-nosed Howie shared with snot-nosed Bernie in Miss Form's fifth-grade class as he grabbed at the front of his trousers and whispered that he had seen Mary Clooney's underpants when she bent over. Peter wouldn't have been interested in Mary's underwear but he was definitely into his pistol. I think all three of them had that in common. "It's loaded!" he whispered, and giggled once more.

I didn't see Peter Dee again for three years, but I did run into one of his lackeys about a month later. When I asked how Peter was doing I was accused of deserting the guy and admonished for blowing a big opportunity. I was told they were about to start construction on the movie sets. "It's going to be a fantastic picture!" he added with a triumphant smirk. "Have you seen the script?" I asked. "No, but . . ."

Six months later I ran into him again. He seemed genuinely shocked by the news he had to relate. Peter Dee had been arrested. He had been involved in one of the most traditional of white-collar schemes: "hanging paper." He'd been opening bank accounts all over town with the same five thousand dollars he had been initially given. He would write a flurry of checks and then withdraw the original deposit before the transactions could be posted to show that his balance had been depleted. Unbelievably, it wasn't the banks who had nailed him. Dee had managed to talk his way out of every situation there. He was that persuasive. But the company from whom he had leased the stretch limo—the one that Mickey Cohn and Jimmy Hoffa had supposedly given him—was less gullible. Month after month he had given them "rubber," and it was they who had finally called the bunko squad.

I went to see his wife. I told her I didn't think he belonged in jail. I felt he could be better helped in a mental institution, and I volunteered to testify to that effect. I was never called upon but he was eventually sent to the psychiatric hospital at Camarillo anyway. I guess one could say that saner heads did finally prevail.

Probably the most satisfying thing that came out of this period of my life was a liaison I established with one of Peter Dee's students, a former Miss USA. As the title would suggest she was exceptionally attractive. She invited me up to her place one evening, and thus began a relationship that was extremely short on conversation. Heavy breathing seemed to be the thing we shared best. We never actually had a date. That is, we never went out to a restaurant or a movie or for a walk in the park. She had an attorney boyfriend who provided her those diversions. Nor did I ever buy her flowers, a box of chocolates, or a greeting card. There was a casino manager in Las Vegas who was writing some pretty sizable checks to cover the bon-bon side of things. In one of our rare dialogue exchanges she told me that he had mob ties and was a dangerous character. I filed the information right there at the front of the cabinet drawer next to "Bruno the Meat Mangler."

Because of the other men in her life, I had difficulty at first in grasping what it was she saw in me. Money, of course, was not a consideration, and since we spent so little time talking I figured she'd have to be telepathic to determine that I had a poetic soul or a sense of humor. What was left seemed absurd but the facts did seem to be pointing in that direction. Could it be . . . ? Was it possible . . . ? Well, really, there just wasn't any other explanation . . . yes, yes, it had to be so . . . *I was a boy toy!* Even if that expression was unknown at the time the concept wasn't. I can't tell you how much I reveled in that knowledge. For the first twenty-four years of my life I had labored under the impression that I was kin to the bell ringer at Notre Dame, and now this beautiful lady's attention was giving me a whole new self-image. Superficial, you say. Absolutely! Beneath me, you sneer. Not a bit. At that point in my life the limitations of this relationship were the very properties required to boost my confidence. I had always had a preoccupation with my physical appearance, and if as a result of this tryst I didn't actually grow several inches I knew at least that the hump between my shoulders was forever gone. Pity, then, that it all ended rather abruptly.

The last time I saw her she told me she had "given me up." An odd turn of phrase, I thought. Perhaps she meant she was giving up on me. An odious conclusion, and one I was reluctant to draw. No, that wasn't what she meant. Evidently, the casino mug had gotten wind that there was a boyfriend here in L.A. and demanded to know who it was. Obviously it was the attorney, since he was the one with whom she had been seen in public. However, since she needed to eat and take walks in the park, she made the pragmatic decision to name me. She had given my name up to him. I think she felt genuinely bad about the decision and I think she might have been willing for us to carry on under deep cover, but the prospect of doing so and getting caught and having my knees broken was all the deterrent I required. We stopped seeing each other after that, but even so I stayed away from dark alleys for a long time.

TEN

"The Sky Above, The Mud Below"

THE NEXT SEVERAL YEARS WERE A SUCCESSION OF CONTIGUOUS HIGH points and low points that made me feel that I was both establishing a beachhead in Hollywood while at the same time being caught in an undertow that was sucking me out to sea. But what's new? Every actor goes through this. It's the schizophrenic nature of the business. Therefore, although the stories that follow are unique to me, you are quite safe in applying a generalization; every performer can recount episodes similar, if not in actual text certainly in flavor, to the biographies of their lives.

I had finally broken in to prime-time television with bit parts on the television series *The Untouchables* and *Combat*. Neither experience was noteworthy except that Robert Altman, who would later direct the films *MASH, Nashville,* and *The Player* among others, was at the helm of the *Combat* show. I asked him if I could add a stutter to the character, a nervous stockade guard, and he shrugged his shoulders as if to say "be my guest." If I knew then what I know about him now I probably could have gotten away with improvising a monologue in which I overlapped myself as well.

The first featured role I had in television came late in 1962 as Lee Marvin's son in an anthology series called *The Great Adventure.* Lee

Marvin, as every film buff knows, was a powerful actor, and the star of many movies including *The Man Who Shot Liberty Valance, Cat Ballou,* and *The Dirty Dozen.* This job typified in microcosm my whole career. Usually splendid occasions and disastrous ones happen independently over the course of many job experiences, but for me the one-hundred-and-eighty-degree spin of my fortunes occurred over a period of six working days. I cannot tell you how much I have regretted the role I played in them.

The character I performed was the first of a series of ethnic parts in which I was to be cast. Marvin and I were Armenian grape growers trying to get our harvest to market by wagon but were being sabotaged by the railroad, which wanted us to ship our produce by train. These stories were all supposed to be authentic tales taken from American history. The event must have had great resonance because two years later I caught an episode of the TV series *The Big Valley* about two Greek date-growing brothers who were trying to get their harvest to market by wagon but were being sabotaged by the railroad, which wanted them to ship their produce by train. My old script was in a drawer and within reach. Sure enough, I was able to follow right along with the story and predict the dialogue, word for word, before it was spoken. I guess a story worth telling is worth telling twice . . . or even more. (Hey, what about one for *Dr. Quinn, Medicine Woman* about two Jewish bakers, a rabbi and his guilt-ridden son-in-law, trying to get their matzoh to market by wagon . . . well, maybe not.)

But I digress. The script described the boy I was playing as being fourteen years old, but since there was no dialogue reference to his age we were able to ignore that fact. Except, that is, for the one piece of business where the writer had Marvin's character boost his son into the wagon. I told Lee that if he tried it I'd have him killed. Which brings me to my relationship with Marvin and the whole point of this story.

I've always felt awkward around boisterous, bigger-than-life personalities. There is an unpredictability about them that makes it hard for me to relax in their presence. I'm usually a little anxious that they may go off the deep end without warning and I won't be prepared to deal with it. (Ironically, the one time I was exposed to that kind of extreme behavior the perpetrator was a quiet restrained performer with an eye-blink twitch who totally lost his mind in front of a theater full of people. But more on that shortly.) That's not to say that I wouldn't love to have the kind of freedom to be outrageous that they possess. Not necessarily to wear lamp-shades at parties but as a character element to draw upon for the right role. Lee Marvin was just such a man. He loved to drink and party and thoroughly enjoy himself in any part he was playing.

My reaction in the presence of such a person is to become stiff, cerebral, and consciously more articulate. There is no way I can play their game without feeling phony and so I end up in a diametrically opposite posture. I add all this preamble by way of explaining that despite the fact that I demurred on his invitations to hop on his motor-cycle after each day's shoot and go drinking with him and his pal, the actor Keenan Wynn, and despite the fact that I must have come off as an uptight and somewhat aloof pain in the ass, Lee saw past it and decided I was going to be his buddy. I couldn't have been more tickled. I loved all those stories about hard drinkers and hard livers and bar-room brawlers in John Ford movies, and here I was locking arms with an archetype.

In fact, the best compliment he paid me on the set had nothing to do with my acting. We were returning from lunch one day when I remembered that I'd left part of my costume in the trailer. I started back, calling out to Lee to tell the director I'd be a couple of minutes late. "FUCK YOU!" he shouted at me, and kept walking. Now, to those of you who are again rolling your eyes skyward, let me say that although an epithet such as the preceding is usually a call to arms, it can less frequently be an expression of bonding. Such was the case here, and I basked in it.

I was feeling so good about things, in fact, that at the end of the last day of shooting I approached Marvin with what I truly believed was an innocent request that he would warmly greet. I told him I had a problem, and he immediately invited me into his dressing room to dis-cuss it. I explained that I was dissatisfied with my agent and wondered if he could recommend someone else. The people with loved ones on the *Titanic* might have borne the news better than Lee did mine. It was like one of those old variety acts on *The Ed Sullivan Show* where the mime wipes away the manic smile with a sweep of his hand and presents in its place an exaggerated mask of tragedy. That was exactly how abrupt and to what magnitude his mood shifted.

Even though I hadn't anticipated it I knew at once what had hap-pened. He had decided in his mind that I had been setting him up for this one moment since the first day on the set. By asking him for a favor I had deceived and betrayed him. It was extraordinary to observe this tough, man's man, hero-villain of TV and movies appear so incredibly vulnerable. I couldn't have felt more guilty than if it had been me who had elbowed aside women and children to jump into one of the *Titanic's* lifeboats. He looked down at the floor, his chin resting heavily on his chest. His eyes remained averted throughout the exchange that followed.

"My God, I really disappointed you, didn't I?"

"No . . . no . . ."

"I don't know what—"

" . . . except when I was doing *M-Squad* in Chicago a lot of young directors came to me looking for jobs and I gave them a shot. But when I came out here and couldn't get any work none of those assholes were ever in when I called them."

"And you equate me with them?"

"No . . . no . . ."

But the truth was that he did. He had obviously thought of these people as friends and they had let him down. And now I had done the same thing. And he was right. When I saw that we were getting along well I figured I would ask him for a favor. It *had* been in the back of my head from the beginning and I *was* trying to take advantage of his good nature. I just didn't see it in the Machiavellian terms that he did. Now we were both staring at the floor. I could not find one word to speak.

"Come on, let's take a walk." He finally broke the silence and started out of his trailer. I was on his flank immediately. We were shooting at the old Republic Studios in Studio City. It was a sizeable piece of real estate and we proceeded to walk the entire perimeter. During the whole time not a word was spoken. What was he thinking? Obviously, I had called up ghosts for him. It wasn't just me but a long list of people he felt had let him down. I hated that now I was to be counted in their number. I won't make Lee Marvin out to be a saint. But he was a marvelous actor and the debauchery notwithstanding, I don't think you can be that without being at risk to a wide range of deeply felt emotion. He had offered me friendship and I had plundered the offer. I had hurt him, and it made us both sad.

We arrived back at the dressing rooms and stood facing each other. After a bit he stiffly put out his hand to me. The sun was going down behind him. I couldn't see his face clearly. It was probably for the best. The handshake felt formal, without any of the warmth we had shared on this job. He turned and went into his trailer. We never spoke again.

✸

During the Christmas holidays of 1962 I went to a party at an apartment given by an actor cum bartender I had known from The Raincheck Room. I met a young actress there. She was small and slender, but the fragility of her appearance was offset by very large, brown, intelligent eyes. She didn't like comparisons but her resemblance to Audrey Hepburn was unmistakable. It occurred to me immediately that she was extremely bright and we talked together a good part of the evening. I asked her if she would be interested in auditioning for an actors workshop I had heard about called Theatre East. She consented, and we chose a scene from what was then an audition staple, *Winterset* by Maxwell Anderson.

We were both accepted into the group but, curiously, we didn't start dating immediately. As time passed, however, we saw more of each other and I began to think that there was a future to this relationship. I found myself saying the words "I love you" out loud. I was told the feeling was reciprocated. A day came when I had to cancel a dinner date because of a bad head cold. She dropped by anyway, lugging a mammoth roast beef sandwich for me. It was a simple gesture but I was enormously touched by it. I don't know why, but on such things is destiny sometimes shaped. We were married in 1965. Her name is Judy Levitt and we have been together now for over thirty-three years. She is just as beautiful today as she was the day we met.

I was at Theatre East about a year when I began to develop a well-known clinical condition called Dramaturgical Dermatology. It's when the itch to perform is only being satisfied on a skin-deep level. The orientation of the workshop was not toward play production as much as it was toward scene exercise. There's nothing wrong with improving one's skills in a class situation so long as attention is being paid as well to moving one's career along. I was spending so much time preparing scenes that would only be seen by other workshop members that I felt I was setting myself up for a potential trap. It is the kind of thing I referred to early on: When the comfort level of a cozy and cloistered classroom environment makes it attractive as an end unto itself as opposed to a means to an end.

And so I went looking for a theater company that produced plays for the public, where I would not only get a chance to be showcased for the theatrical community but where I could perform in full-length plays with sustaining characters before live audiences. "Live audiences" are the operative words here, and my attempt one dark and stormy night to decapitate a member thereof is the eventual purpose of this story.

But first: The Company of Angels was a theater company established in 1961 by actors for the very reasons I enumerated above. Vic Morrow, best remembered for the television series *Combat* and for film roles in *The Blackboard Jungle, Deathwatch,* and *Twilight Zone: The Movie,* and for the ghastly and reprehensible way in which he was killed during that picture, directed the group's first show. Leonard Nimoy was scheduled to direct another production, but that didn't work out. But Richard Chamberlain, later to be equally famous as television's *Dr. Kildare* as well as the star of *The Thornbirds* and motion pictures including *The Three Musketeers, The Four Musketeers,* and *The Five Ladies Leaping* (well, not that one), did work with the company. (Although it is totally irrelevant, I feel compelled to announce that although he has done much excellent work Richard Chamberlain also starred in the single worst movie I have ever seen, *Alan Quatermain and the City of Gold.* There, I said it. Now back to the story.)

I stopped by the theater on a day early in the rehearsal of the play *Blood Wedding,* the work of the Spanish writer Federico García Lorca. The play is a modern tragedy about a mother who has lost all her menfolk except her youngest son in feuds with another family. On the day of the youngest son's wedding the bride runs off with her lover, who happens to be a member of the rival clan. The bridegroom vows vengeance, goes in pursuit and, naturally, since it's a modern tragedy, the two suitors battle to each other's death.

It was a study in *one* degree of separation when I met Vince, the play's director. He saw the zippered sweater I was wearing and immediately became apoplectic. "Where'd you get that?" he hissed at me the way only Italians in a jealous rage can hiss at you. The sweater had been a present from an actor named Jonathan, whom I had met at The Neighborhood Playhouse.

At the time I was living in New York Jonathan and Vince were both dating a lovely young actress named Louise Sorel. She had also gone to the Playhouse and had been a student with Jonathan in the class below mine. Louise would later star in the soaps *Santa Barbara* and *All My Children* as well as guest star in the third-season *Star Trek* episode "Requiem For Methuselah" as Rayna Kapec.

Evidently, Louise had come home late from a date with Jonathan in the dead of winter and found Vince, very upset, in his shirtsleeves waiting for her on the front step. Louise, being of a giving disposition, offered Vince the zippered sweater she was wearing but failed to tell him from whom she had gotten it. Mollified, Vince went home, took off the sweater, and then found Jonathan's name stitched inside. Displaying passions not unlike those in Lorca's *Blood Wedding*, he ripped it up into many small pieces and vowed vengeance. Jonathan and Vince never did cross paths, and Vince's rage went unabated.

But now here I was wearing what appeared to be the exact same apparel. I didn't look anything like Jonathan and I hardly knew Louise but the look on Vince's face spelled "modern tragedy" and "if-you-can't-heap-havoc-on-the-right-sucker-his-buddy-will-do" all over it. Hold a magnifying glass up to the theater and you have Life. Frankly, I think Lorca would have balked at the unlikely coincidences that occur in real life. I braced for a battle to the death for a crime I never even had the pleasure of committing. However, seeing that he would have to suspend disbelief to justify the urge for retribution Vince, always with a good sense of story structure, decided finally to abandon his vow. And thus it was written that blood would not splash from these warriors' veins and mottle the grassy carpet of the Spanish woods that day.

I hadn't made the connection before but now that I think about it, the "Return of the Zippered Sweater" episode, just like my "Well of Loneliness" episode, follows closely in the tiny but crazed footsteps of the malevolent "Talking Tina."

I assume now that Jonathan's generosity to both Louise and I was a consequence of owning several dozen of these exact same garments and finding no other way to dump them.

After the smoke had cleared Vince asked me if I would play a small role in the show that he had not been able to cast. I was told that it could serve as my audition into the company. I agreed.

The part was that of the Young Woodcutters. Lorca had written it for three actors to perform in the manner of a Greek chorus, commenting on the action as it unfolds. Vince had had trouble getting one actor for the Woodcutters let alone three, so he reduced the chorus to two and had me play the two that remained. I did this by utilizing a mask for the second character. Judy, my girlfriend and future wife, was an artist as well as an actress and she made the mask for me out of papier-mâché. It was about the size, shape, and weight of a Frisbee.

Vince also decided that the character should move in a dramatic modern-dance fashion. I had never thought I'd be able to employ anything Martha Graham had attempted to teach me but apparently there were those misguided audience members who, having seen the show, actually thought I was a dancer. One guy even asked me for a date. Among the cast members was Vic Tayback, with whom I developed a lasting friendship. Vic, of course, was the short-order cook in both the film *Alice Doesn't Live Here Anymore* and the television version, called *Alice*. His distinguished career also included feature films like *Bullitt* and *Papillon*. He also played the mobster boss Jojo Kreko in the *Star Trek* original series episode "A Piece of the Action." Tayback, was by the way, one of the great underrated talents in the business. Years after *Star Trek* I saw him perform admirably in the theater at levels that far exceeded the challenges he was offered in film.

Also in the cast was Eden Marx. She was Groucho's wife at the time and when he came to see the show she asked him about my work playing two characters—one with and one without the mask. In the inimitable style that was his calling card Mr. Marx replied, "Oh, you mean the kid with the puppet?" 'Tis better, I think, to be lampooned by the best than suffer praise by Siskel and Ebert.

Another player in our group was Edward Le Veque, one of the original members of the Keystone Kops from the silent movies. Ed was already an older man when he worked in this show and not quite as alert as he once had been. Still, he was a very personable fellow and effective in the role of the Bride's Father. However, one night as we were all lining up for a group entrance to the second-act wedding party Ed whispered to me that he couldn't remember any of his words. The opening speech he had was along the lines of "Everybody come to the wedding, we are going to have a wonderful time, help yourself to the food and drink," that sort of thing. Then there was additional dialogue as he exchanged greetings and comments with the individual partygoers. I explained to Ed from my vast knowledge of theater lore that it would all come back to him the moment he stepped on stage. "Do you really think so?" he asked me hopefully. I nodded sagely. This from the actor who knew backward and forward that "last but not least is tin" and who could say "I opened the skylight" with six different inflections.

Our cue arrived, and laughing loudly we all stepped out on the stage together. Ed raised his arms, smiled triumphantly and began his speech: "La-la, la-la, la-la-la-la!" You know they say that Greta Garbo could have gotten away with reading the telephone directory and still make an audience weep. She didn't have anything on Mr. Le Veque. "LA-*LA*, LA-*LA*, LALALA, LA-LA, LA . . . . *LA*!" He was on a roll now, bursting with enthusiasm, full of energy, how could you not like this guy? Those of us on stage were managing to keep our laughter pretty much in character although I'm not sure any wedding is supposed to be that funny. However, when characters approached him with their individual dialogue from the text and he still replied "La-la, lalala," we totally lost it. Everybody was cracking up and quite literally falling down. For all intents and purposes that evening's performance was down the drain. Ed never noticed. I'm quite sure that he felt, and I'm not sure I disagree, that this was his finest hour.

Unquestionably, my worst hour came during this same production. It haunts me still. One of the cardinal rules of theater is that actors do not mingle with the playgoers before the play or during the intermission. Not only is it bad form but it can be crazymaking if you are disposed in that direction. To begin with I was having a new tic problem. It was a precursor to the rapid eye blinking that I would later acquire and which remains with me sporadically to this day. In this case, as soon as I would set foot on the stage my eyes would start to close. I went through whole scenes stumbling into furniture while simultaneously struggling to raise my eyelids. Before, I had been able set aside my various twitches when I was performing, but this new manifestation was a direct result of it.

So I wasn't in the best frame of mind when I made the mistake of stepping outside for a breath of air as the audience was arriving. The night itself wasn't actually dark and stormy as I suggested earlier, it was only my brain that was clouded and in a tumult. I was certainly not of a disposition to treat with equanimity the conversation I overheard by a group of college-age people:

"Should we go see this thing?"

"I don't know, what else is there to do?"

"I just know it's going to be fucking boring."

One of the problems was that, according to the Actors' Equity Union, the rule enabling us to charge admission would ultimately cost us more than we could earn at the box office. Consequently, we didn't charge admission but relied on a fishbowl. The problem with that is the public then views the work as free theater, and how good could that be? There were those in our audience disposed to think that way.

I was incensed by their comments but said nothing, and marched back into the theater. The play was about to start and I was determined to put away my anger to chew upon later. I believed I had succeeded. I didn't realize that later was sooner than I thought.

The theater was small and the playing area was only about three feet from the first row of seats. When I make my first entrance it is to appear in the woods spinning and leaping about in all manner of choreographed movement while foretelling with and without mask the tragic history and gloomy future that would soon be revealed. To light my way through the treacherous night I carried a torch. The torch was actually a foot-long lit candle, and I spent many hours inventing ways to incorporate its use into the spectacular dance I had created. Which, by the way, I had to pray each time would not send me crashing into the spectators, because I couldn't keep my eyes open long enough to see where I was going. I must tell you that I took the whole thing very seriously. I was definitely thinking Nureyev as I bounded onto the stage.

I had no sooner made my first grand jeté then I heard a whooshing noise that was certainly not part of the play. I looked down at my candle and saw it flickering. I spun into a pirouette and heard it again. The flame from the torch was doing its own dance but not in accompaniment to my own. "Whoosh!" I heard it again and this time I identified it. It was a wind a-blowing, one distinctly laced with the smell of garlic. "An ill wind that bloweth no man good," sayeth John Heywood. Maybe in his time that was a strong statement. Where I was coming from those were words to rock to sleep a colicky baby. For you see, what was happening was that some fucker in the first row, one of the college-age students, *was trying to blow out my candle!* When I realized the source of this wind and what its intent was my reaction was to reap the whirlwind. In other words, I simply lost it—totally—like few actors on the stage ever have before. I stopped the show and screamed at the audience: "THIS ISN'T A MOVIE HOUSE, IT'S A THEATER! EITHER RESPECT THE ACTORS OR GET OUT!" By any standard, that was bad. Far worse was that at the same time I flung the mask I was carrying at the audience. Naturally, someone quite innocent was hit by it. It is inconceivable to me today that even with my psychologically induced blindness and the kids' crass comments and my generally paranoid disposition I could have so completely lost control. This was truly a moment of insanity. Lest you nervously begin flipping the pages now for other such examples let me assure you that I have never again behaved that extremely.

After vilifying the audience I momentarily left the stage, relit the candle, reentered, and finished the scene. God knows where I got the balls to do that! It was only after I completed my part in the play that I was able to grasp the enormity of what I had done. I was, as I should have been, humiliated and not a little scared. I was sure that madness was descending on me. I was becoming a crazy person. But if that was so of me then what of the audience?

I left word for our director that I would not come out for the curtain call, I was simply too ashamed. He came backstage and told me that I had to go on, that it was in the tradition of the theater that I do so. That argument alone would not have convinced me but I suddenly saw that remaining in the dressing room was an act of cowardice and, if nothing else, the derision of the crowd would be penance that might, in some degree, assuage my guilt.

The only moment of self-respect that I could look to that evening was when I stepped to the apron and bowed and faced unflinchingly the obscenities hurled at me by the crowd . . . except that when I bowed what came back was a standing ovation as enthusiastic and rousing as ever I have heard. I should have been grateful, I suppose, but the thought flashed in my head that the inmates were definitely in charge. It just goes to show that no matter how deranged your behavior is there will always be people who will somehow construe it as an act of courage and inspiration.

Although I didn't really need it there was one member of the audience, a bit more jaundiced than the others, who put it all in the proper perspective. I was standing in the theater after the show looking at the place where I had hurled the mask when he entered.

"What do you do nights when no one is sitting in that seat?" he asked dryly.

I had a sleepless night and climbed groggily out of bed the next morning. I went to the local convenience store, within a block's walk, and brought back a cup of coffee and a newspaper. I was hoping the sports section would lift my spirits. I was trying very hard not to think about the state of my mental health but with almost no success. Was I really flipping out? Was last night the first step toward modeling a very tight-fitting white jacket with wraparound sleeves?

The sun had risen bright and warm and I decided to do my reading on the front step of my bungalow. The kitchen of the bungalow in front of me was just a foot to the west of where I was sitting. A middleaged school teacher lived in that cottage. For the longest time I had assumed she had a roommate because I had heard two voices coming from the dwelling. The manager finally explained that "Martha" talked to herself occasionally. With time I came to realize that Martha did more than just talk to herself. There were heated discussions in two different voices frequently ending in tears. Martha appeared to have two distinct personalities and was definitely a candidate for a clinical study.

Sure enough, I could hear her beginning again through her kitchen window. A surreptitious peek between the open curtains revealed that the ensuing dialogue was performed to the accompaniment of breakfast preparations. The conversation started out very much the same as it did every morning.

"I don't want to go to school today . . ."

"You can't earn a living unless you go."

"But I'm sick!"

"Your mother was sick every day of her life but it never stopped her . . ."

I was taking it in but I was still wallowing in self-pity. I mean, really, how much worse off was she than me? Wasn't I doing a play where I spoke in two voices? How long before the pencil-thin line of reality would rub away and I would begin believing that I really was two different people up there?

"Don't talk to me about Mama!"

"I'll say any damn thing I please!"

Okay, Martha, I was thinking. Right now you're crazier than me but at the rate I'm going—

"Tell her, tell her! She has to go to school, right?"

"But I don't . . ."

"She's right, she's always right! You listen to her!"

"But . . ."

"No 'buts' about it, we know what's best for you!"

The coffee spilled from my hand. If only the Yankees were as hot as the steam rising from the stain on their box score. I was shocked but no less grateful. Bless Martha, bless her. She had shown me that beyond the forbidding mountain there was a green pasture where daisies and petunias and geraniums opened wide their petals and promised a better tomorrow. I might be a little whacko but I could never match Martha. I had had a moment of disorientation and screamed at the audience but I knew that I lacked the madness quotient to babble in *three*, count 'em, *three* different voices at once. Martha and her multiple personalities were a beacon in the night showing me the way. It was as if they were saying to me:

"Give it up honey . . ."

"No matter how hard you try . . ."

"You'll never be as nuts as we are."

Feeling a lot better, I went inside and took a nap.

I am frequently asked what was the one event in my career that did most to change my life. The assumption going in is that it must have been *Star Trek*. Of course, *Star Trek* was the principal player in shaping my destiny, but to find the initiating occasion one has to go back three years before *Star Trek* to a casting call in 1964. Joe D'Agosta, who starred in one of the episodes of *Strange Loves* and later cast the *Star Trek* series, was at this time casting a series called *Mr. Novak* at MGM. The stars were James Franciscus, who went on to star in movies like *Marooned* and *Beneath The Planet of the Apes,* and Dean Jagger from *Twelve O'Clock High, Executive Suite, Elmer Gantry,* and seventy others.

The series was about a high school and the student problems tackled by the teacher, Franciscus, and the principal, Jagger. Joe called me in to read for the part of a Russian student who had been raised by the state but had defected and was now having a tough time adapting to the less rigid, more open society of the American classroom. Alexi, still spouting the party line, was uptight, inflexible, and opinionated. The acting choices seemed simple. And my own assessment was that I pretty much nailed the audition. This was corroborated by Joe, who called me later to tell me the director really liked what I had done. It seemed that it was in the bag. This was the first guest-starring role I had had a chance for and with each hour that passed I found myself wanting it more and more.

Two days later I still hadn't heard anything so I called D'Agosta to find out what was going on. The script was requiring a lot of rewrites and with time on his hands the director was continuing to see young actors even though I was still number-one on the list.

Another stressful night ensued as I waited for the call. The following day, Thursday, came the bad news. An actor named Gregory had read for the part. He had a major motion picture credit on his resume, which was certainly more than I had but he also had a totally different take on Alexi's character which, as it turned out, the director "loved." (I use the preceding word advisedly.), Gregory, as the expression goes, could have been the supreme potentate in the kingdom of Fey, and he played the part with a great deal of flamboyance. When it was described to me how he flew across the room, smashed into walls, and cried a lot I knew we were on different wavelengths.

My callback was for Friday and it was between Gregory and me. He went first and I could hear the wailing through the walls. I then came in and did the uptight, brittle, state-indoctrinated school boy that the director liked so much the first time. My audition was so different from my competitor's that he definitely had a clear choice. As it turned out, however, that wasn't what he wanted. He asked me to try it again but this time to make Alexi more emotional, more bizarre, more neurotic. I knew instantly what was going on here and it really pissed me off. Despite the fact that none of those elements were in the character I might still have tried it if it had simply been the director's vision. But knowing that what he was asking me to do was simulate another actor's interpretation was too much to swallow. I told him I could not in conscience do what he was asking. He replied that he really needed to see it done that way. The implication was obvious. Still I demurred. He gave me a tight-lipped "thank you" and turned his back. I knew I had lost the part before the door had closed behind me.

As actors do, I played over and over in my mind what I might have done to salvage the situation. I could think of no other action I could have taken. Particularly when I learned that the director had Gregory as a house guest that weekend, ostensibly to work on the part.

The show had been scheduled to shoot on the following Monday. I waited until Wednesday and then called Joe. I wanted to come in and watch this young man work. Maybe there was something I had missed. Maybe, after all, I could improve my craft by observing his performance. Joe was surprised I didn't know that the episode had been postponed. Dean Jagger, who had a major role in this story, had taken ill.

Six weeks later the show was put back on the schedule. The original director was now not available. I read exactly one line for the man who replaced him, Michael O'Herlihy, who proceeded to tell me then and there that I had the part. I'm sure one line couldn't have told him much, but Joe had obviously done the advance work. I think Mr. O'Herlihy had been predisposed to believe that a brittle, anal-retentive Russian was exactly what the part called for.

The performance went well. I did not disgrace Joe for having put his faith in me. Three years later Mr. D'Agosta called me in for the part of another Russkie—this time on a television series called *Star Trek*. Just think, if Dean Jagger hadn't become sick the navigator of the *Enterprise* might have added to his talents a keen sense of fashion design.

Later that year I was cast in a guest-starring role in the anthology series *Alfred Hitchcock Presents* at Universal Studios. It was the best part I had to date. The show was called "Memos From Purgatory" and was an adaptation from a collection of short stories with the same title by Harlan Ellison. Ellison, as almost everyone knows, was the teleplay author of the award-winning *Star Trek* episode "City on the Edge of Forever." Purportedly, the material from "Memos" was autobiographical, which made for interesting casting when James Caan was hired to play him. Jimmy was under contract to Universal at the time but not yet a major motion picture name. The experience was notable for several reasons.

I was the leader of a gang that included Tony Musante *(Once A Thief, The Incident, The Detective)*, Zalman King (director of *Wild Orchid*, and *Two Moon Junction*, and producer of *9 1/2 Weeks*), and Mark Slade *(Voyage to the Bottom of the Sea*, the character of "Blue" on *Blue, The High Chaparral*). Along with Caan, some of whose credits have already been listed, this was a group of five actors who went on to achieve considerable prominence in the biz.

The director, Joe Pevney, was enamored of my work and on several occasions during the shoot told me I was headed for stardom. Although it never quite happened, he was instrumental in getting me a steady gig. Pevney was one of the two alternating directors of *Star Trek's* second season and was present when I auditioned for the role of Chekov.

During one scene in which I interrogated Caan I was supposed to backhand him. The idea was to just come close and let the camera angle make it appear that the blow had found its mark. Unfortunately, I came more than close. I was wearing a ring, and I clipped Jimmy's lip with it. The shot was a close-up of him and only my hand was on-camera. The blood flowed liberally and I stood there horrified. I was sure that the director would stop the action but Caan wouldn't have it. He continued his dialogue, prompting me to do the same. His performance took on a heightened intensity. I found myself a spectator admiring his work. Generally speaking, solid performances are the result of preparation, focus, and innate talent. Once in a while a good shot in the mouth does the trick.

Once Jimmy and I were coming back from a break. We were walking leisurely toward the soundstage when the assistant director appeared frantically waving at us to hurry. Reflexively, I started to break into a trot. Caan grabbed my arm and pulled me back. "Stars *never* run," he said to me. Well, it worked for him.

During this same period I had the principal guest role on an episode of *The Lieutenant*, a TV series created and produced by Gene Roddenberry. Gary Lockwood, who would guest in the second *Star Trek* pilot episode, "Where No Man Has Gone Before," was the star of *The Lieutenant*. About eight years later I had a recurring role in the Canadian television series *The Star Lost* starring Keir Dullea. So, for you trivia buffs out there who needed to know, I am the answer to the question "Which Star Trek actor worked with both of the leading actors of perhaps the best science fiction movie of all time, *2001*?"

★

Judy and I set our wedding date for July 1965. We would leave immediately thereafter on a honeymoon that would last about twelve days. About a week before, an old friend of mine from Fieldston High School, Ken Geist, called me. Ken was the only person from that period with whom I had consistently remained in touch over the years. The fact that he had also chosen a career in the theater was certainly a plus to our enduring friendship.

At the time, he was an assistant to Gordon Davidson, the Executive Director of the UCLA Theatre Group. When the operation moved from the university to downtown Los Angeles some time later it became the Centre Theatre Group, Los Angeles' most successful theatrical organization. Under Davidson's guidance the company has consistently produced many first-rate original works that toured nationally and/or played New York.

Ken was calling me in to read for a play called *The Deputy* by Rolf Hochhuth. I was touched that he had thought of me. It is my experience that there aren't many times in a life when, unsolicited, people extend themselves to others out of loyalty. For years after, I made it a point to bring it up whenever I saw him and thank him for his kindness all over again.

The audition went well enough and I had reasonable hope that I would be called back for a final reading. In 1962 Syd Pollack had made his second overture to employ me in another production for this same group. It was a play called *P.S. 193* starring James Whitmore. That effort failed because of an organizational policy prohibiting the use of actors who were not yet members of the stage union, Actors

Equity. In almost every other company in the country an invitation to join an Equity production meant an invitation to join the union, but not so here. I still did not have my union card when I came in for *The Deputy,* but the group's rules had changed in the interim. This time the problem was time or, more precisely, timing. The days were passing, my wedding and honeymoon were approaching, and I still had not heard about a callback. The longer I had to wait the more I wanted to be part of the cast. The more I wanted to be part of the cast, the more interminable the wait and, of course, that's when it seems Fate designs to make it as tough as possible on actors. Nothing comes easily, but under these circumstances one can not hope for success without a barefoot run over burning coals or a naked swim in a state of tumescence in a river of alligators.

Ken was keeping me apprised of what was going on but he couldn't speed up the process. Our wedding day came and went. We took off for Yosemite, Las Vegas, and San Francisco. I was bolting into phone booths on each stop along the way, calling Los Angeles for word. A honeymoon is supposed to be the most carefree occasion of one's life and here I was as much in knots as if I were staring at the phone in my apartment. As it was, we cut our trip short by one day when the call finally came. I must say that Judy was incredibly understanding considering what event it was we were celebrating.

I got the part. It was actually three small roles. A Jewish refugee, a Catholic monk, and a Nazi sergeant. *The Deputy* was a very powerful and somewhat controversial piece of theater that examined the failure of the Roman Catholic Church to involve itself in the plight of the Jews under Hitler's reign. The work centers on one humanitarian priest who helps hide Jewish refugees and tries in vain to rouse the Papacy's interest in their plight. In the end the priest himself becomes a prisoner and joins the others in the march to gas chambers.

The cast Davidson chose was quite strong, and as the picture in the photo section will attest included several people who went on to roles in *Star Trek* original series episodes. Robert Brown played the leading role of the priest and was later seen as Lazarus in "The Alternative Factor." Joseph Ruskin played Galt in "Gamesters of Triskelion," William Wintersole was Abrom in "Patterns of Force," Ian Wolfe played Septimus in "Bread and Circuses," and Richard Carlyle was Lt. Carl Jaeger in "The Squire of Gothos." Just to confirm that the *The Deputy* was an equal-opportunity employer, Alan Napier, the tall

Sarah and Isadore Koenig. There were good times too.
(*From the author's collection*)

The Koenigsberg family around 1908. My father is at far right. (*From the author's collection*)

Playing in *The Devil's Disciple* at Fieldston High School in 1954. I think I had my lines written on my palm. (*From the author's collection*)

As Orin in *Mourning Becomes Electra* at Grinnell College. I was sooo sensitive! (*From the author's collection*)

"THEATRE REVUE"

"PART ONE"

Directed by DAVID PRESSMAN *and* MORDECAI LAWNER

Assisted by BERNARD HIATT *and* ERNEST LOSSO

Choreography—DEBORAH ZALL • *Musical Direction*—ROYAL HINMAN

SCENE I: ACTORS' OUTING .... Walter Koenig & The Company
"Where Do We Go From Here" & "Beatniks' Lament"
by Mordecai Lawner & Jacques Press

SCENE II: ACTORS' LOFT

1. "Hamlet" .... Dabney Coleman & John Harl
2. "Romeo and Juliet" .... Harold Baldridge & Margot White
3. "Audition" .... Mary Bayes, Jean Hale & The Company
4. "Peer Gynt" .... Charles Maggiore & The Company
5. "Dance" .... The Company

SCENE III: ACTORS' HEAVEN

Heavenly Producer .... Walter Koenig
Heavenly Secretary .... Jessica Walter

1. "All 'er Nuthin" .... Dabney Coleman & Margot White
2. "Spoon River" .... Brenda Vaccaro
3. "Younger Than Springtime" .... John Harl
4. "Spoon River" .... Joseph Della Sorte
5. "Where is the Life" .... Daniel Jaramillo
6. "Spoon River" .... Margaret Cathell
7. "Always True To You Darling" .... Roslyn Dee Cohen
8. "Let Me Entertain You" ... Lucia Cucullu & Joseph Della Sorte
9. "Shy" .... Shirley Dalziel
10. "Everything's Coming Up Roses" ... Shirley Dalziel & The Company

SCENE IV: "ACTORS LOFT" .... The Company

"Don't Be Afraid To Dream"
by Robert Bolfird

Incidental Music for "Part One" devised and played by Ernest Losso,
Robert Simon, Robert Sudenberg & Frank Liebermann

INTERMISSION

"A MIDSUMMER-NIGHT'S DREAM"

by

WILLIAM SHAKESPEARE

(Our Version)

Directed by DAVID PRESSMAN

Assistant Director—RICHARD EDELMAN • *Musical Direction*—ROYAL HINMAN

CAST

Theseus	Christopher Lloyd
Egeus	John Harl
Lysander	Paul Crosse
Demetrius	Robert Corpora
Quince	Walter Koenig
Snug	Daniel Jaramillo
Bottom	Victor Resnevics
Flute	George Constant
Snout	Joseph Della Sorte
Starveling	Charles Maggiore
Hippolyta	Margaret Cathell
Hermia	Pamela Wylie
Helena	Jessica Walter
Oberon	Robert Jundelin
Titania	Margaret Foster
Puck	Serena Stewart
Fairies	Roslyn Dee Cohen, Shirley Dalziel, Jean Hale, Brenda Vaccaro & Margot White

SCENE.—Athens, and a Wood not far from it.

Production Supervision—PAUL MORRISON

PRODUCTION STAFF—FIRST YEAR STUDENTS

Production Manager	Thomas Portelli
Stage Manager	Leonard Frye
Lighting	Ronald Pollock and Robert Saddenberg
Sound	Judith Burkett & Marcia Levant
Costumes	Marylee Matthews & Judi Smiley
Properties	Jane Hunt & Rosalie Posner
Crew	John Law & Douglas Reid

SECOND YEAR STUDENTS

Margo Annulai	John Harl	Victor Resnevics
Harold Baldridge	Daniel Jaramillo	Serena Stewart
Mary Bayes	Robert Jundelin	Brenda Vaccaro
Margaret Cathell	Walter Koenig	Jessica Walter
Roslyn Dee Cohen	Frank Liebermann	Margot White
Dabney Coleman	Christopher Lloyd	Pamela Wylie
George Constant	Jean Hale	Charles Maggiore
Robert Corpora		
Lucia Cucullu		
Shirley Dalziel		
Joseph Della Sorte		
Margaret Foster		
Paul Gross		

Neighborhood Playhouse production of *Midsummer Night's Dream*. Can you find Jessica Walter, Brenda Vaccaro, and Chris Lloyd in the picture? (*From the author's collection*)

As the "Woodcutters" in *Blood Wedding* on a night I didn't throw the mask at someone in the audience. (*From the author's collection*)

With James Franciscus
on the *Mr. Novak* show.
My first Russian. (*From
the author's collection*)

With Lee Marvin in *The Great Adventure* before I
screwed it all up. (*From the author's collection*)

With Zalman King and Tony Musante on *The Alfred Hitchcock Hour*. I played "Tiger," a psychopathic gang leader and possible distant relative of *Babylon 5*'s Mr. Bester. (*From the author's collection*)

On the set of *I Wish I May* with Tony Franke, the director. (*From the author's collection*)

"Who Mourns for Adonais" episode
with DeForest Kelley. "Doctor, I tink
dot bird iz goink to nest in my vig."
(*From the author's collection.* ©
Paramount Pictures)

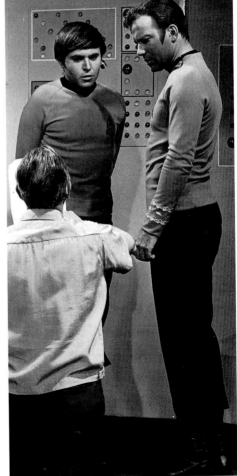

Shatner and Koenig on the TV series.
Bill: "Pleeease shoot this over my
shoulder so that Walter can have a
richly deserved close-up." (*Courtesy
of Richard Arnold Collection*)

Judy was working next door on *Mission Impossible*. This publicity shot shows to what depths I would sink to get work. (*From the author's collection*)

With Keir Dullea in *The Star Lost* series. I'm the gold-costumed alien, "Oro." Oro—gold, very subtle, right? (*From the author's collection*)

A rare moment of somber adult reflection. (*From the author's collection*)

The cast of *The Deputy*. Ian Wolfe (second row, left); Richard Carlyle (second row, right); Joe Ruskin, William Wintersole, and Robert Brown (fourth row, from right) all appeared later in episodes of *Star Trek*. Alan Napier (rear, center) was later Alfred the butler in the *Batman* TV series. (*From the author's collection*)

Playing "God," as a Puerto Rican towel attendant in the play, *Steambath*, with Terrence Locke. (*From the author's collection*)

Mark Lenard and I in *Box and Cox*. He wasn't *supposed* to be breaking up, but I'm just so damn funny! (*From the author's collection*)

On the set of *The Wrath of Khan* with Paul Winfield. The hoist is attached at my crotch and doesn't feel nearly as good as my expression indicates. (*From the author's collection: Bruce Birmelin*)

"The Gang of Five" celebrating Leonard Nimoy's *Star Trek* directing debut on *The Search for Spock*. (*From the author's collection: John Shannon*)

It takes a village to raise a movie. (*From the author's collection: John Shannon*)

With Nichelle Nichols. This is either "Ken you tell me vhere da nuclear wessels are?" or "Officer, vhat heppened to dot lady's head? From *Star Trek IV*. (*From the author's collection: Bruce Birmelin*)

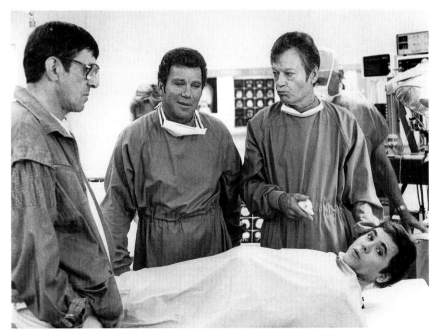

From *Star Trek IV: The Voyage Home*. DeForest: "I'm for pulling the sheet over his head and calling it a day. What do you think, Bill?" (*From the author's collection: Bruce Birmelin*)

From *The Voyage Home*. (*From the author's collection*)

From *Star Trek: Generations*. Yea, Whoopi! (*From the author's collection*: *Elliot Marks*)

With Mark Lenard in the play, *The Boys in Autumn*. "Come on, Mark, if you really try you can look as silly as I do." (*From the author's collection*: *Matthew Campos*)

From the TV episode, "The Apple." Chekov didn't always *not* get the girl. (*Everett Collection*)

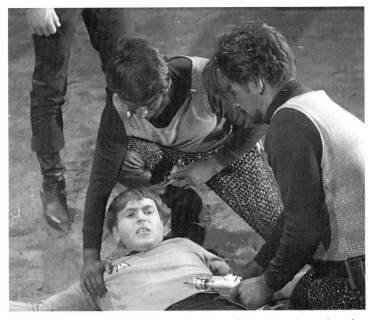

From the TV episode, "Day of the Dove." Chekov in pain—what else is new? (*Everett Collection*)

With Bill Shatner and George Takei on the set of *Star Trek: The Motion Picture*. Bill: "I believe in share and share alike."(*From the author's collection. © Paramount Pictures*)

From *Star Trek VI: The Undiscovered Country*. (*From the author's collection. © Paramount Pictures*)

From *Star Trek V: The Final Frontier."* (*Everett Collection*)

This is either the Ceti eel-boring-a-hole-in-my-head scene from *Star Trek II* or I'm singing "The Indian Love Call" from the operetta, *The Red Mill.* (*Everett Collection*)

Judy and Walter at home. Aw, gee.
(*From the author's collection*)

Danielle and Andrew.
Double aw, gee.
(*From the author's collection*)

With Bruce Campbell aboard a space craft from the film, *Moontrap*. At least this time we had seat belts. (*From the author's collection.* © *Magic Lantern Productions*)

With Jimmy Doohan from *Star Trek: Generations* in costumes from a scene that never made it into the final cut. (*From the author's collection: Elliot Marks.*)

Judy outranking me on *Star Trek VI: The Undiscovered Country*.
(*From the author's collection: Gregory Schwartz*)

As Bester from *Babylon 5*. (*Byron J. Cohen © Warner Bros., used by permission*)

From *Babylon 5* with Jeff Conaway as Zack. (*Byron J. Cohen © Warner Bros., used by permission*)

Publicity shot with Jerry Doyle as Garibaldi from *Babylon 5*. (*Byron J. Cohen © Warner Bros., used by permission.*)

At the *Babylon 5* convention in Blackpool, England, with producers, actors, and crew. You have no idea how much money I had to pay these people to strike this pose. (*From the author's collection: Alasdair.*)

At a convention quoting a fan: "Could you please sing 'Hey, hey we're the Monkees,' Mr. Jones?" (*From the author's collection: Donn R. Nottage*)

In a fan-made Bester uniform at Blackpool walking through the audience. A magical moment for me. (*From the author's collection: Alasdair*) fellow in the back row, went on to portray Alfred the butler in the *Batman* television series.

The production was very successful and the run was extended twice. Nevertheless, there was a very uneasy feeling that pervaded the backstage area. Rumors persisted and with time grew more wild that we were to come under siege by the American Nazi Party. As I said before, the play exposed a lack of humanitarian leadership by the Papacy and was, therefore, a source of controversy. We had been told on a couple of occasions that that particular night would be the one on which they would storm the theater causing chaos and destruction. That it didn't happen either time was not a source of comfort. It only meant that it gave them more time to build an arsenal and prepare a strategy thick in sanguinary intent. From night to night the tension rose exponentially. And then we got word that this particular evening, a Friday I believe, was definitely the night it was all coming down.

A scene in the first act had Jacobson, the character I was then playing, go to the apartment of an SS officer who was secretly sympathetic to the persecuted Jews. There is a knock at the door and I hide behind a folding screen upstage center. The priest enters and an impassioned dialogue between the two men ensues. I could see them through the space where the hinges separate the panels of the screen. So heated was the exchange that the air turned moist with a saliva spray that neither actor in his respective rage could contain and which rose and hung between them in the amber jell light like a dark cloud.

And then, suddenly, there was another knocking. But this one didn't come from the door to the set. It was instead a pounding, a pounding with great force against the large metal door behind the stage that led to the outside, to the real world where Nazi uniforms aren't costumes but badges of dishonor and where the guns that are carried in gloved hands do not shoot blanks.

"OPEN UP!" came the cry. "OPEN UP!"

I looked out at the two actors. The air between them was very clear. Their mouths had gone dry. There would be no more spittle this night. They continued the dialogue nose to nose but now it was by rote. There was no intelligence in the words. They stared vacantly at each other. The look in their eyes said "Gone Fishing, Room to Let— Unfurnished."

"OPEN UP!" came the cry, louder than before, and now I'm wondering whether the actors will improvise some excuse and leave

the stage. And then what of me? I couldn't just slip out from behind
the screen and tiptoe into the wings. They could say, "We will discuss
this further in the library" and exit, but how the hell did I justify
leaving? Believe it or not, this concern carried a weight equal to the
fear of being riddled by machine gun fire. And then, just as I became
certain that my fellow performers were about to flee and desert me,
the cry from behind the metal door was heard once more. It echoed
in the verdant valleys and atop the purple mountains and across the
rolling whitecaps.

"OPEN UP . . . OPEN UP . . . THIS IS CHICKEN DELIGHT!"

Somebody in the cast had ordered a late dinner.

⚡

I told Judy when we got married that we had only to earn six
thousand dollars a year to get by. But 1966 was proving to be a fallow
year. Nothing would grow in "the mud below," and the mucky stuff
was rising past my kneecaps. The "sky above" seemed further away
than ever. If I had known that one experience early in the year would
foreshadow a fruitless campaign to obtain employment I might at least
have managed to reduce some stress in my life. It's probably better to
know that your career is going nowhere than merely suspect it.

I was called in to read for a guest role on an a TV series about the
exchange counter at a department store. The production company
involved was Levy, Parke and Lavin, named after the three guys who
ran it. I don't remember which was which but they were all there when
I auditioned. The show was a comedy but you couldn't tell it by the
scene I read. My character was returning an engagement ring that his
girlfriend had refused. My speech was along the lines of "She thinks I'm
a pipsqueak, a runt, a midget, knee-high to a grasshopper, a Lilliputian,
a shrimp, and a pygmy." This was the most self-deprecating dialogue I
had ever read, and in order to take the edge off it I tried for a light-
hearted rendering that suggested the guy was truly bewildered that his
girlfriend would say these things to him. One of the production team,
Levy, Parke or Lavin, I don't recall which, was extremely short and was
quite obviously the author of the piece. After trying unsuccessfully
against almost impossible odds, I might add, to make the material
funny, the short producer pointed at me accusingly and asked how
tall I was. I really think he was trying to cover for having written an
autobiographical sketch that had more to do with catharsis than it did
with laughs.

Usually I would add an inch or two but this time, knowing what the part called for physically, I was scrupulously honest. "About five foot six," I answered. The guy who had asked the question jumped up and was instantly at my side measuring himself against me. His head barely rose above my shoulder. "Oh, no," he said disdainfully, "I'm five-seven, you must be five-ten!" According to him, you understand, it wasn't that the piece lacked humor, it was just that I was the wrong size to play it.

As I said at the beginning of this story it's a pity I didn't read the signs. I mean, how good could it turn out to be when the first time out of the box I don't get hired because I'm too tall?

◼

When 1967 rolled around the mud began to feel like quicksand. It was time to take matters into my own hands. I wrote a script called *I Wish I May.* I invested six thousand dollars that I had saved, raised another eighteen thousand from an investor named "Big Don" Tarzwell, and commenced to shoot a movie starring my wife, myself, and an actor named Gus Trekonis. Gus was dating Goldie Hawn at the time. (They later married.) She came to our house one day to view dailies (the film we had shot the day before) and halfway through became incredibly anxious to leave. The story was supposed to be a comedy about three young actors trying to make it in Hollywood and how they keep deluding themselves that success is just one interview away. I like to believe that the material was just so incisive and poignant and painfully funny that she saw her own career struggles registered there and found it too close to home to watch. Actually, I think she was bored out of her mind and needed to escape just to stay awake. Despite the film's weaknesses there were some very good things about it. Judy's performance was marvelous. She looks back on it now and doesn't like the slightly ditzy character she played. I do believe, however, that if the picture had received some big-time exposure she would have gotten a lot of work from it.

Since I was the producer I had to put all the elements together. This meant that in addition to raising the money I had to rent the equipment, hire the crew and other actors we used, find the locations to shoot and help build sets toward that end, and generally worry about everything twenty-four hours a day. My performance definitely suffered, as did my emotional equilibrium. Three days into filming the footage came back from the lab out of focus. I was devastated. Everyone's salary was deferred, so I couldn't really scream at people who were working for nothing.

I went to see my brother, who had finished his residency in New York and was now back in L.A. in semi-private practice, his wife and child with him. I told him that the whole thing was too much for me and that I was going to quit. He told me I couldn't give up after only three days of shooting. It was true, of course. I just needed to hear it from somebody I trusted.

We resumed the next day. The first thing I did was make an essential change. I asked Tony Franke, who had been our sound engineer, to take over the direction. It was the best decision I could have made. At that point I had known Tony for about six years. He was then an actor and had been featured in that classical piece of cinematic Americana, *The Blob* with Steve McQueen. He would go on to even greater heights in *McHale's Navy Joins the Air Force*.

Tony was patient and knowledgeable. I kept giving him more and more responsibility and he handled it all extremely well. If nothing else, the experience launched him on a career that has taken him all over the world as a sensitive and gifted documentary filmmaker.

We were able to get ninety percent of the picture in the can within a thirty-day period. The last ten percent took over a year to get done. In between I would be cast on *Star Trek* and Judy would become pregnant.

I was burned out by the time we got to post production and Tony handled all of the editing himself. One of the last official acts I performed was to locate and hire the musicians to compose, score, and play the music. It was a group called the Lewis & Clarke Expedition. The band's leader, Michael Martin Murphey has become a very successful country singer. His song "Wildfire" crossed genre lines and became a huge pop hit.

We finally got the last shot during a break in the *Star Trek* schedule in 1968. Judy was seven months pregnant at the time. Gus was no longer available and we used another friend in his place, making sure that his head was always bowed so the audience wouldn't be able to see his face.

Someone told me about an exhibitor in Dallas. He specialized in low-budget exploitation horror movies but he invited me to show the film to him and his associates anyway. I flew it in and a screening was set up for that same afternoon in one of the movie houses they owned.

There were about six of us there. The lights dimmed. The story began. The comic situations unfolded. The jokes were revealed. The only sound heard for the next ninety minutes was the hum of the movie projector. Doctors performing lobotomies on their mothers get bigger laughs. I began hoping that was the case here—that all these guys had been under the knife and were incapable of recognizing humor. You can tell I was getting pretty desperate.

The lights came back on. I kind of slunk down in my chair waiting for the searing critique to begin. The leader, a Dutchman, as I recall, said we would not discuss the film until we got back to his office. Maybe I was wrong. Maybe he just wanted to think about it, let it gestate, maybe he was cooking up an advertising campaign and a distribution strategy to help sell the picture, maybe the Dutch just don't laugh audibly. You can tell I was getting pretty desperate.

Not a word was spoken during the car ride back. I knew how all those guys named Paulie "the Pigeon" felt when the wise guys in the fedoras and bulky topcoats invited them for a little ride. At the same time I kept hoping against hope that this was all some kind of gallows humor and at the end of the trip there would be a big cake and a bottle of champagne. You can tell I was getting desperate.

We sat around a long conference table. Still, not a word had passed anyone's lips. Finally, the Dutchman leaned back, leaned forward, made a couple of adjustments in the crotch area, and spoke. "The first thing you must do is change the title. *I Wish I May* stinks!"

Okay, okay, I can do that. Anything if it would help make a sale, I thought.

"I would call it *The Blood of the Vampire Monkey* . . . ."

There was no beat between the first half of the sentence and the second but still, in my mind, I managed to sandwich in an explanation: He really does think the picture is funny and this is his way of showing me that he enjoys a good laugh.

" . . . and then I would burn it."

I looked into his face. It was carved from rock. It belonged at Stonehenge. What was it Don McLean sang in his song, "American Pie"? This was "the day the music died." I don't think one needs to interpret the word "music" literally. It's a metaphor. Feel free to substitute the word "laughter." I had put a great deal of work into this film. We all had. I had fantasies about its triumph that were better than those I had about pitching for the New York Yankees. And this guy was telling me to burn it!

I got on the plane for the return trip to L.A. annihilated, disconsolate, and feeling very, very lonely. To evoke the proper mood, a good screenwriter would *not* place this despondent producer on the night flight back in a row by himself with the single reading light casting mood shadows across his face while the passengers in the other rows slept contentedly with just a trace of a smile on their lips. That's what's called playing the scene "too much on the nose." The sense of the producer's defeat and feeling of isolation is more tellingly experienced if there is conflict—forces in opposition—in the scene. So what the good screenwriter does is place a hyperactive traveling salesman who wouldn't recognize a funeral if he was sitting on the casket next to the miserable producer and proceed to tell him nonstop every cornball joke he ever heard . . . for three-and-a-half hours. So the producer doesn't only have his own trials to contend with—he must suffer the manic assault of a creep who probably thinks that chemical warfare is a good thing because it refers to what competing pharmacies do when they lower their prices. Now you have the circumstances that set the groundwork for a dynamic feeling of alienation that the good writer sets out to achieve. And thereby hangs the scenario played out at my expense on the flight back. It probably would have been overkill to have the gremlin from the William Shatner *Twilight Zone* episode break through the portal, rip me out of my seat, and make me dance with him on the tip of the wing. On the other hand, exaggeration for the purpose of emphasis is sometimes a good thing.

We did explore other venues through which we might gain a distributor. For a brief time it looked as if we had found a company, but that possibility fell through and in the end we didn't find a market for *I Wish I May*.

The final punctuation to this story is that several months later I was called to testify in closed chambers before the Securities Exchange Commission regarding the solvency of the corporation I had formed to make this picture and whether, in fact, a picture was ever even made. The worst insult is not to suggest that you have made an inadequate film but that you have not made a film at all! We were ultimately vindicated on both counts.

For all of the problems, the frustration, the stress, the disappointment, the lost money, I found making the movie an amazing experience that I would not have missed. We put together a feature film with a beginning, a middle, and an end fully scored, dubbed, and edited, and we did it for twenty-four thousand dollars. As an integral part of that production, along with Tony and Judy, I still consider it one of the undertakings in my life of which I am most proud.

ELEVEN

"The Russians Are Coming, The Russians Are Coming"

IN THE LATE SPRING OF 1967 JOE D'AGOSTA MADE THE PHONE CALL that changed my life. "Can you come in this afternoon to read for a part on *Star Trek?* The money isn't great but the character may recur." By now I was a veteran of the television wars. When you're told that the money "isn't great" it probably means that it's close to the minimum they can legally pay you, and when it is said that the part "may recur" it usually means that somebody's lying through his teeth. *Star Trek* was about to begin its second season, but the only thing I knew about it was what I had perceived in thirty seconds of channel surfing: The boulders were made out of styrofoam. How good could a show with phony rocks be and how long could it last? I figured that if, indeed, I got the role it would be work for two or three days and then my life would resume as before.

I arrived at Gene Roddenberry's outer office and was handed a scene from the episode "Catspaw" to look over. At that point, they hadn't settled on the name Chekov and I was wondering why a character named Jones would speak with a Russian accent. I began to suspect that this might be something more than the usual audition situation when Roddenberry, Pevney, D'Agosta, and Gene Coon, the other *Star Trek* writer-producer at the time, traipsed past me on their way to the inner office. In the past I had usually read for just a casting person and the director, but this show's entire hiring personnel were now in attendance. I began to examine the lines a bit more seriously. That's always a mistake because as soon as you do that the pressure mounts and so does the stress level. I found myself fumbling in my pocket for a card that had been given to me by a friend who said that the chant written on it would bring me luck. To this day I can't believe that I bought into that. "Nam myoho renge kyo," said the card. "Keptin I'm not daht griin," said the dialogue. I began alternating chant and dialogue out loud. "Sehr, dah sheep iz about to blow owp . . . Nam myoho renge kyo . . . I yem not afraid sehr . . . Nam myoho renge kyo . . ." I was on a toboggan, out of control, flashing across the frozen tundra toward a precipice. "Nam myoho renge kyo . . . Vhat veal ve do, keptin? . . . Nam myoho renge kyo..." If only I'd had a lipstick and a bathroom mirror; "STOP ME BEFORE I CHANT AGAIN!" would have been my scrawled plea. And then by providence a shadow fell across my script page. I veered to the left, hit a snow bank, my sled capsized, I came to a skidding halt. There was a man looking down at me, staring at me. Well, staring at my head actually. My first thought was that he was a doctor inspecting my skull for blunt instrument trauma. What else would cause such feverish babbling?

"You're going to need some help," he said coolly.

Tell me about it, I almost replied.

"You're here for the part of the Russian?"

I nodded.

He leaned closer. "Your hair is thinning in the back. You better come with me."

He introduced himself as Fred Phillips, the head of the makeup department. He hustled me out of there promising that we would be back before I was missed. We got to his trailer and he whipped out a can of something called Nestles, Streaks and Tips. The brown spray covered the island of withering follicles at my crown and thus began my life of deception on *Star Trek:* I was thirty-one at the time not the twenty-two Chekov was listed as, I was born in Chicago not Russia, and the resolute assault of male-pattern baldness was, at least temporarily, obscured by the magic of the paint can.

Not only had we returned in record time but I was now far more composed than I had been before. Bless Fred Phillips and his bag of tricks.

The assembled executives were properly sober and restrained as

I began the audition reading opposite Joe D'Agosta. I brought to the lines the sense of jeopardy the scene called for and added the character element of someone trying to appear more in command than he actually felt. There was a long moment of silence when I finished. I figured I must have taken their breath away with my powerful interpretation. At last Gene Roddenberry spoke. "It was nice, Walter, but can you make it funny?" I was flashing back to the *Mr. Novak* audition when the director asked me to bring to the role qualities which were totally inappropriate for the character. This was different, however. On that occasion I had been asked to mimic another actor's performance and I had found that extremely offensive. This situation was not unlike a common classroom exercise where the participants try to establish relationships and communicate objectives without the use of real words. "Dobble-dobble-dobble-blah-blah-blah" that kind of thing. The idea here in front of this group of people was not to let the dialogue stand in the way of the intention. To justify what I was about to do I decided that Jones/Chekov was going to treat the situation as lightly as he could in order to dispel his own fears. "Hey, keptin, guess vhat. Dah sheep iz about to blow owp!" I clicked my teeth, winked, puffed my cheeks and ended with an idiotic ear to ear grin. The only thing I didn't do was cross my eyes. They laughed. Fred Phillips was called in. They wanted me to model some different hairdos. The bald spot had gone undetected but I had cut my hair short for *I Wish I May* and they were after the Beatles/Monkees look that was then so popular. Fred and I drove over to the Max Factor Makeup Company and returned with three women's wigs—blonde, brunette, and redhead. I was praying they wouldn't choose the blonde one because it looked really awful and, if I got the part, it might mean that I'd have to dye my own hair when it grew out.

I could take all of this seriously only because they were discussing the advantages of one coiff over another in a manner so filled with importance that I was put in mind of Roosevelt, Churchill, and Stalin at the Yalta Conference in 1945. My God, if the right decision was that crucial who was I to question the severity with which they tackled it? And then, as if we had been in a solar eclipse and had now passed through it, the scene brightened dramatically. Gone was an ambiance that had been gray and cool, sober and restrained. In its place was a hot and flashy mood of uninhibited hilarity. These heretofore pensive and deliberate men were now chasing around the room, giggling hysterically, bobbing and weaving, all in an effort to stick the different wigs on each other's heads. I kept thinking, they have to hire me now. They sure as hell wouldn't want it known that behind the austere walls of Paramount Studios post-adolescent crossdressers had formed a cell and taken up quarters.

They said nothing to me about getting the part but I was asked to return to my station in the outer office while they deliberated. That in itself was unusual. Generally you go home and wait and wait and wait for a phone call that may or may not come. And if it does come all that means is they want you to come back for another audition and then another one after that, and if the ulcer you have developed hasn't total- ly eaten through your stomach lining by then they'll have you come back once more. Given these circumstances, I really began to feel I had it knocked. Why else would they have me hang around? And then my heart sank. Another actor came through the door. His name was Tony Benson. Curiously enough, we had worked together playing French Resistance fighters on an episode of a short-lived TV series called *Jericho*. He was a talented guy and apparently the choice of Gene Coon, the only one of the decisionmakers with whom I had no prior history. Tony went in to read and—he never came out. I swear to you, *he never came out!* At least not past me. A half hour passed, then an hour. The secretary left.

An hour and a half passed. I was still sitting there. The outside light was at half mast. The shadows in the room were growing longer. Where was everybody? Where was *anybody?* What I didn't know was that there was an exit to the hallway from Roddenberry's office as well as the one I was in. Everybody had departed through that door. I was ready to think that this was some kind of gigantic malicious joke at my expense and that I'd have to dodge a crescent moon and slip past the security guards at midnight to escape from the Paramount lot. And then a *Star Trek* wardrobe person appeared and with hand on hip looked me over a bit petulantly. "Oh, alright, come with me," he said, spinning on his toes and heading out the door. I could tell he was not having a good day.

We arrived at his workspace and before I knew what was hap- pening he had dropped to his knees and shoved the back of his hand between my legs. I was more than a little shocked. He read the panic in my eyes. "Well for goodness sakes, if you're going to do this part you're going to need a costume, aren't you?" I then saw the tape measure in his other hand.

Don't ask me what happened back at Roddenberry's office. I guess everybody assumed that someone else had told me that I had been cast on *Star Trek*. I have no idea what it means but I somehow find it fitting that I learned of the most significant event in my career, an action that would change the next thirty years of my life, from a man parked on his knees in front of me with straight pins between his teeth and a hand under my crotch.

The first eight weeks at my new job was like the eight days of Hannukah when a gift is supposed to be given each day. I had not been offered a contract for the series and so I had no guarantee I'd be working from show to show, but each new week would come and there would be another script to learn. I loved the surprise of discovering each time that I'd be in yet another episode.

The cast was uncommonly friendly. James Doohan (Scotty), Nichelle Nichols (Uhura), and DeForest Kelley (Dr. McCoy) made me feel instantly welcome. It is a tribute to them, I think, that I wasn't made aware of concerns they had regarding their own status on the series. I was never treated as an interloper or as a threat to their portion of the pie. I had met Leonard Nimoy (Mr. Spock) earlier on an audition for a small film he was involved in called *Deathwatch*. I had been recommended for the part by Bob Ellenstein, who was later chosen by Nimoy to play the president of the Federation in *Star Trek IV*. I mention it now to drive home the sense of what a truly small community Hollywood is. Ultimately, everybody has worked with somebody who's worked with somebody who's worked with Kevin Bacon.

I didn't get the part on the film but Leonard had been courteous, and so he would remain *almost* ever after in the thirty years of our relationship. My first weeks with him on the *Star Trek* set were no different. Bill Shatner (Captain Kirk) was obviously the leader of the troop, and his mood established what the emotional tone on the set would be. He brought to his work a contagious ebullience and a sense of fun. There were a lot of laughs on the show. If he hadn't been there there would have been far fewer.

The protracted stay of George Takei (Mr. Sulu) on the film *The Green Berets* meant that his return to *Star Trek's* second season was delayed. No doubt, I was assigned roles he would have played had he been there. He writes in his biography that my presence, therefore, was a source of considerable annoyance. He does himself an injustice, I think, or he's an even better actor than I had imagined. I was never aware of the animosity he says that he harbored toward me.

The emotion that best describes those first few months on the series was delight. I had a steady job, an occasional acting challenge, and a semi-happy environment in which to work. Each day brought with it a sense of adventure. I had few complaints.

Well, I might have been a trifle more relaxed if Marc Daniels, the director who alternated with Joe Pevney during the second season, had been a bit friendlier. I keep reading in everyone else's books about what a keen fellow he was. I imagine it's so, but I never saw it. Actors' sensibilities can be very acute. Performers expose themselves emotionally to degrees that are not demanded of others. To do this they have to lower their defenses and, consequently, their protection against blindside assault. They are out there being very very vulnerable. The public twitters about mollycoddled actors, the prima donnas who demand excessive attention, the ones who are labeled "difficult." The fact is that good actors are an open wound, and the way you treat an open wound is to sanitize the atmosphere. Disallow the bad air, welcome in the good. Keep discord to a minimum, reinforce a cordial supportive environment. I did several shows with Marc before I ever saw him smile. That precedent-setting occasion was during a scene I was doing from the episode "I Mudd" by Stephen Kandel in which Chekov sits on a throne between two voluptuous androids and says, "This place is even better than Leningrad." Up until then I assumed that, in his eyes, everything I had done sucked. It was why I said it was a *semi*-happy environment.

There was another notable occurrence on this particular show. Joe D'Agosta had been instructed to find young attractive female twins who could play robots. He actually spotted a couple on Hollywood Boulevard and gave them his card. They had no acting experience and ended up with non-speaking extra roles on the episode.

There was much snickering among members of the crew on the second day of the shoot and I found myself eavesdropping. The fashion of the day was miniskirts, and Joe's discoveries were apparently doing far more than their part in wearing revealing attire. This was determined in the cafeteria by the best boy, two grips, and a gaffer, who simultaneously choked on their hard-boiled eggs when the girls, in their civilian garb, bent over to get a better look at the salad bar. Neither was wearing underwear.

For some reason still inexplicable to me I decided to enlighten these misguided ladies. I went into a lengthy sermon about professionalism and self-respect. They couldn't possibly hope to be taken seriously as actresses, I told them, if they continued to dress in such a breezy manner. Their eyes grew bigger as I droned on, and I began to realize that they were underscoring my remarks with little gasps, rapid head bobbing, and much "oohing" and "aahing." They focused on me as if I were an astrophysicist explaining spectrum analysis of electromagnetic wavelengths. Such concentration! Such a desire to comprehend! Was it really possible that this was all new to them? When I was done there was a moment of profound silence. Not unlike the moment, I was hoping, just after the apple plunked Newton. They stared at each other. "$E=mc^2$," their look seemed to say. "Can we get back to you on this later?" is what their lips actually formed. Surely, I was being put on?

Nope. They cornered me before I left the studio that night and explained that they had given my words a lot of thought. They had washed off their stage makeup, but I was prepared to attribute the dark shadows under their eyes and the pale cast to their skin to the rigors of this thinking process.

"We decided that what you said makes a lot of sense and we wanted you to know that from now on we're definitely going to wear panties."

After Harlan Ellison's "City on the Edge of Forever," "Who Mourns for Adonais" was the second-most emotionally evocative show, I believe, that we did on *Star Trek*. Charles Dickens wrote about little people who had to deal with struggle, betrayal, and loss. Gilbert Ralston, the author of this story about the god Apollo, took the position that the bigger they were, the harder they fell. And there is, indeed, something heart-rending and tragic in seeing the mighty deposed. I'm not sure this episode has received the credit it deserves. Certainly Michael Forest's portrayal of a deity in despair occupies a place in the pantheon of excellent performances by *Star Trek* guest actors.

Little has been said about my work on this show but I, no less than Michael, had to reach deep into my soul and in an almost Herculean manner draw forth a performance that would have about it the ring of truth. The reader pauses for a moment and unsuccessfully scans his memory for the exquisite theatrics to which I allude. If you're looking for broad strokes you won't find them. My work is very subtle. Mainly it's being able to walk past the incredibly gorgeous Leslie Parrish in that incredibly provocative costume she is wearing and not once drop my tricorder.

In the second-year episode "The Apple" by Max Ehrlich, Chekov gets to kiss the girl, thus forever putting to rest Sydney Pollack's Gypsy prophecy that osculation was not in the cards. The object of Chekov's affection is Yeoman Martha Landon, played by the very attractive Celeste Yarnall. I was feeling rather flattered by the aggressive way she grabbed hold of me until I realized that she was positioning my body so that it is her face that dominates the camera frame. I guess that's what you call the tricks of the trade.

I never understood why the story "A Private Little War" conceived by Jud Crucis was commissioned, and why Gene Roddenberry went on to write the teleplay. Here we were trying to espouse a philosophy which held that in the twenty-third century all civilizations would be better served by a decrease in weapons use. Yet the driving statement in this episode was that the balance of power between feuding sides was best achieved by a mutual buildup of arms. It seemed reactionary to me and out of touch with our desire to deal with topical issues in an enlightened manner.

On the other hand, I was tickled by the fact that on this episode I was finally able to help an actor get work. Ever since my experience with Lee Marvin I had promised myself that if I were ever in a position to assist other performers I would do so. There was less nobility in it than you might think. If ever I was to exculpate myself for exploiting my relationship with Lee it would be by a selfless act in a similar context. Mainly, I was after a way to discharge my guilt. On such twisted motivations do actors find employment. Arthur Friedman, my instructor at UCLA and longstanding friend, was also an actor who went under the name of Arthur Bernard. I had already brought several other actors to the attention of D'Agosta and his assistant who I thought might be right for parts on our series. With Arthur it finally clicked, and he ended up playing the king of the hill people in "A Private Little War."

After it was determined that there would be a third year for *Star Trek*, Gene Roddenberry invited me to his Beverly Glen home to discuss my contribution in the new season. He showed me a memo endorsed by Herb Schlosser, the President of NBC, and Mort Werner, the NBC Vice President of Programs, suggesting that Chekov be more heavily involved in the upcoming episodes. I felt good about that. I felt even better when he presented me with a copy of an Inter-Department Communication that he had circulated among the various executive personnel under his command. The first page was dated April 18, 1968 and was titled "Kirk, Spock and other Continuing Star Trek

Characters." His prefacing comment was as follows: "The continuing challenge and sometimes problem to all of us is that of keeping our various characters growing, individualistic and orchestrated . . . *alive!*" He then went on to discuss the ways in which the characters could be enhanced. In this epistle he devoted as much space to Chekov as he did to Kirk and Spock. I excerpt it here:

Chekov

We may well find our most important secondary character this season, certainly one which might give us our best entre to youth, is Chekov. The studio has been sufficiently impressed by the volume of Chekov fan response to sign him to a contract, one of the few secondary characters we have so optioned in our third season.

Most of us (because of our own ages) tend to forget that Kirk and Spock and the others actually seem rather "middle aged" to the large youthful segment of our audience. We badly need a young man aboard the Enterprise—we need youthful attitudes and perspectives. Chekov can be used potently here.

Too often in the past Chekov has been simply the young man, who keeps saying "Russia invented that first!" This was never really a good joke anyway—in fact runs rather counter to the broad international philosophy we've always tried to build into *Star Trek*. If we do continue to use that as a continuing joke, lets make certain that it does come off as good humored fun rather than appear to be a stupid chauvinistic attitude from the writer or producer of the episode.

Our original plan all along (and one we never really accomplished) was to play Chekov as an extraordinarily capable young man—almost Spock's equal in some areas. An honor graduate of the Space Academy. But even though verging on genius, his youthful inexperience and tactlessness, his youthful drive to prove himself, his need of approbation, his quite normal youthful need for females, and all of that, keep getting in his way. Kirk realized his ability and can play something of the "father image," alternately slapping his down and lifting him up as wise Captains do when they have a young Ensign with the potential of someday becoming a fine ship Captain. Referring to something in the previous, an interesting continuing joke and one with which a youthful audience can relate could very well be Chekov's constant interest in young females, his continuing failures and frustration in that area—certainly a quite common experience for all young men at that certain time in life. It can have the double advantage of pointing up to the audience the existence of pretty yeomen and other attractive females aboard our vessel.

Gene Roddenberry

I was over the moon, as they say in both astronautical and bovine circles, upon reading this directive. Judy has recently reminded me that towards the end of my first season on the show I had become increasingly restless. A lot of the later episodes had me popping in for one day and uttering such deathless prose as "Keptin . . . ?" and "Hmmm," and when there was a real burst of inspiration, "Aye, aye, sahr." I was beginning to think about not returning even if we were picked up for a third year. (Judy argued that I proceed with caution in coming to a decision.) Then came Gene's missive and I thought that everything was going to change.

I remember the precise moment when I learned that it wouldn't. I had roped Jimmy and George into doing a layout with me for a teenage magazine called *Fave*. They posed us astride horses for the session. The genius behind the shoot was the hard scientific fact that preadolescent girls adore horses and if you sit *Star Trek* actors on these animals you have the equestrian equivalent of bubblegum-flavored ice cream. Mounted thus, someone informed us that NBC had changed our third-season time slot from Monday at 8:00 pm to Friday at 10:00 pm. I knew instantly that this would have dire consequences for Chekov. My character was created to appeal to the age group between eight and fourteen. By ten o'clock the lower end of this age range is tucked between the sheets and the highest end is out cruising the local soda shop. Learning that Roddenberry, feeling betrayed by the network, had withdrawn his promise to actively produce the show in the third year was only the final nail. He had written the directive boosting Chekov's involvement in the series and his presence would assure its enactment. But now he was gone.

There is no evidence that more tellingly states my sudden change of fortune than the third-season script for the episode "Spectre of the Gun" by Lee Cronin (aka Gene Coon). It was our version of the Gunfight at the OK Corral. In it Chekov beams down with the major *Star Trek* performers, is tightly involved in the action, gets the girl, and is a tragic foil when he is shot and killed (albeit only through the next commercial break). The point is, this story was written before the network had done a bait-and-switch and relegated us to the graveyard shift. I truly believe that had all things remained constant Chekov would have become a far more valuable addition to the cast. It is not a huge leap then to expect that the feature films would have reflected this change in status as well. It is a capricious business that we actors are engaged in. Careers have changed on incidents far less significant than the one NBC was responsible for. I told myself at the time that my bad luck was no worse than what any other actor endures, and I tried to sweep my disappointment into some neglected corner of my brain where the dust bunnies would disguise its presence. Despite my best efforts, I've been known to whine with considerable frequency about the lost opportunity for the Russian navigator. I guess I need a better broom.

Speaking of "Spectre of the Gun," it was for obvious reasons one of my favorite shows. Beyond my own self-interest, however, I felt it had a very distinctive style and a tremendous feeling of atmosphere.

The budget to shoot the episode as originally conceived had been considerably trimmed. So instead of a fully realized set a sparse surrealistic one was created. This, in turn, dictated changes in the way the story was shot, the pacing, and how it was edited. The result was a program that was eerie and mystical and conveyed better than most of our efforts that preternatural forces were at work. It was one of those serendipitous occasions when an obstacle acts as catalyst for improving the product.

I did have one problem with the script's logic and I brought it to the attention of Arthur Singer, the story consultant at the time. To whit: according to the teleplay, once the *Enterprise* crew understood that the "shootout" was an illusion, they could not be harmed by the Clanton Gang's guns. That would explain why Chekov, who was shot before this information was learned, died when fired upon. It does not explain why our adorable ensign was back inverting V's and W's at his old station on the bridge by the end of the show. Singer did not seem terribly pleased to see me. After some prodding he admitted that the writing staff had the same concern, couldn't resolve it, and finally decided to ignore it. Since the only option consistent with the story's structure would have been to leave Chekov dead I decided not to pursue my complaint any further.

One final addendum to the story: Chekov assumed the role of the outlaw Billy Claiborne in the show. Claiborne's girlfriend was Sylvia. Sylvia was played by actress Bonnie Beecher. Bonnie Beecher was the girlfriend of Hugh. Hugh was my compatriot in crime back in New York. This crook thing has a way of sneaking up on you and never letting you forget it.

The third-season episode "Let That Be Your Last Battlefield" with a story by Lee Cronin again and teleplay by Oliver Crawford guest-starred Frank Gorshin as Bele and Lou Antonio as Lokai, two black-and-white cookies whose colors were mirror opposites. My sense was that Gorshin couldn't quite decide which one of the many actors he had so ably impersonated in his club act he was going to be in our show. Additionally, they both had to deal with makeup that was missing only a big red nose to put it in a more believable context. But none of that is the reason why this episode is memorable for me.

The active participants in this story are Bill Shatner and our director, Jud Taylor, a man cut from a different bolt of cloth entirely. On this particular day the setup called for the Gorshin character to be on the bridge to the far left of the turbolift as you're looking at it. A group of us had gathered and were facing him. Captain Kirk made his way through the crowd to the front and traded words with the hunter from the planet Charon. (By the way, I don't think "Charon" was ever pronounced the same way twice in a row.) At this point, the turbolift door opened and out popped Lokai, the being that Bele was pursuing. We all turned around to look at him. This put our stalwart leader now to the rear, behind us. It is understandable that Shatner would find the positioning awkward, and in rehearsal he reversed direction and pushed through us again to confront the new arrival. Taylor felt that the action was too similar to what Bill did with Bele and declined to shoot it that way. Whether you consider it a Shatner birthright or source material for jokes, the star of our group was always nearest the camera frame, and he saw no reason to make an exception now. The exchange between actor and director heated up and they moved off to discuss their artistic differences privately. Even at a considerable distance it was obvious that the temperature between them was still rising. The point of this story is that I, personally, in all the shows and years I have worked with Bill have *never* seen another director go toe to toe with the formidable frontiersman of space. Soon they were yelling. And then Shatner was decisively marching toward his dressing room. "COME BACK HERE!" shouted the intrepid director. Insert here the two-word expletive phrase that comes first to mind as rejoinder from our dearly departing captain.

I found this confrontation fascinating. Frequently, the star of a television series is the one who exercises the most power on the set.

Directors come and go on a weekly basis, but the lead actors are there for the duration and, as the saying goes, they're the ones who get the big bucks. You don't mess with the stars. In this case, Taylor can at least lay claim to a partial victory. If you haul out your old tape of this show you'll see Kirk standing next to his command chair as first Bele and then Lokai enter the bridge. All the action takes place in this configuration. Kirk does not get to push through the crowds like Moses parting the sea, so that round belongs to Taylor. On the other hand, Shatner avoids the precedent-setting situation of appearing on his own show as a background player.

"Miri," written by Adrian Spies, was one of the more successful first-season *Star Trek* episodes. It dealt with children who contract a deadly disease when they reach puberty. In an effort to replicate that success Roddenberry encouraged writers to come up with another children-oriented story for the third season. Although "Spock's Brain" by Lee Cronin is generally conceded to be the worst of our third-season efforts I mark the decline and fall of the *Star Trek* TV series from the fifth episode of the third year, "And The Children Shall Lead." The casting of Melvin Belli, an attorney and non-actor, in the pivotal role of an evil entity was an act of aesthetic corruption. The man was absolutely dreadful. He read his part the way people read nursery rhymes to very small children. Worse than that, however, was the machinations involved in the casting process.

Belli was cast because he was a friend of Fred Freiberger, our third-season producer, or because his name was well-known and it was believed his appearance would boost ratings. In either case, we were operating from a deficit position. If Belli was the guest lead because of his friendship with our producer then certainly we had unfurled the white flag of surrender and shown the world that we had given up on the series. If he had been cast to attract more viewers then, ultimately, the effect was the same. In that case it would be an act of desperation so transparent that it could only signify that we had lost faith in our product.

NBC had pulled a card from the bottom of the deck and at the eleventh hour had abandoned us to the tenth hour on Friday night. Given that graveyard time slot, we all knew the show was in trouble as we began the third season. But whatever happened to "going down with the ship," "fighting to the last man," or, at least, "standing tall in the saddle"?

It seemed to me that Belli's appearance was a clear act of capitulation, and if we didn't have any more faith in the show than that, what could we expect from our audience? A sidebar to the story is that in hiring a "personality," a *good* actor, possibly pumping gas to make his rent, was deprived of an opportunity for employment.

"The Way to Eden" was one of our least-successful third-season efforts. My relatively heavy participation in that show came indirectly from a two-page note I had written to Fred Freiberger about how Chekov's character could have greater dimension in third-season stories without subverting the text or the involvement of other characters.

I was standing in a corridor of the *Star Trek* office building when Freiberger came up to me from behind. He tapped me on the shoulder, and without breaking stride says "Read it, forget it." Nevertheless, Dorothy Fontana's original story called "Joanna" was later totally overhauled on our producer's orders and a sensitive story about Dr. McCoy and his long-absent daughter became, in part, about Chekov and his former hippie girlfriend.

I'm certainly not complaining about the added dialogue and the greater opportunity the teleplay accorded me as an actor but I'm not so sure Chekov was pleased. Since when did the slightly smartass, fun-loving ensign become an anal-retentive Establishment sympathizer? Irina, his former love, wants to go to Eden and all the Russian can do is wag his finger at her. Give me a break. Chekov would hit the ground running and be bobbing for apples before the shuttlecraft had touched down and bumped up against a coconut tree.

Adding insult to character assassination was our very nervous director, David Alexander. He had to get the last shot by twelve minutes after six on the last day of the shoot. Why did he have to get the last shot by twelve minutes after six on the last day of the shoot? Because the budget was cut on all third-season shows and he was promised another directing gig if he didn't go into overtime by more than two increments of six minutes. The union rule was that overtime be measured in six-minute units, and the studio decreed they would pull the plug on any *Star Trek* episode that went past the two-unit mark.

It was standard operating procedure that, if possible, scenes with Bill, Leonard, and De were to be recorded first during the day so they could get out early. I had no problem with that. They were the stars, they had the most work to do on the show, and they were the ones who would most benefit from a short day. As a relative newcomer with a light load I was frequently around when the director yelled, "That's a wrap!" "The Way to Eden" was no exception. Except that the six o'clock hour was about to bong and David still had two shots to get. One of them was with me and Mary-Linda Rapelye, who played Irina. He decided to do the other one first and turned to me with hands trembling and sweat beading on his forehead. "Block the scene and get it ready to go!" he said. "We'll shoot in five minutes!" "Me?" I said to him, not quite believing that he wanted me not only to stage the action but position the camera in the scene between the Russian and his hippie ex-girlfriend. "You're an actor," he barked back, as if being an actor and being a director had somehow become interchangeable. There was no room for discussion here, and when he returned in five minutes the scene was staged and ready to roll. We got it all in the can by eleven minutes after six. My contribution notwithstanding, David Alexander did not get another show to shoot.

Back in 1965 I'd run into Peter Dee in the street. I had not seen him in three years but his conversation acknowledged none of that. It was as if we had been talking continually since then and our discussion had been interrupted only by the time required for an eighteen-wheeler to loudly rumble by.

". . . so I'm going to Schwabs tomorrow to meet with the top executives at CBS. They could be of help to you. You want to come along?"

"Uh . . . sure."

After all I had gone through with him how could I possibly have said yes? "Asshole" is the term that most quickly springs to *my* mind. How about yours? Well, I didn't go after all. I managed not to be home when he came knocking at my door. But the fact that I bought into his fantasy again even for a minute shows to what extent we actors will go to avoid a mundane reality. Another example:

By 1968 I had acquired another manager. I believe he, too, spent time in the lockup after our relationship terminated. At this point, though, he had connections with Colgems, which was the music branch of Screen Gems, which was the television arm of Columbia Pictures. He set up an audition for me with the objective of getting a record contract. The composer of the music I was to sing was Michael Martin Murphey. It was how I met Michael and how he came to score *I Wish I May*. I took the song home and practiced it at least three or four hours a day. The more I practiced it the better I felt I was getting. I was at the point where I began to suspect that I had missed my calling. I was a little bit country and a little bit rock and roll and one hell of a singer. I finally recorded the song in my bathroom where I felt the sound, bouncing off the walls, would give me the acoustics required to do it justice.

At the meeting a half dozen of the top Colgems executives were huddled around the tape recorder. The order had been given that no calls would be put through. I pushed the button. I won't keep you in suspense. It was worse than awful. It was worse than all those dreams of being ten years old and standing naked in the schoolyard, worse than all those dreams actors have of performing before two thousand people and not being able to remember a single line. It was the most embarrassing three minutes of my career. How could I have not known how bad it was? Wasn't I the one guy at the Neighborhood Playhouse they wouldn't let sing? Wasn't it Santayana who said "ignore history and it will bite you in the ass"? You know the answers to all those questions, but what you may not know is that unlike the rest of the world self-delusion is an important component in an actor's personality. If he were to coldly calculate the odds for success in a business with ninety thousand members in its union, where the average income is less than three thousand dollars a year, where as far as employment is concerned there has *always* been a Depression, then he would never choose to enter it. But actors do ignore the odds because secretly, they believe that the statistics don't apply to them. Now if that isn't self-delusion I don't know what is. But if they didn't feel that way the American family would have to entertain itself, and how much can you really do with shadow puppets on the living room wall?

The music audition was a disaster, but this same manager did get me booked into a theater to do a play called *Make A Million* by Norman Barasch and Carroll Moore. The problem was that the play came in the middle of *Star Trek's* third season and meant I would have to miss a month's shooting in order to do it. I petitioned for a leave of absence and was given it readily. I was now under contract to the studio, which meant that if I was to appear for even one day in an episode they'd have to pay me a week's salary. My request gave them a good excuse to use actors not under contract to do the day jobs I would otherwise have been assigned. They were disposed to think this way now because the attitude was, as I've said before, one of surrender. We weren't going to be picked up for a fourth season anyway, so what did it matter?

By the way, since the word "contract" has entered the narrative I should tell you that my salary as a free-lance actor for my first season was ten thousand dollars. That's for the whole year. Under contract during the 1968–1969 season my salary increased to eleven thousand dollars. That's for the whole year. My son was born in August of '68. I received the following telegram from Gene Roddenberry:

> MR AND MRS WALTER KOENIG:
> WILL GIVE HIM SEVEN OUT OF THIRTEEN
> IF HE WORKS FOR MINIMUM.
> CONGRATULATIONS AND LOVE,
> GENE RODDENBERRY

Yeah, so, Gene, what's your point? Actually, for that time the money wasn't bad. It just wasn't the megabucks that people always assumed it was.

By leaving for a month I lost the opportunity to do three episodes that had been written with Chekov in mind. They were subsequently rewritten for George Takei and I like to think that because of my departure he was getting back some Star Trek exposure he had lost when his return from *The Green Berets* had been delayed.

I took off for St. Charles, Illinois to do the play on September 1. We opened after a week's rehearsal at the Pheasant Run Playhouse. Judy and my infant son Joshua Andrew (later to be known as Andrew) flew in for the opening. That month at the theater was one of the happiest periods of my career. Not the least of which was that my family was with me. Most of the cast were professional actors from the Chicago area and they were all quite good. The other actor from L.A., however, was Jackie Coogan, and I've never had more fun than I did working with him. Coogan, as everyone knows or should, played opposite Charlie Chaplin in the great 1921 silent film *The Kid*. He went on to play a series of roles that established him as a terrific child actor. When we met his career had already spanned nearly fifty years and included his run as Uncle Festus in the television series *The Addams Family*.

Besides being great fun, the play was invaluable to me in another way. Coogan was determined to enjoy himself. He did more shtick than the Three Stooges and the Marx Brothers combined. He *started* with the kitchen sink and then began throwing things in. After a disastrous first night in which I was very tense I decided that Coogan's road was the right road. I loosened up . . . a lot. There was an unspoken contest between us as to who could be the more outrageous on stage. Jackie was a compulsive scene stealer, but he'd tip his hat if I could find a way to steal it back. The audience ate it up but no more than the two of us.

What I learned for the first time was how to totally relax on stage. It's amazing how inventive you can become when the stress is absent. In the past my best work was done in spite of myself. This time I had my own full approval to have a ball.

A week before we opened the sister theater to Pheasant Run had opened the play *Born Yesterday.* Jackie and I were invited to the premiere and then on to a restaurant for a party afterwards. The star of the show was Betty Grable. She started her career in the thirties and starred in almost forty films. Among them were *Million Dollar Legs, Mother Wore Tights, That Lady in Ermine, Call Me Mister,* and *How to Marry a Millionaire.* She was the runaway champion of movie star pinups for our fighting forces during the Second World War and as such was famous around the world. Certainly, at this point her career had already peaked, but you couldn't take away from her the impressive list of her past accomplishments. I mention all of this because of what happened that night.

There was a radio personality in Chicago at the time (and if I could remember his name I would identify him here) with the manners of a pig. Part of his gig was to attend openings of new shows and interview the stars afterwards. He was at the restaurant too and had Betty Grable, Coogan, and myself beside him on a small stage area holding microphones as he conducted a live radio interview.

He started with some sleazy questions about whether Betty and Jackie still had the hots for each other, since they had been married briefly when both were kids. Grable was immediately flustered. Coogan, who could be very ribald, tried to set the tone with a gentlemanly response. The radio host wouldn't be dissuaded and kept poking at them. It got more distasteful the more he tried to bully the actors. I thought it highly unprofessional. For all the years they had put in, for the great body of work they had produced, for their ability to endure in such a fickle business, respect ought to have been shown.

He then turned to me. "I bet you never even heard of Betty Grable" he said. "On the contrary," I replied. "Ms. Grable is one of the most sought-after actors in Hollywood." I went on to explain that she had an offer for a Broadway show, a film in Yugoslavia, and another in Paris as well as being at the center in a tug-of-war between competing networks who desperately wanted her to headline several new television series. Betty Grable looked at me dumbfounded. Coogan hid a smile behind a glass of beer. Of course I was making it up as I went along but I was pissed at the guy and really needed to put him in his place. I was prepared to cite chapter and verse of Grable's additional job offers for another ten minutes when he interrupted me. He knew I was putting him on but contradicting me on the air would make him look like a bigger shit than even he was prepared to be. "Tell me," he asked, "is that what all the starlets wear in Hollywood?" He was referring to an Edwardian double-breasted jacket I was wearing that had been a gift from my wife. It sounded like one of those comments you make when you are ten years old and you run out of arguments so you resort to insults. I certainly wasn't above retaliating in kind. "Actually," I replied, "this jacket was inspired by styles from around the turn of the century, whereas your jacket is only twenty years old." I then walked off the stage and returned to the table where my dinner was waiting.

I was headed for the bathroom just as the rest of the interview was ending about twenty minutes later. Betty Grable was standing in front of me. She put her hands to my face, kissed me on the lips, and said "Baby, you got class." It was a terrific moment.

I returned to *Star Trek* in time to finish out the rest of the year. It went pretty much without incident. The only person who held out hope that there would be a fourth season was Jimmy Doohan. He couldn't believe that a show this good with such a vociferous fan base could be canceled. He insisted we would be back and, of course, he was right. It just took ten years longer than he thought.

When I think back now on my two years with the *Star Trek* television family, it's the little moments that seem to have most indelibly become a part of my consciousness:

Discussing pets with Deforest Kelley. He had a dog at the time. I had a dog. We were nuts about our dogs. Discovering what a genuinely nice man he was. Appreciating his ability to move effortlessly between the Shatner-Nimoy camp and the rest of us. De thought that there would be great things in store for me beyond *Star Trek*. He believed I'd have a big future in the business. I loved that faith. I regret that I wasn't able to live up to it.

Nichelle Nichols kidding me about my "big hair" during those six weeks when I wore a woman's wig. A feeling of total acceptance by her from the first day I stepped on to the soundstage. Going to some bizarre evening event that Roddenberry set up that was narrated by Burgess

Meredith. Nichelle danced for the audience and didn't miss a step when her dress strap broke forcing her to complete her performance one-handed. What a trouper.

Jimmy Doohan's candor. His willingness to talk about the most personal things in his life. The sense that he either didn't care what you might do with the information or that he was trusting you with his private thoughts and experiences. In either case, I was flattered to be taken into his confidence and never abused it.

Sharing ideas with George Takei about issues of a socio-political nature. Discovering happily that we shared much the same views. Being educated by him in the world of business. Coming away from those talks knowing that no one would ever have to worry about Mr. Takei's financial future.

With Leonard Nimoy there was a moment that stands out like a frieze in high relief against a background of uniformity. Our relationship was a succession of salutations in which I would say "Hi" and Mr. Spock would say "Hello." Did he really need to be the Vulcan *all* the time? Maybe so. I mean, just look what that character did for him. On the other hand, Leonard's talent being prodigious, I betcha he could have gotten into character for his scenes without spending every waking moment as the Vulcan. There was one day, though, at the beginning of the third season, when he called me into his dressing room. He had just viewed dailies and felt that a word of instruction was called for. It was Leonard speaking now, not the half-alien. He cautioned me in more tactful terms than I use here that my performance was in danger of becoming too broad to be believable. In essence, I was playing for the camera. I was embarrassed by this revelation but not resentful. At least I didn't think I was. (It's amazing the nuts you store away to chew on later when the weather turns inclement.) I thanked him for his input. I took it to heart. Far better to be constructively criticized by the actor than to suffer the impersonal cordiality of his alter ego.

When I was cast in *Star Trek's* second season I came aboard as the new guy. I was fairly naive. If there were power plays going on I was not very aware of them. I did once hear Leonard heatedly say on the phone that he was going to take his ears off and go home. And I was aware that scripts whose first drafts were written to feature supporting actors had a way of changing focus to concentrate more on the leads. Also, Captain Kirk had a penchant for stepping forward in any group scene so that he'd have to be shot in a "single." But from where I was coming these things were not important in my life. I was working on a series. I was getting reasonably steady work. I was grateful for the opportunity.

But in keeping with this synopsis of small moments, there was an incident early on that I had with Bill Shatner. We were sitting around a table rehearsing "Who Mourns for Adonais." There was a reference in the script to Ulysses. I suggested that in this context it would be more accurate to use the name Odysseus. Shatner agreed and it was changed. To this point, I really hadn't spoken to him much, but emboldened by my success with the name change I mentioned having seen Bill perform on live television back in the fifties. My lips were pursed for the compliment to follow but he shot me such an icy look that the tip of my tongue went numb. He had construed my comment to imply that I had remembered seeing him when I was just a little kid. These days that is said to me all the time. I'm never insulted by it. But that wasn't my intention anyway. I guess he didn't know at the time that I was just six years younger than him. The thing that made such a trivial incident memorable for me is that it was the first time I had seen beyond the commanding, fun-loving television-star personality. Chip away the many applications of well-polished veneer and discover beneath it the raw material from which we all are made. It would be twenty-nine years before I would see it so exposed again.

Again and again I am asked in the most reverential terms what Gene Roddenberry was really like. The questioner's tone precludes all but one acceptable answer. I can come closer to satisfying that need as a result of my experiences with him on the TV series than in the course of the years that followed. This is not to suggest that our relationship soured later, on only that I was enormously grateful to him during the run of our show and chose to perceive him in the most flattering light. Certainly, our conversation after the second season about my involvement in the coming year was a high point for me. I also remember that his infrequent appearances on our set seemed quite special. For me there was the sense about it of a visiting dignitary. I bought into it completely. It didn't hurt that he was always genuinely friendly, and in our brief individual moments together I never sensed any employer-employee posturing.

Dorothy Fontana, our most important story editor, was a total enigma to me for the longest time. She seemed removed from the conviviality of the *Star Trek* company and from me most particularly. It was as if she had probed my psyche and discovered some singularly objectionable character trait concealed there. (I was disposed to think in such terms.) That was my assessment at the time. And, of course, it was simply a case of subjective judgment on my part and on hers a personality that ran very deep in still waters. I didn't know then what a caring and loyal associate she really was. It would take the years of contact following the series to conclusively decide that my earlier concerns were unfounded.

Bob Justman was an associate producer on *Star Trek*. He was a quiet, sensitive man whom I grew to like without ever really knowing. I do remember that when he left the show before the series was canceled he made a point of stopping by and telling each of us about it personally. I was touched by that, by the respect that he showed us. It made me feel more important in the scheme of things than I did generally. It also made me feel sad. He seemed to genuinely care about the people and the show and that the decision to go was very hard for him.

TWELVE

"Trouble in Paradise"

THE CALL FROM GENE RODDENBERRY CAME IN THE SPRING OF 1969:
"We've been canceled . . . it's been a pleasure working with you . . .
hope we can do it again sometime." His tone was upbeat, and for a
moment I dug my fingernails into his parting words, clinging to the idea
that this was not the end of my career.

But then the days and the weeks and the months went by and the
phone never rang. Whatever attempts my agents were making to secure
me employment were not working. It wasn't as if I had been auditioning poorly, there simply were no auditions. I was not being asked to
interview. There were several explanations. To be sure, typecasting
entered into it. The image of the Russian navigator was a hard one for
the film industry to shake. But there was also the conundrum of my
physical appearance. For years I had been playing characters that were
ten years younger than I was. Now, if you stood me next to a twenty-
year-old, the difference in our ages became quite apparent. At the same
time my face didn't register the maturity of a young doctor or attorney—roles that I had hoped I could graduate into. It was a case of borrowing from Peter to pay Paul. I had traded on my juvenile appearance
to get work during the sixties, but now as the seventies descended I was
paying the price for good skin. Of course, to stop there would be to
only address part of the problem. The biggest issue was supply and

demand. There were just too few parts for too many actors, and Hollywood was always looking for new faces.

As bad as I had it, think about the plight of actresses in this town. There are about one fifth as many roles for women as there are for men. In general, an actress's most profitable years are late teens through mid-twenties. If she hasn't established herself by then the odds against success grow exponentially. The "business" can dry up for a young leading man, but he can come back a decade later as a middleaged charmer or as a character actor. When the petals fall from an ingenue's career the roots wither. The reason the exceptions come so readily to mind is because they are distinctive for their small number.

There were no statistics, however, that I could draw upon for consolation. The days were interminable. The weeks insufferable. The stagnant breath of last night's depression hung in my nostrils the morning after. I could think of no reason to get up. There was a one-year-old who needed attention and a beleaguered wife who not only had to deal with the mood swings of her child but those of her husband. It wasn't pretty.

I was never a drinker and I didn't do drugs or smoke, and overeating wasn't an option, but there are more than four ways to pack an artery. Emotionally I was a mess, and I'm sure that the stress of all that emotion contributed to the heart problems I would have twenty years later.

And then, because ultimately I do feel that I have what it takes to separate the men from the toddlers, I found the means by which to pull myself from the muck and wade to shore. What I needed was structure. An objective. A reason to get out of bed every morning. I began to write. It was a novel. A satirical fantasy about a group of losers who are the last people on Earth and from whose stumbling beginnings civilization starts anew. While I was writing it I felt it vitally important that it get published. I was putting in five hours a day and nothing less than bestseller status would satisfy me as a return on my time and effort. When I was done I showed it to four people aside from my immediate family. Two science fiction writers liked it a lot. Another science fiction writer and a literary agent disliked it a lot. George Clayton Johnson, one of the two who was supportive, was the writer on "The Man Trap" Star Trek episode and co-author of the novel Logan's Run. He gave me the title for my tome, Buck Alice and the Actor-Robot. I made a couple of stabs at getting it published but what I discovered was that, in this case, the process was far more important than the result.

Writing the novel put some order in my life, and provided me with some emotional balance. Never was there a creative project whose principal benefit was so therapeutic. That I did sell the book nineteen years later is beside the point.

I did do a couple of plays during this period. One was *The White House Murder Case* by Jules Feiffer and the other was *Steambath* by Bruce Jay Friedman. The first was a very dark comedy indeed. I played a CIA agent who is exposed to poisonous gas on the battlefield, which causes him to fall apart, literally. By the end of the play I'm holding my penis in my hand . . . at about eye level. On closing night during the curtain call I tossed the dildo into the audience. I don't know who caught it but I noticed that of the several hands that reached for it all of them were flashing nail polish.

In the Bruce Jay Freidman work, I played a Puerto Rican towel attendant in a steambath who believes he is God. Another comedy. If you were sitting close to the stage my performance was very good. I was going through my quiet period. No more tics, you just couldn't hear me beyond the fourth row. The reviews for both plays were pretty good, particularly from those critics in rows A through D.

By 1973, when my daughter, Danielle Beth, was born, we were nearly broke. I wasn't making enough money to receive medical insurance through the Screen Actors Guild. In those days all you had to earn was a thousand dollars during a whole year to qualify. Residuals counted, but by then the *Star Trek* residuals had run out. At that time there was a finite number of repeat airings for which you would receive compensation. A segment of the public thought we were getting rich on the reruns. Tain't so, Magee.

I had three experiences with television movies during this period. The first one was a "mercy" role, as in "mercy" when sex is a charitable event. Roddenberry had gotten wind of my financial woes and offered me a job on a movie of the week (MOW) called *The Questor Tapes*. As I indicated, the part was almost nonexistent, but it was two weeks' employment and I was grateful for it. The other two were far more significant in my life. In one I got cast and in the other I did not. Strange as it may seem, the one in which I worked left me with a badly damaged ego while the one I lost did much to bolster my self-esteem.

Goodbye Raggedy Ann was written by my friend Jack Sher. He also carried the title of producer. He knew of my economic situation and wanted me in the picture. The story was about an actress and the men in her life. I read the script and told him that the part of the actress's agent was one I could do justice to. He agreed, and I then read for the director, Fielder Cook. He also screened some previous film work of mine. The verdict was that I was very good but not for this role. He had in mind a slick, dapper, sophisticated kind of character, someone more along the lines of George Hamilton. I couldn't argue with that. George Hamilton I'm definitely not. Even though he was the writer-producer Jack did not have the final say. That was the province of a hyphenate of a different caste, the *executive* producer-director, Mr. Fielder Cook. I thanked him for his time and was prepared to move on.

Jack Sher being a very good friend felt worse about this than I did. There was another character I could play in the story, a guy who delivers chicken dinners to a party hosted by the actress. Jack knew he could get me this role. It was very small and I wanted no part of it. But I was broke, you say. Shouldn't I be willing to take anything? I know I've spoken about an actor's vanity before but what we really suffer from is a shifting self-image. When we receive approbation we feel worthy. When we perceive events as belittling, we feel demeaned. (Oh, sure, there are mature performers out there, but obviously I'm not talking about *them*.) My circumstances notwithstanding, I felt accepting such a part was too humbling; it was, in effect, a threat to my sense of self.

Jack was persistent. He even suggested that we rewrite the character together and make him more interesting. I couldn't turn that down. He came over to the house and I sketched for him a guy who did the chicken thing to pay his bills but was really an actor. With every dinner, he handed out a playbill of the Little Theater production he was working in. He was ballsy with just a hint of used car salesman about him. Also, making him an actor opened up the possibility of a scene with the woman who played the actress. Jack went away and wrote it just as we discussed. Fielder Cook said he was overjoyed to have me aboard.

Mia Farrow played the actress. Hal Holbrook played her neighbor-confidant and John Colicos from the *Star Trek* episode "Errand of Mercy" played the rich boyfriend. The part of the agent had not yet been cast when production started. I really thought everything was going to be okay . . . and then I got into my white delivery boy uniform with the pointy white hat. When you're an actor and you step before the camera you're supposed to come to it with only the clothes on your back. Nothing in your history that doesn't apply to the role you're playing has any place on the set. *Please leave all emotional baggage in the docking area.* I looked in the mirror and I knew I was sunk. That someone then asked me for a thigh and someone else for a breast only meant that my feet were encased in cement and I had plunged to the sandy bottom. I was absolutely humiliated. I could make no distinction between playing a delivery *boy* in a movie and feeling that the downward spiral of my career had rendered me as impotent as a boy in my real life. The role was a mocking affirmation of the sorry state of my affairs.

You cannot quit a movie. *You just can't do it.* Trust me. I did the next best thing. I withdrew—both physically and emotionally. I stayed in my dressing room unless I was called for a shot. Mia Farrow wanted the cast to be all one big family. She felt it would help the production. Everyone was to sit together and eat together. It would have been nice to get to know her and Hal Holbrook and Fielder Cook and the others. I couldn't do it. The word was getting out I was a little weird. Cook misread my moodiness. He assumed it was because I hadn't been chosen to play the agent. He reiterated that although that role hadn't been cast yet the actor who played it would probably be my diametric opposite. The explanation was a kindness on his part that went unacknowledged by me.

I was ticking off the days, dying for it to be over, dying to take off that fucking white pointy hat forever and go home. And then that thing happened to me that predictably does. I got over it. I stopped being threatened by the character's servitude and I began seeing it for exactly what it was, just a part. For the transition to occur this way is not good drama. When people change psychologically there should be some external incident that sets it in motion. Something the audience can see happening. How do you show a person reaching a point of emotional saturation, exhausting his reserve of self-pity, and then deciding to again join the living? You don't. But that's what happened nevertheless.

It was my last day on the film. There would be a take after lunch of me driving up to the party to deliver the chicken dinners. We had filmed the party and my small scene with Mia days before. It was lunchtime now, and everyone had congregated on the hillside of the home that had been rented for the exteriors. I sat down with the other folks. See, I wasn't totally bonkers after all. I started a conversation with Ms. Farrow and then Jack Sher came onto the scene bursting with good news. They had signed the actor to play the agent. It was . . . Martin Sheen. So much for all the healing I had done. No one is a bigger fan of his than me, but if he looks like George Hamilton then I look like Cesar Romero. I know he had a bigger name than I did, but the "agent" was not the part that carried the picture and, in this case, my interpretation would have been just as credible as his and, to boot, we weren't that far apart physically. I wasn't feeling sorry for myself anymore. I was just damned angry. Cook came up to me at precisely that moment to discuss the shot we would be doing. I said not a word but he looked into my eyes, saw the fury there, and fired me on the spot.

The word went out that I was nuts and that CBS, the network which would run the film, would never hire me again.

I would love to tell you that my behavior on *Goodbye Raggedy Ann* never repeated itself. It didn't . . . for seventeen years. Then we made a picture called *Star Trek" The Undiscovered Country*. But I'll get to that in time.

✶

During the seventies I changed agents several times. Each agency was smaller than the one before. I was working from the theory that being a big fish in a little pond was better than being one of many in a vast sea of talent. The problem was that I finally landed with a theatrical agency so small that there was no pond. I was belly up in the morning dew. My gills were sucking foam. My flippers were flapping in the mist. Well, you get the idea.

In the time I was with him he provided me with one interview. And although the experience didn't change my life it did affect my psyche. Believe it or not, this time it was a good thing.

I went to the Universal Studios lot to meet Bert Remsen, the casting director. A word about Bert. He may be the only casting director alive whose face you'd recognize. He also may be the only casting director who has concurrently had a successful career as an actor. You'd know him by his strong eastern seaboard accent and the signature cane he always carries.

The part I was brought in for was probably the most talked-about role in the most talked about television movie of 1976. Bert ushered me into the office of the director, Tom Gries. I had met Gries before in regard to a screenplay I had written which he was interested in directing. I had written the principal character, a Native American, with Marlon Brando in mind and Gries, who knew him, agreed to hand-deliver it to the actor's house. As it turned out, Brando wanted to do movies about Indians, not play them.

Gries was cordial but not very receptive to Remsen's notion of casting me in the picture. The director said he knew me as a writer and couldn't shake that image. That was rather ironic. At the time I had been writing for only five years but had been a professional actor for sixteen.

I left undaunted. There had to be a way I could get him to let me read. I knew they were having a hell of a time casting this part, since they'd seen practically every actor on the West Coast who was even remotely right for it. *And I knew I could play this character.* I called in my big guns, Jack Sher and Joe D'Agosta. They each called Gries on my behalf and, a bit grudgingly, he saw me a second time. Again he said he didn't think I was right for the role but he gave me a few pages of the two-part script and told me to study the monologue where the guy addresses the court in his own defense. He very specifically told me not to memorize the scene and not to try and sound like the real person about whom this film was being made. I was to come back in forty-eight hours.

I knew that there was a documentary playing around town that was a record of the heinous acts this man had perpetrated. I went to a drive-in where it was playing armed with a tape recorder and recorded every word he spoke on film. I think right from the beginning I had an intuitive understanding of the character's homicidal nature. (This from a person whose most violent acts have been to grab a few people by their shirt fronts and once to throw a plate of spaghetti across a room.) But what I needed now was to secure the physical behavior. I didn't have footage on him but I did have my audiotape. And so I did exactly what Tom Gries had told me not to do. I listened to his voice again and again and again. By the time I was to go back in I had the dialect down, and I could recreate the timbre and the pitch and the pattern of his speech. I also memorized the scene, an effort Gries told me expressly not to make.

I came to the audition in sneakers. The character was shorter than I was and these were the only shoes I had with no heels at all. Gries greeted me rather perfunctorily. I asked if I could take a moment to "get into" the part. The director nodded and sat down behind his desk. He had been in the middle of writing something when I entered and now resumed the work. I was standing just in front of his desk, only the breadth of it separating us. And then I began.

"I never went to school, you know . . ." These are the only words I remember now from the speech. It didn't take much more than that to notice a profound change come over the director. His pen stopped moving, but he didn't look at me immediately. His face remained down but his focus had changed. He was *listening*. I was a third of the way through when he very slowly lifted his head. I sensed he felt that something extraordinary had been captured in this room and that if he moved too quickly it might escape and disappear. Whether I was right or not it gave me an overwhelming feeling of dominance. I *owned* Tom Gries, he was *mine*. Our eyes met and locked. I wouldn't let him go. I understood totally the enormous power that the man whose character I was portraying had over his disciples. It made perfect sense to me that these people would go out and kill for him. You could certainly say that my imagination was running wild, that it was all in my mind, that none of it was true . . . except that when I was finished, when the last words were spoken, Tom Gries, still staring at me, whispered, "My God, that's Charlie . . . that's Charlie Manson!"

The four-hour television movie was called *Helter Skelter*. It was adapted from Vincent Bugliosi's bestseller by J.P. Miller. Gries was very excited. He talked about my getting fitted for a beard and a long wig. He told me to hold tight. To stand by. He would be getting in touch shortly. I left there feeling incredible, knowing that I had put it all together, that I had accomplished with this audition everything I had set out to do. I could not beat myself over the head on this one. I was good. It was now in the hands of the gods.

I didn't get the part. It was true I was the best actor for the role on the West Coast. But there is also an East Coast. Elia Kazan (he of the suspect politics, and the brilliant director of *Gentlemen's' Agreement, A Streetcar Named Desire,* and *On The Waterfront* recommended a young performer in New York named Steve Railsback. I would have liked to bitch that Railsback missed the mark. That he didn't have it. I couldn't. His performance was superb.

There are those among you who will ask, why would I even want to play such a reprehensible individual? Let me tell you. The monster lurks within us all. It's buried deep within the catacombs shackled to a wall, and in the lives of most of us it never sees the light of day. But it's there. And knowing that it's part of me—as it is all of us—what a rare opportunity to give expression to it, to examine it, to process it, and in the course of doing so to not injure so much as a waterbug.

I also wonder from time to time what road my career might have taken had I won the role. But as crazy old King Lear said, "That way madness lies."

In a ten-year period starting around the early seventies I had a total of thirteen options on or productions of scripts I had written. Of these, five were shown on television, a sixth was a pilot that was made but not screened, a seventh was a television episode that I was paid for but which was not made, and an eighth was an ABC movie for which I received partial payment. The option money on the projects that never saw a reel of film were substantial.

The first screenplay I ever wrote was called *Phantasm*. Yeah, I know, there were several horror movies with that title, but mine, a psychological suspense story, was the first, and not from the blood-and-guts exploitation genre. At various times Julie Christie, Ann Bancroft, and Cher all expressed an interest in playing the principal role of the psychologist. Years later, when it was resurrected, Sharon Gless from *Cagney and Lacey*, an in-demand actress at the time, was also a candidate for the lead character.

The first time around a former CBS network executive named Jerry Adler and his partner, who also represented him at a literary agency, optioned the screenplay for a motion picture. Jerry would be my producer thereafter. They worked hard and came close but couldn't quite interest a studio to fund a production. When their option was about to expire they took it to NBC for a possible movie of the week. They liked it enough to pay me another option fee for an additional six months. For the uninformed, an option is a payment that is a percentage of the sale price. It gives the investor the exclusive right for a designated period to pursue production of the property.

There was no word from NBC for the entire six months, but then on the very last day they called to re-option, and now they were really hot to go forward. There was only one problem. They couldn't find a copy of the script, so could we please send another one over? I should have known then that I wasn't dealing with the swiftest intellects at the network. By now Jerry Adler and I had become good friends. We had been to each other's homes. Jerry's wife, Arlene, had made dinner for Judy and me. After about two weeks we were called in by NBC to discuss a rewrite of the script. This is standard operating procedure. Even if there were such a thing as a perfect script to begin with, it would *have* to be rewritten. Hold the tablets Moses brought down from the mountain at a certain angle and you'll see it chiseled there. I know for a fact that there are several thinly disguised references to it in the King James version, and for those of us steeped in Islam one need only read between the Archangel Gabriel's lines to Muhammad to know that the holy law of the rewrite is the immutable word of God.

I was, therefore, not offended when we were asked by the network executive in charge of this project to discuss the improvements that were needed. When we arrived at his office we were told by his beaming secretary that he was in conference with Stanley Robertson down the hall. We ambled down there and waited in Mr. Robertson's outer office. This was the same Stanley Robertson who made several ill-advised attempts to control the *Star Trek* series when he was the NBC program manager for the show. In accordance with the Peter Principle, he had since become Vice President of Motion Pictures for Television at NBC. Most currently, as we could clearly hear behind the closed door, he was screaming epithets at the man we were supposed to see shortly. The volume at which these chastisements were issued and the uninterrupted flow of them was, if nothing else, testimony to impressive lung capacity and a limber tongue. Unfortunately, one could not but suspect that our meeting, which was next up, might not start off on a very good footing.

I can't recall the chap's name but I do know that those who worked directly under Robertson in the MOW department were referred to as his Lieutenants. The lieutenant in charge of *Phantasm* staggered from his boss's office and led us to his own. His secretary gasped when she saw him. From her expression now, as opposed to before, I gathered that neither of them had anticipated the attack he had just sustained. I remember reading about GI's in Vietnam who had picked up booby-trapped dolls that exploded in their faces. There were no physical injuries on our guy but he wore the accompanying shock like a body bag.

We sat opposite him in his office. He was very quiet. I tried to break the ice with a comment about the antique oak furniture in the handsomely appointed room. He came alive for a moment but then as he checked his surroundings his expression evaporated into wistfulness. It was as if he suddenly realized that he might lose it all. Jerry finally broached the subject of the rewrites. The lieutenant seemed to pull himself together. He began: "Yes, what I'd like you to do . . ." And then he stopped. Just stopped. His jaw went slack. His eyes glazed over. His hands hung limply in his lap. His clothes suddenly seemed too large for him. It was as if he had vacated his body and the shell was settling, shrinking. He sat that way in total silence for half a minute. I looked over at Jerry but he made a small gesture for me to remain quiet. I was perplexed but fascinated. How long could this possibly go on? And then, without any acknowledgment that he had been orbiting the moon, he finished as if there had never been an interruption " . . . and we'll talk some more when you've made those changes." We got up to leave and he smiled a little more courageously now. The whole experience had the feel of something surreal. I was thinking Pinter or Ionesco or Pirandello. We shook hands and exited stage left.

What happened next is very sad because it involves betrayal. I couldn't begin rewrites until I knew what it was they wanted changed, and a week had passed without word from the network about having a *real* story conference. I felt particularly in the dark because all the information was being funnelled through Jerry and he wasn't returning my calls. Another week went by and he phoned to explain that a meeting was taking place, but it was a preliminary one and I wouldn't be needed. He promised to call as soon as he got back. He didn't. I phoned him the following afternoon. He wasn't available to take my call. *On the third day He visited upon the Pharaoh's people a plague of frogs . . .* and on that day Jerry rang and invited me to his office.

I walked in suspecting nothing. It turns out that my partner had made a deal with NBC to bring in another writer. That in itself is not unusual. Writers are always being hired to rewrite other writers. And, besides, I was unknown to them. However, my contract stated that I had the right of refusal on any first rewrite, and that was as inviolate and as spiritually inspired as all the other things about writers fixed in stone and parchment.

I was definitely pissed off and I told him on the spot that I was putting him, his literary agency, and NBC on notice that they could not proceed without me. There was namecalling after that and a countersuit was threatened, but in the end the network didn't want any part of a writer controversy and was prepared to drop the whole project. My agent then called and asked what my bottom line was. He said the film would not get made at all if I wasn't prepared to negotiate. I'm hardly a businessman, but off the top of my head I came up with a proposal that would compensate me for every fraction of credit I lost on story and teleplay. In other words, if I had to share story credit with the new writer I'd then be paid more. If I lost story credit entirely I would receive a still higher fee. The same thing with teleplay. I also asked for an additional immediate payment for not being given the privilege of doing another draft of my own work. I assumed my demands were as outrageous as I intended them to be and that I would be turned down. They bought the whole package. I was stuck with letting someone else rewrite my work. That was galling. Far more difficult to swallow was my associate selling me out. That was extremely painful.

Time has a way of making us wiser and more temperate. I understand better now where Jerry Adler was coming from. He had invested his own money in the first option and well over eighteen months of his life trying to jumpstart this movie. At the same time, he was being pressed financially. Ultimately, it couldn't have seemed like a very big thing to him to have another writer come in when such exchanges were a common transaction in the industry. After all, I would still be paid amply for having written the original screenplay. What ultimately was the big deal except pride of ownership? All that notwithstanding, I would never have done it to him. But then again, we all march to different drummers—some, perhaps, just a bit more haltingly than others.

Oh yeah, they turned down the new writer's revisions. The story wasn't made. The script reverted back to me.

The first television script I sold was for an anthology series called *The Class of '65*. The show was loosely based on a bestselling book called *Whatever Happened to the Class of '65?* by Irving Wallace and David Wallechinsky, and was about a real-life graduating class at Pacific Palisades High School in California. The stories on the series were, of course, fictional. I got the job based on sample work from a couple of features I had written, and from the fact that I looked young enough to make the lie credible that I too had graduated from high school that year. Even as a writer, physical appearance was still playing a role as to whether or not I would gain employment.

Despite the producer's first words after hiring me ("Don't fuck this up, my whole career depends on it"), this assignment was my most satisfying television experience. There was no story editor on the show. It was just the producer and me, and all the changes that were made were done by me. Basically, I had written a script that was just too long. I had a ninety-minute story for a fifty-two-minute slot. I had to keep whittling it down, whittling it down. I never thought I could pare it so much and still have it make sense but somehow it did hold together.

Meredith Baxter Birney was one of the leads having taken time off from her hit series *Family Ties* to guest on this show. She thought I wrote well for women and recommended me to the producers of *Family Ties*. After *Class of '65* I went to work for them. It was there I learned a rather startling fact about television. *Family Ties* was considered one of the more literate shows on the air, and yet the departure point for each story idea was its resemblance to some well-known movie. The m.o. was to take a successful motion picture concept and remake it in their own image. I found this tack rampant within the industry. I had assumed that originality was the cornerstone of art. What I was learning was that everything was built on a foundation of familiarity. "Go with what has worked before" could well have been television's rallying cry. The story that the producers had me write was based on the film *Brief Encounter*. After I handed in my final draft it was rewritten by the company's writing staff. When I saw it on television it bore little resemblance to what I had done. It bore even less resemblance to *Brief Encounter*.

I wrote an episode for the television series *The Incredible Hulk*. I was paid in full but the show was never produced. I sometimes listed it as a credit because it should have been produced and would have been produced except for the clash of wills—the executive producer's and mine.

The order in which a freelance writer sells a story is as follows: You meet with those in charge, producers, story editors, writing staff, etc, and you "pitch" a story idea. Nothing is down on paper. Depending upon your reputation and how well structured your concept is, this meeting can last five minutes or as long as a half hour. More than one story idea at a time can be pitched at these sessions.

Should your story meet with the company's approval you will then be given the assignment to retell your story in outline form on paper. Again, depending on your writing style, this can be as short as four or five pages or as long as twenty. For this work there is a fee. If your outline is accepted you will then write the first draft of the teleplay. This work has all the action, description, and dialogue that would be in a complete script. Another fee accompanies this submission. The production entity then has the right to request a second draft of the script and a "polish" after that to get it into a final shooting form. There is one last payment that is attached to this part of the job.

When I went in to pitch my story for *The Incredible Hulk* I was met with much cordiality by two young women who were the line producers on the show and the male story editor. This was one time my *Star Trek* background seemed to play in my favor. They were all fans.

The story I told was about the Hulk appearing in an Appalachian village. It was a cloistered community without access to the outside world. My inspiration was a newspaper article about just such a community discovered in New Jersey, of all places, where the people were a mix of African-American and Native American. In my story they were mountain people with strong religious superstitions. To them the Hulk was a manifestation of the devil.

Everyone liked the story a lot. I was given the assignment to write the outline. They were overjoyed with the outline and, in fact, inquired about my availability to take over as story editor since the man holding that position was moving up. I hesitated. I had a hard time seeing myself working all day in an office rewriting other people's scripts. I knew we could use the money but now that I had broken through as a writer I thought I could earn enough writing my own stories. I kept stalling, and they finally gave the job to someone else. But that's okay. I did have the go-ahead to write the first draft.

I turned that in and waited to hear what changes might be wanted on the second draft. One of the producers called a few days later. She sounded a bit cooler on the phone but said that their plans were to go ahead with my script, and we arranged a time for me to come in.

There was another person there when I arrived. His name was Ken Johnson and he was the executive producer of the series. He had been off directing a two-part *Hulk* episode and hadn't been available at our first meeting. I noticed that the two young women were considerably more restrained than they had been before. Johnson was an ex-Marine who was known to be a tough guy and a talented writer. He told me that they would move forward with my script but wanted to change the locale from Appalachia to Mexico. He felt that it was not reasonable to believe that such a secluded community as I described could exist in the United States. (Like a guy who turns into a green monster could.) He mentioned the Census Bureau as somehow being proof for his contention. (Now there's an organization with a history of accuracy!) I tried to point out to him that I had culled the idea from a newspaper article but I could see that the door was swinging shut. I told him that I couldn't in good conscience place the story south of the border. My sense was that doing so would vest it with ethnic implications. By placing the events in a Mexican village we were tacitly validating the idea that only such people would be ignorant enough to believe that the Hulk was the devil.

"You mean you won't write it that way?" he asked me.

"I can't," I replied.

"Click," went the swinging door.

He was angry now and he turned to his producers. "Who gave an okay on this story anyway?" he demanded.

My understanding is that these two ladies were making around three hundred thousand dollars a year as writer-producers of the series. That's a lot of money to let something like principle stand in the way of. They immediately replied that I had not written the story I had sold them in my pitch. "It was supposed to be like Shirley Jackson's 'The Lottery,'" they bleated. I tried pointing out that they had enthusiastically purchased my outline and they had only to compare the two to see that my teleplay was just an expansion of that. I never got through it. I was being shouted down. Jesus Christ, another damned argument, another fight! Did this happen to other people as often as it seemed to happen to me?

"Mr. Johnson, these two women are lying."

I could hear the safety bolt sliding into place. The door had not only been slammed shut it had been securely locked. Johnson wasn't about to do anything but defend his employees. I'm sure I would have done the same. He stood up but didn't extend his hand.

"I guess that's it then," he said.

"I guess so," I replied.

At least they didn't hate me in the barrio.

Among my first adventures in the onionskin trade was writing for the animated *Star Trek* series. Gene Roddenberry had read *Phantasm* and although he felt it "needed work" (if you were to take Shakespeare's name off of *Hamlet* and Arthur Miller's name off of *Death of a Salesman* and Tennessee Williams' name off of *A Streetcar Named Desire* nine out of ten executives in Hollywood would say that the scripts "needed work"), he felt it was good enough to offer me an assignment on this new hybrid form of our show.

My concept was about cloning an army of giant Spocks to keep peace throughout the universe. It was called "The Infinite Vulcan." Dorothy Fontana was the associate producer and it was with Dorothy I worked most closely. I found her to be supportive and helpful. It was about then I learned just how inaccurate my impression of her from the series days had been.

Roddenberry was the executive producer. He felt that since we had this unique medium at our disposal we should add exotic elements that wouldn't otherwise be available to us. And so it came to pass that in a distant galaxy on a planet even farther away there existed a troop of talking vegetables that looked a lot like artichokes and pomegranates. I thought that the whole thing was rather silly, but it wasn't an important enough issue to fight about. I even called one of the root bearers a Retlaw Plant (hold it up to a mirror) to go along with the gag. Gene required a great many rewrites, the reason for which neither Dorothy or I could fathom, and I was quite weary of the whole thing by the time I was finally done with it. I was later invited to write a second episode but decided to pass on the opportunity.

I won't take you through the whole odyssey of my experiences as a television writer but since this is for posterity I should detail the one that finally tipped me over the edge.

There had been a couple of successful motion pictures between 1974 and 1977 about a wonder dog named Benji, and the decision had been made to turn the property into a TV series. Benji was the most anthropomorphic creature to ever grace the animal kingdom. He could do anything humans could do only much better. This dog could check the personal ads in the classified section of the newspaper, make the phone call, go out on the date, and if it didn't work out still have the recourse of licking himself to satisfaction.

The television series had not yet aired so several writers at a time were called in to have explained to them how the show would work. I was in a room with three other writers. We all had our notebooks and pens. The producer, part of a husband-and-wife team, was nothing if not committed. To help better explain Benji's behavior he took on his persona—literally. He showed us how the dog's tongue lolled out of the side of its mouth when it was trying to tell its masters about the retarded boy who fell down the well, how it panted in emulation of the locomotive bearing down on the old drunk passed out on the train tracks, how it howled in empathic pain for the pregnant young housewife trapped in the attic just after going into labor. And then, and so help me I'm not exaggerating, he leapt onto his desk, sat back on his haunches, steepled his front paws, raised his eyes to heaven and in a whimper as divinely inspired as any utterance from Mother Teresa, prayed that Grandpa would recover from his colon blockage. This guy was hilarious. Of course it was beyond ludicrous, but if you came to it with the right approach—say, after scarfing a half dozen Prozac—there was certainly room there for a humorous interpretation.

I turned to the other writers, expecting them to share my feelings of incredulity. If I had considered the performance of the producer bizarre it was nothing compared to the behavior I now witnessed. They all had their wet little noses in their notebooks feverishly writing down every pant, whine, growl and saliva drip that emanated from Benji, the Man-Faced Dog as it hunched atop its office desk in religious ecstasy.

Come on, boys and girls, surely we're not taking this stuff seriously? Oh, but they were, and then I was seized by the thought that I might some day be them. It was a chilling notion. The other writers talked about getting together for coffee afterwards but I begged off. I had a funeral to attend. Actually, I felt as if I was just coming from one—my career writing for television.

I was working on another novel in 1976 and I was paying Susan Sackett, Roddenberry's executive secretary, to do a professional typing job on it. (To this day I can't spell.) She showed it to Gene, who then asked me to collaborate on a novel he was writing. He was calling it *Star Trek II* It was, in part, a story about an entity that believed itself to be God. Roddenberry had previously submitted it as a screenplay to Barry Diller, the Paramount Pictures chairman, as the basis for a feature film. Diller didn't like the religious overtones and declined to go forward with it.

Gene had been writing on it for a month and had sixty-eight pages done when he handed it over to me. I did another eighty-three pages in the two months that followed and handed in the finished manuscript in December. His initial reaction was very enthusiastic. He was delighted with what I had done and although it was more like a novella than a novel he was looking forward to its publication.

A few weeks went by and Susan called to say that he was abandoning the project. I assumed that he had re-evaluated my work, found it wanting, and decided not to have it published after all. I've only recently learned that my efforts were not a mitigating factor. It all had to do with Gene's relationship with Paramount Pictures and the fact that a deal to produce a new *Star Trek* TV series rendered publishing the book superfluous.

I still have the material. It's not a bad story. Anyone listening?

I spent a considerable time during the seventies and part of the eighties teaching acting and directing in the UCLA Extension Division, at The Sherwood Oaks Experimental Film College and in private classes. I also taught a course employing acting techniques at the California

Institute of Professional Psychology. The curriculum at this school was considered postgraduate and was geared toward slightly older students who were seeking their Master's and Doctorate Degrees in psychology. When I interviewed for this job I was told that a new era had dawned in the classroom and that I should be prepared for vigorous and heated exchanges with the students. Was I secure enough, I was asked, not to feel threatened by a student body that might challenge my every word? Could you comfortably change your program if the class demanded it? "Absolutely!" I replied, assuming that I had the flexibility and maturity to cope with such a situation.

The course I designed was geared toward increasing self-awareness in these future psychologists with the use of acting techniques. My theory was that intuition was as important a tool in helping clients as was all the book learning they had been exposed to. The more they understood how they personally responded in a variety of situations the better equipped they'd be in dealing with the psychological processes of their patients.

I remember in particular one exercise I gave the class. It had a very dramatic effect on them as it did, subsequently, on me. I had called a student at home and asked him to spend the next class session laughing to himself and smirking at another student. He was instructed to tell no one else of this. I then called the person who was the subject of the smirking and asked him to simulate profound grief during the entirety of our coming meeting. He was not informed about the other student.

The class convened with both my participants playing their roles to the hilt. Within a very short time the tension was thick enough for the executioner's axe. In fact, without knowing what was going on, everyone was becoming so furious with the smirker that a beheading was not out of the question. I did not provide them an opportunity to discuss any of this, having given them an assignment that required their total attention. At the same time, I conducted the class as if totally unaware of what was transpiring. The stress in the room continued to grow, however, and when I felt it had achieved critical mass I abruptly called for a coffee break.

During this time out my griever explained sotto voce to those who had inquired that the wife of a former student, loved by everyone who knew her, was dying of cancer. I had left it up to my lugubrious performer to come up with his own motivation and this was the story he had concocted. I called the group back to order and my other actor resumed his act of laughing and smirking. At this point a half dozen of these students, who had chosen a career in which helping others achieve emotional stability was a primary objective, rose from their chairs prepared to throttle the life out of my first accomplice. I called a halt to things at this point, explaining that I had conceived the scenario they had just played out. Their wrath now turned on me. "How irresponsible!" "How unprofessional!" How this, how that. Fists were shaking, threats were being hurled about getting me discharged, and through it all I must say I've never comported myself with greater equanimity. "Curious," I said low enough so that they had to quiet down to hear me, "that throughout this deluge of emotion I have heard not one expression of relief that this woman you all know is not sick after all. What you're pissed about is being had. That you think you've been made fools of. This is not a right or wrong response," I said, "it's a human response. One which you might do well to catalog. It might help you some day in understanding where your patients are coming from." The room quieted down, the point was made. Such maturity, such wisdom. Was I good or what? Wait. It wasn't over yet.

The following week's homework was to read through a one-act play by Arthur Miller called *A Memory of Two Mondays* and create a personal history for the character from the play that I assigned each of them. The idea was that the history would help explain the character's motivation.

I arranged the seating in a circular configuration when next we met. I wanted everyone to be able to see everyone else. Face-to-face confrontation heightens the immediacy of the situation being addressed and encourages spontaneity in those involved. At least that had been the rule of thumb when working with real actors.

As it turned out, each of these people were the actor's equivalent of somebody with *all* thumbs. I sat back flabbergasted as one after the other read their roles as haltingly as grade schoolers. I knew there were serious defects in our educational system but I had no idea the decline was that steep. My patience was fast eroding. Still another person stumbled over words and I slammed closed my copy of the play. "What's the matter with you people? Didn't any of you look the material over before coming to class? You read English like it's a third language."

One of the brighter students in whom I had taken some pride then mumbled something under his breath. I asked him to repeat it. Reluctantly he blurted out that they weren't supposed to be actors anyway, they were psychologists. Before I even had a chance to react a classmate added that what I was teaching had no place in their post-graduate curriculum. With this a third student dropped her script on the floor and shoved it under her chair. So did a fourth and fifth. In a whisper loud enough for me to hear, my prize pupil told the person at his elbow that I was probably here because I couldn't get work as an actor. There were about fifteen people in the group. Emboldened by the first few the rest now packed their scripts away and sat facing me defiantly. This was really my worst nightmare. I had become an actor to be loved, and everyone in this room now hated me. Captain Queeg, Captain Bligh, and Captain Nazi had nothing on me. Panic clutched at my throat. I could think of no way out of this.

"Why do we have to do this shit anyway?" said someone who had not spoken before.

"Yeah!" came the chorus emphatically.

I remembered the interview that I had submitted to for this post: "Are you secure enough not to feel threatened by a student body which challenged your every word? Could you comfortably change your program if the class demanded it?"

"Absolutely!" I had replied then.

"Because I'm the teacher here and you'll do as I say. Now pick up your goddamned scripts and we'll start again!" is what I actually said. Up until the last statement, about acting being "shit," I hadn't considered the response I had just made to be an option. But I had spent twelve years at my craft by that time and I wasn't going to let it be so easily denigrated. Sometimes you've got to go with your gut and maturity be damned because, quite remarkably, one by one they all opened up their copies of Miller's play and began reading again. This time they read with fluidity and precision. Obviously, I had been wasting my time being a tolerant, understanding teacher in the past if just screaming at students could improve their skills so miraculously. Also quite obviously, I didn't have a clue as to what had actually been going on. It turned out they had been scamming me exactly as I had done them the week before. Each of their actions and comments had been planned. They wanted to see what *my* behavior would be under pressure. They assured me there was no right or wrong response, just a human response. One I might do well to catalog for future reference. Where had I heard that before?

At the end of the semester I graded them and they graded me. We all gave each other high marks.

In 1975 I got wind of correspondence that Gene Roddenberry had sent to the cast alerting them to the possibility of a new Star Trek project. It turned out to be the *God-Thing* screenplay that he and I later converted into the short novel. James Doohan had mentioned the communique to me in a conversation but since I had not received such a letter I was a bit concerned. I called Susan Sackett who told me that I was being paranoid and that of course Gene had mailed one to me too. However, since he was currently out of the country she couldn't absolutely confirm it. Why wasn't I reassured? Perhaps because I had already been left out of the animated series and only found that out when a fan informed me of it at a Star Trek convention. Dorothy Fontana had given a talk at the convention where the announcement was made. Apparently, she and Gene had gotten their signals crossed, each thinking the other had told me. Learning it from a fan was quite possibly the most embarrassing Star Trek moment I have ever had. When I mentioned to Gene how awkward it had felt he dismissed my complaint with a display of irritation.

And so I waited for Roddenberry's return with more than just a little apprehension. He called me on a Sunday when he got back and explained that not including me in the communique had not been an oversight. The story he had in mind was going to take place three years before the five-year mission. Since it was now six years later and I had been, to begin with, playing a character who was nine years younger than I, I would now have to play Chekov at a time when I was eighteen years older than the ensign. He didn't think I could pull it off and I agreed. In passing, he asked how I would feel about playing Chekov's father. I thought the idea an interesting one but also suspected that it might easily be forgotten once shooting commenced.

We later heard that Barry Diller, the Paramount Pictures Chairman, had rejected the story line for the film. We were back to square one but at least a story taking place in the past was not now being contemplated. I was back on a level playing field, or so I thought.

1977 rolled around and there was fresh talk about reactivating Star Trek, first as a television movie and then as a TV series. In anticipation of a new weekly show, Roddenberry created a *Writers/Directors Guide* that sketched how the characters should be written and what direction the story lines should take. It was passed out to all concerned parties. Once again I had that old sinking feeling. The character synopsis for the Russian navigator was definitely underwritten—far more than for any of the other crew. Bearing in mind that I had already been dispatched from two Star Trek projects, I don't think my anxiety was unfounded. The other *Star Trek* actors like to joke about my pessimistic view regarding Star Trek's survival from one film to the next and my involvement therein, but twice burned you start wearing a psychological disposition heavy in fire retardants. I sent Roddenberry the following missive.

Gene Roddenberry   8/12/77
Star Trek
Paramount Studios

Dear Gene,

Having read the WRITERS/DIRECTORS GUIDE I must admit to a vague feeling of concern. I am not able to determine whether Chekov's new duties will be beneficial to his character's development and increase his exposure on the series or will prove to be disadvantageous serving to bury him somewhere within the vessel's innards for the greater part of the show's run.

Rather than make an appearance at your door with my doe-eyed and tattered children in hand I have conceived of a literary device that I think can preserve my personal dignity and the integrity of Chekov's character.

Of all the profiles drawn for the continuing characters in the writer's "bible", Chekov is the only one for whom idiosyncratic behavior defining personality has not been included. On the other hand, the statement is make that "The Captain's safety is Lt. Chekov's responsibility too . . ." With that in mind I conceive Chekov as a young officer who takes his job of protecting the Captain very seriously. Should Kirk be in danger or suffer an injury Chekov would suffer self-recrimination and guilt. This could make for an occasional touching scene between them. More to the point, however, Chekov's "mother henning" his Captain could add a bit of humor that might evolve into a running piece of business. Not only would the doting lieutenant be a mild irritant and consequently a good foil for Kirk to play off of but there is inherently good comedic value in the smaller, albeit serious minded, Russian offering to fight Kirk's battles for him.

I'm not suggesting that in this relationship we have the nucleus for an hour episode but what I am saying is that it is the kind of device that may be slipped into most any story without subverting plot nor redirecting emphasis away from other characters.

Chekov's chauvinism ("Inwented in Russia") although sophomoric did serve the purpose of a "handle" for audience identification. I believe that the kind of slightly disproportionate sense of responsibility I have described for Chekov in his dealings with his Captain can serve the same purpose for him in the new series.

      Best,

      Walter

Shortly after this, word started spreading that the project was again stalled. I did not have a direct line to what was going on and could only speculate that there would be no Hallelujah Choir, that *Star Trek's* resurrection was still a miracle or two away.

Then, during the second week of November 1977, the following letter arrived at my home.

November 9, 1977

Mr. Walter Koenig

Dear Walter:

WELCOME BACK ABOARD!

After two and one half years of struggle here at Paramount, with STAR TREK's return on and off again almost monthly, I have felt somewhat battle-weary and pessimistic until recently. But I believe we are now going to make the opening STAR TREK II film!

When the film is made and with our STAR TREK sets and paraphernalia bought and paid for, the return of the weekly series to television has to be considered almost a certainty. Will let you know more about the television production dates as soon as Paramount's front office agrees on that schedule. Meanwhile, we are accumulating the first dozen episode scripts.

I think you'll like out new production staff, our director Bob Collins, our producers Bob Goodwin and Harold Livingston, our cameraman Bruce Logan. And of course you'll find many familiar names and faces among staff and crew who have returned to join us in the new production.

Just to prove that I never ask anything I'm not willing to do myself, I'm on a diet too!

                    Warmest of welcomes,
                    Gene Roddenberry

GR:ss

The *Star Trek II* film to which Roddenberry alludes was to be a television movie that would segue into a new television series. Even though it carried the same title as his film proposal of 1975 it was not the same story. The TV movie and the series that would follow it were to be the flagship programming for Paramount's plan for a fourth network.

It was now 1978. We were all getting primed for the new series. To be sure, Leonard Nimoy wouldn't be joining us, but everyone else had signed aboard including a new Vulcan officer named Xon. Events thereafter changed with so much frequency and at such an alarming pace that I never did meet the young fellow who was to play the new character. I remember being called in for a costume fitting one morning. At this point, we were still scheduled to wear our television outfits from the sixties. Bill Theiss from the series days was again in charge of wardrobe. Most everyone in the cast had already been in for their fittings when I arrived. I chuckled smugly over the gossip that several of our group would need to have their uniforms altered appreciably. Never chuckle smugly. There is no lasting mirth when you're up against the god of girth. I had been back less than an hour from my wardrobe appointment when I received a call that any final fittings which had been scheduled were now canceled. Not postponed—canceled. The filming was off. As a devout believer in the "other shoe" credo (I know, but it's been at least a hundred pages since I last mentioned it), it's not beyond me to believe that my cockiness in the wardrobe room, at the very least, abetted the collapse of the project.

Actually, from what I could gather, we were dead as a television series because Paramount discovered it could not be competitive as a network with the Big Three. ABC, CBS, and NBC lowered their rates to advertisers, in effect undercutting the Studio and forcing it out of the network market. That determination and the unprecedented success of *Star Wars* made Paramount rethink its options. It was finally announced that a big-budget *Star Trek* feature film would be made instead.

That this enterprise was back on and then off and then back on and then off again during the spring of 1978 probably lends itself to an analogy that could most accurately be described as "projectus interruptus." There is a condition with a slang monicker that sometimes affects the testicles when sexual congress is adjourned before a session is completed. In our case, as many times as we were on and off, feeling "blue" would not be an imprecise way of describing our state of health as well.

THIRTEEN

"Back to the Future"

MY FIRST BOOK, *CHEKOV'S ENTERPRISE* WAS A BEHIND-THE-SCENE journal of the making of *Star Trek—The Motion Picture*. There are only a few things that I would add to that account here.

There are three gossip items that people always circulate about an actor. Number one: he is really gay. Number two: he really wears lifts in his shoes. Number three: he really wears a hairpiece.

"Hi, I'm Walter Koenig and beginning with the first Star Trek movie I've been wearing a rug for the last nineteen years."

"Hi, Walter, have some coffee and a hair restorer."

Why don't I feel cleansed by this admission? Probably what I need to do is find *somebody somewhere* who is also a longtime user and ask him to come over and hold my follicles.

George Takei, Nichelle Nichols, and I were originally contracted to work five weeks in the Star Trek feature film. Because we operated under a "favored nations" clause, which meant that our basic salaries were the same, I do not feel it appropriate to tell you what I was paid. I would have no objection otherwise. Suffice to say that with payment penalties for postponements and with a protracted shooting schedule that had me personally on the payroll for sixteen weeks I earned more than four times what was originally agreed upon. The studio got wise after the first movie. For succeeding pictures they proffered contracts that were for the run of the film up to a total of ten weeks. They were still obligated to pay overtime, but there would never again be the unexpected bounty that came with the first motion picture. In fact, although each succeeding project included a raise, it was sufficiently modest so that I didn't actually earn more than I did on the first one until we made *Star Trek IV: The Voyage Home* in 1985.

My experience on the first Star Trek picture was generally a good one. Principally, it was good because it was so novel. As many times as it was stalled, I had little confidence that it would actually be made, so every favorable experience on the shoot took on added dimension. In fact, many of the conversations that the cast had, at least at the beginning, concerned how unbelievable it seemed that we had risen from the ashes to flap around in the stratosphere once more. That Leonard Nimoy joined us after all was more of the same.

Perhaps the strangest thing about this motion picture, which few other films can claim, was that we began shooting without a concluding act to the story. I believe that the movie's artistic downfall can be attributed to this circumstance. We painted ourselves into a corner and didn't know how in hell to get out. The main problem as I see it was that the character of the V'ger entity was not clearly defined from the beginning. Initially, it was an antagonist bent on destroying all us carbon-based units, but because there wasn't an overview of the story a resolution to the jeopardy had not been worked out. By the tenth or twelfth week Bill Shatner and Leonard Nimoy began participating in the story conferences.

These meetings were taking place on mornings when we would have otherwise been shooting. Because Robert Wise, our director, was also in on these discussions the rest of us were left to munch bagels and speculate on the fate of what had begun to look less like a journey to the stars and more like a star-crossed journey. The script was now in the hands of far too many people, each with a vested interest in seeing it go in a particular direction. Achieving a consensus under these circumstances was particularly difficult. It was a fait accompli that any decision finally rendered would be a compromise that diminished the quality of the film.

What happened was, V'ger underwent a psychic transformation. Instead of this formidable foe that threatened our existence, it became a being that was seeking a higher level of enlightenment. Sort of Buddhism for the astral boonies. That would have been okay except that in an action picture there should be a dovetailing of events toward a dramatic climax, a tension that keeps the audience on the edge of its seat and holding its breath. I don't think anyone would argue that we totally missed the spaceship on that one. In *Star Trek—The Motion Picture* the last moments of the story were designed to create a wide-eyed, slack-jawed sense of awe. My guess is that unless you're doing a story about the Resurrection that is not the way to end a movie. As the saying goes about hindsight, it's easy to pontificate eighteen years after the fact, but still . . . there must have been somebody in that room who knew, when the decision was made, that the third act might bring down the curtain but it wouldn't bring down the house.

At the same time we were making *Star Trek—The Motion Picture* both the *Mork and Mindy* and *Taxi* television series were shooting on the lot. Franklyn Seales was one of the actors who played bridge personnel on our film. Robert Wise released him early from his contract in order that he might star in the adaptation of the Robert Wambaugh novel *The Onion Fields* with James Wood. Franklyn, as we were later to learn, was a brilliant actor. He had attended Juilliard, the famous music and performing arts school in New York, along with Robin Williams, and Williams frequently sat down to lunch with us in the commissary. I was not at all amazed by his machine-gun patter of stories, impersonations, and oneliners because it only corroborated what I already knew; comedians are *always* on. In a sentence: he was funny, likeable, and exhausting.

I was relaxing on the set during a lunch break one day when I became aware of two figures moving cautiously in the shadows. It was Danny DeVito and Tony Danza from *Taxi*. It was delightful to watch them move down the *Enterprise* corridors, through Sick Bay, and onto the bridge. There was reverence here that might better be suited to St. Peter's. Of course, they have both gone on to extremely successful careers, but it was charming to see them in the beginning when the sense of wonder was still fresh.

Chris Lloyd played Reverend Jim on *Taxi* and I thought I'd surprise him in his dressing room. At that point, I hadn't seen him in several years and was anticipating a warm reunion. He answered my knock looking totally befuddled. He hemmed, he hawed, he shook his head as if trying to clear it. I asked if I had awakened him. The question seemed to confuse him. Hey, either I had or I hadn't. We weren't talking here about the Judeo-Christian ethic as interpreted by the Mikasuki Indians of the Florida Seminoles. Yes or no? I suffered through about ten minutes of his rambling and then left, figuring that he must be whacked out on drugs. What had really transpired hit me in a flash several days later. He had been playing Reverend Jim with me. Congratulations, Chris, you can sustain a character even at the expense of an old pal.

Years later he came aboard *Star Trek III* as the Klingon Commander Kruge. We hadn't spoken since that day in his dressing room four years before. He looked at me sheepishly and laughed self-consciously. My sense was that he totally remembered our last encounter. He was on my turf now and I was still pissed.

"Hey, Chris, how you doin'?" Okay, so I'm not good at retribution.

I remember the plane flight to Washington D.C. for the premier of *Star Trek—The Motion Picture*. Jeff Katzenberg, the Paramount executive in charge of our production, sat down next to me for awhile. He was only twenty-six or twenty-seven at the time and had an abrasive personality. I was wondering how long somebody like that could last in our industry. Obviously, I'm a great judge of character. Katzenberg went on to hold the second-highest position at Disney and is now part of the triumvirate along with Stephen Spielberg and David Geffen who make up DreamWorks SKG.

At some point during the flight I got to talking with Gene Roddenberry about the film. We were carrying what was called a "wet print" of the feature to the screening. The expression means that it had only been hours since the final version of the movie had been put together.

Gene was one of the few who had already seen it and in response to my question said that our ten-to-twelve-million-dollar-budgeted picture, which had become a forty-three-million-dollar epic, was a "good" film. Until that moment I had been riding the same high everyone else had been (having conveniently dispatched the problems with the story's structure from my mind). After all, we were going to the nation's capital. There would be limousines, red carpets, and parties. The media would be everywhere. How could we not be a success? But if ever a motion picture had been damned with faint praise it was this one at this moment by its producer. Wasn't it Bette Davis in *All About Eve* who said, "Fasten your seat belts, it's going to be a bumpy night"?

The premiere ended, and the lights went on accompanied by polite applause. I rose from my seat and stood facing Harold Livingston. Livingston was credited as the screenwriter although the battle to keep his vision of the story intact had severely tested him. We looked at each other and simultaneously our eyes rolled heavenward.

The reviews in the Washington papers the next day were brutal. They said that the Star Trek regulars were old, fat, bland, and constipated. Names were named. Everyone was scorched by the critic's wrath except me. Me they hadn't even listed as being *in* the picture. It was the only time in my life that I reveled in anonymity.

I never thought there would be another *Star Trek* film after this one. (You will hear this refrain again in succeeding chapters.) In fact, I bet Jon Povil, a writer and associate producer on *Star Trek—The Motion Picture,* fifty dollars to that effect. I am embarrassed to say I never got around to paying him. I am going to have to do that one of these days. What I failed to recognize was that despite its artistic shortcomings the movie was racking up impressive domestic box office numbers. In fact, not until our fourth *Star Trek* film, *The Voyage Home,* did we surpass the box office tally of the first worldwide.

🪐

As with almost all the features we did I had unofficial sources at either the studio or in businesses related to the studio that supplied me with advance information on the projects and/or advance copies of the screenplays. I read through a preliminary bootlegged copy of *Star Trek: The Wrath of Khan* and perceived an egregious structural error. I phoned Harve Bennett, the very successful television producer who had been called in to replace Roddenberry and to right our ship. He was at first reluctant to see me, implying that he didn't have the time to discuss "actors' problems." I told him that my concerns ran far deeper than that and he scheduled an appointment.

Robert Salin, the project's producer, was there (a very nice man, indeed), as well as Harve, who carried the title of executive producer on this picture. I felt sure that the story point that needed to be addressed was so obvious that my contribution would be to reinforce what others had already pointed out. I was rather surprised to discover that I was actually bringing to the table a fresh perspective. The story as written to this point had Spock meet his end in the second act, long before the climax to the piece. My feeling was that Kirk, Spock, and the *Enterprise* came closer in the public's mind to being synonymous with the concept of Star Trek than anything else. If you remove one of these elements it had better be the dramatic high point of the story. If Spock was going to die it should be in the last ten minutes of the picture.

Bennett was an extremely bright man and had been wooed by Paramount not only for his track record but for his intelligence. Once assigned, he had done his homework assiduously. He screened all of the seventy-nine episodes of the television series looking for a story he could build a sequel on and had made the dead-on absolutely right choice in using the first year show "Space Seed." What he didn't know going in was Star Trek fandom. It was the unseen writer at every story conference. Those involved in the creative process could have their own vision, but ultimately obeisance had to be made to the letter-writing, convention-going, ticket-buying, devoutly committed Star Trek public. He was to learn again and again and ultimately to his defeat just how influential this audience was.

Another draft of the script came down after that and Harve asked me to do a "trekkie run" on it. The pages appearing in the appendix under "Notes to Harve Bennett on Star Trek II" were my response. I have asked that they be published as I wrote them, bad spelling, bad punctuation, bad suggestions, and all. Obviously, I totally blew it on my criticism of the use of "Amazing Grace," but several of my other comments seem to have been taken to heart.

There was one note I did not make. Had I done so it would have eliminated the most glaring inconsistency in the script, but at what price glory? In the story, Khan recognizes Chekov from the "Space Seed" episode—but that show was shot the year before I joined the cast. My concern was that if I mentioned it the decision might be to change the actor rather than change the dialogue. I love George Takei but you've got to take my word for it—I give good Ceti eel scream. I can't imagine the dignified Mr. Sulu being as effective.

I started working on *The Wrath of Khan* a week after the regular cast began. Shooting began aboard the *Enterprise* with the Kobayashi Maru exercise designed to determine how a ship's captain would respond to a no-win situation. Since Chekov was now First Officer aboard the USS *Reliant* he was not involved in this part of the scenario. When I did begin work it was to play opposite Ricardo Montalban as Khan Noonien Singh and Paul Winfield as Captain Clark Terrell. It was a complete joy to perform in the same scenes with these two gentlemen. Neither of them took the director aside and asked for shots to be redesigned. They played what was given them without complaint. They conducted themselves as true professionals. It was very refreshing. The tone for this period in the shooting was established early on when Nicholas Meyer, the director, called us in to his trailer to discuss a scene we had just rehearsed. Nick, in a most guileless fashion, told Montalban that he was playing the action too broadly. I'm sure I winced visibly. I was used to situations where directors tiptoed around the leading actors and would never think of suggesting that they were hamming it up. And Montalban was more than just a leading actor. Not only did he have his own very successful television series but he had also been a leading man in movies for over three decades. After I stopped wincing I held my breath. I was preparing for the tirade to follow.

"Aaah, I see what you mean," came the reply from the noble Latin star. It was not what I had expected. I realized then how conditioned I had become to expecting a more self-serving mode of behavior.

James Doohan, Nichelle Nichols, George Takei, and Walter Koenig have been heard to speak at length about behavior on the set of the various films that have left them feeling victimized. I believe these feelings surfaced strongly during their experience making *Star Trek II: The Wrath of Khan*. The target of most of their criticism has been William Shatner. I offer the following incident as a departure point for a discussion that addresses the problem and asks some questions as to where else responsibility for their grievances might lie.

The setup in question takes place shortly after Kirk, McCoy, and Saavik discover Terrell and Chekov on the otherwise deserted Regula I base. We are in the Regula transporter room about to beam down to the planetoid where the Genesis Device is stored. Bill is standing on the foreground pod and the rest of us are placed in positions around him. I'm behind him over his left shoulder. The camera is facing us. Shatner sees me out of the corner of his eye and tells me to move further left. I inch in the direction he indicates although such decisions are really the province of the director. He is still not satisfied and motions me to move even further left. He obviously doesn't want me behind him. I can only assume he finds my presence a distraction to his monopoly of the screen. But now, it seems to me, if I move any further I will not be in the camera frame at all. I mention this to him and his laugh is laced with ridicule. I'm sorry to say that everyone laughs with him. I don't condemn them. It's a reflex sycophantic response that I probably would have made had I been in their shoes. Nevertheless, I am really pissed. The implication is that in my concern over my positioning I am acting like a movie star and not like an actor.

"Well, I'm only taking my cue from you, Bill." That's what I replied, and to that point I am happy with myself.

"What are you talking about? I don't do that. That's neurotic!"

He is now equally as angry, and it's my turn for rebuttal. But I say nothing. Absolutely nothing. I've got to tell you, I don't think any one of us ever pushed him further than I did then, but it's of no consolation. What a puny effort! I went to bed that night doubled over. My stomach had cramped so badly I couldn't straighten out. Sleep was a myth. I was angry at Bill and furious at myself. If I had thought through my self-condemnation and taken it to the next step then, as opposed to doing it thirteen years later, the history of Star Trek might have been altered somewhat; either from a physical standpoint or an interpersonal one.

See, what I have learned is that the beehive in which we operated was not a function of predetermined genetic destiny. None among us were born to be the queen bee and none among us were fated to be the workers or drones. I don't deny that the environment predisposed the caste system to exist. There were those who were the "STARS" of the film and those who were the "stars" of the film. There were those with the big trailers and those with the smaller trailers. Those with the huge salaries and those who were making one twenty-fourth as much. None of that can be denied. But free will was a viable option even if it was at a cost. How many times during the course of all these films could we have stepped into Shatner's path and said, "This isn't fair, it isn't right that you interfere with the process and deprive us of the acting moments which have been allotted us"? Would it have made a difference? Who knows? If we had been sufficiently vehement could it have affected our Star Trek careers? Possibly. I don't think he would have had us fired on the spot, but could he have interfered with our employment on succeeding films? Perhaps. Would he have done so? We'll never know. And therein lies the rub. The fear of power is often more potent than power itself. We have complained about him to each other and in interviews and at conventions and in books but no one ever looked him in the eye and said, "Cut the shit, Shatner!" And because we haven't, I'm not sure we can be quite so self-righteous about feeling dishonored. In stating this, I do by no means free Bill of culpability. I'm only saying that when transgressions occurred we helped perpetuate them by not taking the personal responsibility of speaking up. Should we have been placed in this position in the first place? Absolutely not. There are many motion picture sets where this kind of behavior does not occur. But when it does you either confront the problem and *possibly* suffer the consequences of a firm declaration of your position or not confront the problem and *definitely* suffer the consequences of a meek response.

Bill Shatner has repeatedly said that he was not aware that we felt the way we did. Knowing his tunnel-visioned approach to his work I think that is possible. If that is true then we must share the burden of guilt with him.

And what part does Nick Meyer play in all of this? He has twice directed feature films for us. Nick is one of the most well-educated and cultured people I have known. He is also a wonderful writer and a disciplined, prepared director who brings his own unique signature to the work. And yet he told me that the most responsible action he could take was to listen closely to what Bill and Leonard had to say because they knew Star Trek better than he did. If Nick had occasionally toughed it out and denied the captain's prerogative would it have made a difference in the greater order of things? Maybe. But would we have had a better film? I doubt it.

Nick didn't just go along with the program because Shatner was the STAR and wielded power. He knew a good idea when he saw one, and the fact is that Bill's ideas were good, they were uncannily good. They did not detract from the story, they probably enhanced the story. They only detracted from the sense of family that the Star Trek crew was supposed to convey; that we were all in this together and that we were each important in solving the problem. But how do you measure the "sense" of something? And even if you could, is it the director's responsibility to take such an ephemeral matter into account? His primary objective is to tell a story well and give flesh and bone to the principal characters. The others get sketched in as best they can. Why should this motion picture adventure be different from any other? There is only one reason, and it's the only reason that makes these questions anything but rhetorical. Star Trek is *not* like other movies. It is unique among film projects because Star Trek truly is an institution. Over the course of three years on television and what would become six features the regular cast did not change.

The public's view over this expanded period was not of Star Trek as a vehicle for two or three star players but one that embraced all seven actors. Not in equal degree to be sure but with a measure of respect toward all that might well be absent in other movie productions. Did Nick see this? No. Did Harve Bennett see this? No. Did anyone at Paramount see this? No. The only people who saw this were in the audience. So I come to the end of this rambling discourse and I'm still asking questions. If the perception of the supporting cast is justified, that we have been ill-used, is there anyone involved, including ourselves, who does not share in the responsibility? I don't think so.

The Wrath of Khan worked so well because of passion, because of emotional commitment. In the first Star Trek movie V'ger was an almost omnipotent adversary. It didn't provoke a lasting sense of jeopardy for reasons already discussed, and because it didn't fall within a recognizable frame of reference. You can fear an enemy without comprehending it, but if you can also identify its motivation, recognize its pain and anger as something you yourself might experience and, because of that, understand to what lengths it would go to seek redress, then you have a threat far more real than provided by any living machine. Khan's cry for vengeance over the death of his mate sprang from human emotion. As an audience we could relate to his passion and understand just how formidable a force it could be. The fury in Ricardo Montalban's performance made believers of us all.

In my opinion the death of Spock is the singularly most affecting scene in all of our Star Trek history. Again, it works so magnificently because of passion. Just as vengeance is a human response, so is love. We understand love and we understand its loss. The emotional commitment between these two men is undeniable and powerful. We recognize this bond and are deeply touched by it. And through the marvelous performances of Bill and Leonard, its dissolution becomes a tragedy as moving for the audience as it is to the crew of the *Enterprise*.

I got off to a very bad start *on Star Trek III: The Search for Spock*. One from which I never did fully recover. I became quite excited when I first heard the picture was going to be made. The Chekov role in the preceding movie had been satisfying, and I assumed that Gene's comments to his staff back in 1968 about expanding the involvement of the Russian character had finally established a foothold. However, I began hearing from my various sources that Chekov's participation was considerably less than it had been in the previous film. Therefore, before signing on, I wanted to read the script.

My agent at the time was Steve. Jimmy Doohan had arranged my introduction to him. Later George Takei came aboard, and for a time he represented the three of us. Harve Bennett invited Steve and I to come in and read the screenplay at the studio. Steve suggested we go in one car.

I admit to being a bit cool when Harve greeted us. I was already anticipating that I wasn't going to be happy with what I read. Harve left us alone with the script and asked us to stop by his office when we had finished. Chekov's part was as eviscerated as I had been led to believe. This was definitely a couple of giant steps backward in his development. Nevertheless, I was prepared to see the producer afterward as he had requested, but Steve had another appointment and asked that we pass on the invitation. It was then I asked Steve to convey to Bennett my disappointment should Harve later call his office. These misjudgments on our parts, Steve not wanting to hang around and my second-hand expression of disappointment, were crucial to what happened next.

Bennett called my agent later that day incensed that we hadn't waited to speak to him. It might have been helpful if Steve had mentioned that it had been his idea to leave, but he didn't. It probably wouldn't have mattered anyway because when my sentiments about Chekov's participation in *Star Trek III* were repeated to him he really lost it. Harve was listed as the writer on the script and I imagine he felt it extreme impudence on my part to criticize the work, even if it were only in regard to my character. I can understand someone taking umbrage at such comments, particularly when the consensus studio reaction was favorable. My argument was with the intensity of his reaction. Steve called me and repeated the blistering attack he had made upon me. I remember two criticisms in particular: I had the worst Russian accent in Hollywood and if it weren't for Star Trek I would never work in this town. I suppose both these statements can be supported, but the intent behind them was so mean-spirited and so obviously designed to humiliate me that I wasn't about to make a judgment based on objectivity. I hung up the phone reeling. I would never have expected that my disappointment in Chekov's role could lead to this kind of vilification. I called Steve back and asked if he thought I should call the producer myself. He cautioned against it. He didn't think he would take my call. And now I felt totally powerless. There was no action I could take to exonerate myself, clear the air, or ask for an apology. I was in the ring with my gloves on but there was nobody to take a swing at. Throughout the whole episode these were the worst moments I had.

And then another phone call came in and provided me the opportunity to counterpunch. The casting office had called my agent and he had then called me. The production company always makes a preliminary salary offer to each cast member. It is understood that this figure is negotiable and would rise, perhaps not to the actor's expectations, but to a more palatable level by the conclusion of contract discussions. In this case, I was told that the first offer was the only offer I would receive. The expression "take it or leave it" was used. In Hollywood parlance this is the unofficial term indicating that bargaining had ceased. You either accept what they offer or you're out of the project, period. This, at least, I could respond to. I still had some use for an athletic supporter; I hadn't been rendered totally impotent after all. "I leave it," I told my agent. Not only had I been kicked in the face, now they wanted me to lick the boot that had done the job. Fat chance!

I called my family together and told them that I was no longer involved with Star Trek. My wife, always supportive, did not try to talk me out of my decision. My son was fifteen, my daughter almost eleven. They nodded solemnly but expressed no opinion. I went to bed feeling rather depressed, but I was able to sleep. Imagine how I would have felt had I backed down?

The next afternoon there was yet another call. The Star Trek company was prepared to rescind yesterday's final offer and make me a new one. It was only for a few thousand more, and on that account it felt somewhat like a pyrrhic victory, but the fact was they had blinked and I had not, and far more important than money was the feeling of self-worth that I had maintained intact.

During the time between the second and third film I had given a magazine interview complaining about Bill Shatner. I can only assume that he read it because he didn't talk to me for several weeks on this new picture. I take no exception to that. In his place, I would have done no less.

I believe Leonard has said that he was concerned about the cast's reaction when we learned he would be directing us in *The Search for Spock*. I won't speak for the others but I was mildly apprehensive. It wasn't that I thought he couldn't do the job, I just didn't know how well the taciturn Mr. Spock would relate to his actors. I use Mr. Spock here advisedly. I had seen far more of him in the years to date than I had Leonard Nimoy and because of that, the Vulcan was my better frame of reference for judging the director's communication skills.

It took me a week or so to learn that Leonard directed actors by omission. If you were doing it right he said nothing. Only if you screwed up did he speak to you. I remember a moment in the story when we wake up outside the temple where the Vulcan high priestess is trying to restore Spock's *katra* (soul/living spirit) to his living body. One of our group yawned and stretched to indicate that we had been asleep. In this context the word "indicate" is an actor's term that implies that the behavior is not real. The performer's gesture was a cliche that detracted from a sense of reality the director was attempting to establish. Leonard yelled "Cut" with more basso profundo that I had before heard. I was standing close by as he approached the actor. In a low voice but with considerable intensity he said, *"Don't ever do that again!"* It was as upset as I saw him get until we were doing *Star Trek IV: The Voyage Home* and I tried to bring a little levity to the proceedings. I'll get to that.

I don't know what conversations took place or what agreements were made between Leonard and Bill before shooting began, but certainly their effect on the set was apparent. Bill's behavior was far more restrained. His tendency to redirect shots was almost non-existent. It looked like their mutual respect was showing.

When I read the script for *The Search for Spock* it felt like the flip side of a hit record: the tune was very similar, only the lyrics were different. In this case, "the bad guys wanting the bomb" was the melody that had already been composed for *The Wrath of Khan* and was being repeated here. However, there was far more to this third Star Trek adventure than I had initially given it credit for. The regeneration of Spock and the transfer of the Vulcan's *katra* from McCoy to Spock were two very interesting elements.

However, critical to the story's success, as it had been in the first two movies, was the way in which the villain was depicted. I do believe we fell short in *Star Trek III*. Central to any good story in any genre is how well-defined and motivated is the conflict. If you have opposing forces of equal strength you have the foundation for a riveting yarn. To make the adversary equal is to do more than just provide it with the capability of blowing you out of the sky. "Equal" here means that it is developed in a way that puts the issue in doubt. Chris Lloyd's Kruge was written as a one-dimensional character. He wanted the Genesis Device because he wanted power. That pretty much explains the Klingon, and being so venal a creature we know going in what will happen to him. The issue is not in doubt and we are, therefore, less involved in his part of the story.

I wasn't doing much talking to Harve Bennett during the shooting of this film. I was still chafing from his attack on me early on and couldn't bring myself to bury it. After I had accepted the second offer and had been welcomed back into the fold I had called Bennett and asked him why he hadn't confronted me directly with his complaints rather than go through my agent. I didn't get a satisfactory answer to that and as a result it took me a long time to shake loose from my resentment.

It was during the preview screening at the studio that I was finally able to disengage from my anger. The picture was better than I thought it would be and Harve's contribution as producer could not be minimized. I gave him a big hug and congratulated him. My relationship with Bennett would run smoothly over the next two films and would only turn ugly again when he began planning for *his* version of *Star Trek VI*.

FOURTEEN

"The Public Eye"

I HAVE MADE PERSONAL APPEARANCES ON BEHALF OF STAR TREK from the mid-seventies up to the present day. During this time I have encountered the following salutations:

"Are you who I think I am?"

"You're Walter Klingon, aren't you?"

"Hey, Scotty!"

"Hey, Sulu!"

"My God, it's you! Could you come over to my table and sing 'Hey, hey, we're the Monkees?'"

("Isn't that the guy from that TV series?")

("Yeah, not the lead, the little guy . . .")

("Yeah, Tattoo!")

"Enjoying your visit to Hampton Court, Mr. Woody Allen?"

Like all of us, I've had my share of unusual experiences at Star Trek conventions and at other public celebrations of our show. Some of them have been funny, others poignant, others ludicrous. Some resonate in my mind because in some tangential way they are tied to other events in my life. For that reason and others, quite a few have been memorable. I offer a sampling here of my adventures on the road.

In the summer of 1957 I got a job as a "package boy" in the world-famous Beverly Hills Hotel. A package boy is below a bellhop in the caste system and, in fact, is so insignificant that he is not even provided hotel raiments. He must work in his own lowly civilian wardrobe.

After being hired I was summoned to an audience with the bell captain, all brass buttons and brocade, and I immediately knew I was in the presence of a person more important than myself. The sneer of contempt, nay, disgust that promptly swept his pan brought to mind that passage from the *The Red Badge of Courage* in which the starving soldiers gobble the undigested corn kernels from their horses' manure. Since I wasn't considered worthy enough to be addressed directly, the minion who introduced us also served as the conduit for his boss's pronouncements. Turning to the fawning lackey he said, "Tell *him* to comb his hair," and when I immediately whipped out a comb he continued in the world-weary way of Roman emperors grown bored with dispatching Christians. "Tell *him* to comb his hair in the *bathroom*." Dutifully the timorous assistant repeated the words to me. It wasn't necessary. Perhaps I had learned Latin in some other state of consciousness, but I had understood the directive the first time.

And so began my hellish employment at this touchstone of luxury living. Not only was this self-important jerk constantly on my ass but I found the performance of shifting feet, left to right, right to left, while stalling for a tip humiliating. If after a package delivery the hotel guest didn't immediately cough up a gratuity I was just as immediately out the door. Between the bell captain's constant harassment and my jingleless pockets I lasted a total of four days.

We now flash forward twenty-seven years. Jimmy Doohan and I are sitting in a handsomely adorned hotel lobby in Charlotte, North Carolina. We are awaiting our stretch limo, the comforts of which will exclude only a masseuse and a jacuzzi, to transport us to our destination. We have also been promised a police motorcade to smooth our path and to shield us from the view of anything our sensibilities might find objectionable. Did you know, for example, that there are people living in the streets in this country?

The occasion is the grand opening of a new Blockbuster video store, and we are being paid far more than our worth (well, mine anyway) to make this appearance. The only condition—one which I had steadfastly refused to accept until now—was that we wear our Star Trek uniforms. Well, what the hell. It will give a lot of people pleasure to see the real Scotty and Chekov. It might even make their day, bring a tear to the eye, give them something to tell their grandchildren about and, of course, they *are* paying us an obscene amount of money.

I am in just such a state of reverie when I feel a persistent and rather impertinent tapping on my shoulder. "You bow'oys ready to tyke mah bags uhp to mah room now?" She is a comely dowager with a tolerant if somewhat perfunctory smile. Jimmy doesn't get it immediately but I'm already on the floor. If only my mom were still alive. She'd be so proud. It's taken me three decades, but at last I've made it! I've graduated from package boy to bellhop—and I have my own uniform to boot. What's more, I'm not going to have to stall to get it—she's holding out a crisp dollar bill to me.

✴

I remember walking my dog, Pan, in the park across from my house. It was before *Star Trek,* about 1965, and the winter had passed. New grass grew beneath my feet and the morning air was fresh and sweet. Despite one of those career lulls which in those days seemed to happen about every thirty minutes I found myself wrapped in a cozy cocoon of optimism. Don't caterpillars turn into butterflies in the spring? If they don't they should. Certainly I felt my time was coming: soon I, too, would soar.

"You're going to hell, man, I'm not shittin' yah, you gotta be saved, man." He looked like a dead branch, ashen and gnarled, that had been kicked from the fire before burning all the way through. He was maybe seventeen. You could see it in his eyes—the severe withdrawal. His body was bare of flesh, rigid and permanently shaped like a crooked "S". I imagined that it was only with the last of his will that he kept it from collapsing into powder and wafting away on the breeze.

"You don't find the Lord, man, damnation will be yours for eternity." He clutched at the leaflets he was carrying as if they were plasma with an IV feed to a vein. If he dropped them his heart would stop beating. His concern was genuine and desperate, his salvation obviously dependent upon mine. If I didn't make it, if I didn't see the light, then he had failed and he wouldn't make it either. He was trying to stuff the tract into my hand. "Please, man, please, open your heart to God, you're full of sin, it's your only chance!"

It was 1980. I was at a Star Trek convention in Phoenix, Arizona. I felt someone grab at me. I spun around. He couldn't have been more than seventeen. He was about five-eleven and weighed maybe one twenty. I started to pull away but I was afraid a bone might break. His, not mine. There was that look again. The ravages of drugs and who knows what else. He buried his face in my palm. I thought I was going to lose a finger but he was only leaving a kiss. He looked up. God help us all, there were tears in his eyes. "If it weren't for Jesus Christ and *Star Trek* I wouldn't be alive today." From eternal damnation in 1965 to blessed healer in 1980. And you thought *Star Trek* was just a television show.

I recounted the story to Bill Shatner. He was underwhelmed. "Well, I don't much care for the billing," he murmured. What a card! But you know what? If you *don't* laugh you could start taking yourself very seriously.

One of the great joys of childhood was Douglas Fairbanks Jr.'s *Sinbad the Sailor* movies. Flavor that with Errol Flynn swashbucklers and you had a fantasy repast to endlessly gorge upon. My friends and I would spring from the low-rising rock formations in the jungles of Inwood Park, roll nimbly on the Kentucky blue, and jump to our feet, our stick swords smartly poised for battle. Hack and slash, tumble and leap all the day long without ever a thought of a truce. It was ecstasy long before we discovered our genitals. The sun would sink in the east before we might ever abandon these great adventures.

But, alas, somewhere along the way, perhaps during the time they introduced trashcans among the forest greenery and built a water power generator and paved roads out of dirt trails and installed high-intensity lampposts, Peter Pan went AWOL.

But, of course, you know that actors never really grow up and so always in the deepest recesses of consciousness lies panting and slavering the thought one dares not think, the daydream that will not die: to be an eye-patched randy pirate one time more, to dangle precariously from the yardarm, to rend the air with a trusty blade, to board the ships of the villainous foe and slay their dastardly kind.

And then George Takei got to play the barechested, foil-wielding swordsman in the *Star Trek* episode "The Naked Time."

Bear in mind, there was no jealousy here. I wasn't even a part of the cast when this show was filmed in 1966, and it wasn't until several years later that I actually got to watch it. Of course, when I did see it it couldn't help but expose to the light my own deeply held fantasy. I reveled vicariously in George's performance. What fun it must have been to play a role like that! How I longed to rub elbows with such an opportunity. And then in 1982, on a trip that started in Orlando, Florida and ended in Dothan, Alabama, I finally got my wish.

As I said before, through two Star Trek movies Jimmy Doohan, George Takei, and I were represented by the same agent. He would frequently book personal appearances that included two or even all three of us together. Such was the case on a miserably hot August day when we began a bus trek from Orlando across the deep South to Dothan, signing autographs at video stores along the way.

The bus itself was a marvel. It had been leased to the musician Prince and his band the year before. The ride was smooth, the air conditioning was perfectly regulated (at least at the start), and there were bunk beds near the middle of the vehicle if someone wished to slide in for a little nap along the way. In the band's case the "someones" must have been the *other* musicians in the group. I would hardly think that Prince would, in a bit of irony, spend time anywhere else but at the back of the bus. Nestled in the rear was a compartment outfitted for royalty, housing a fully furnished bedroom with a waterbed, skylight, stereo system, diffused lighting, large screen TV and a well-stocked bar.

We flipped for the chance to settle in there and Jimmy won. You'd think he would have been in a better frame of mind seven hours later when we finally arrived at our last stop. Perhaps it had something to do with the fact that the cooling system failed 170 miles from Dothan and on a day when the temperature was over a hundred degrees outside it was over 105 inside. Just for the record, I threw up.

We stumbled off the bus ragged and weary. Tempers were short. Even George, the perennial Pollyanna, looked as though he had been broadsided by a runaway truck or a fierce tsunami or the *Star Trek V* screenplay.

The video store in Dothan was small and crammed with perspiring humanity. Again, we were without air conditioning. The two small fans pumping furiously at opposite ends of the room were like jugglers flipping bowling pins at each other. In this case, however, the only thing that flew through the air was the noxious scent of people standing too long in line. Nobody was feeling very cordial, neither the long-suffering fans nor us.

The store owner appeared and asked if we wouldn't mind changing into T-shirts emblazoned with the company logo. Jimmy growled, waved the man off, and went directly to the signing table. He just wanted to get it over with.

George and I welcomed the opportunity to get out of our sweat-drenched shirts and repaired to a little house behind the store to change. It was here that it happened. It was here the years peeled away.

Images of Captain Kidd and Sir Henry Morgan and, of course, Sinbad whipped through my mind. For George it was far more profound. His own shirt had come off and he was reaching for the "Dothan's Dandy Family and X Rated Videos" garment when out of the shadows, perhaps even out of another dimension, an arm stretched forward and slapped into George's hand a fencing foil. I remember a bright white light enveloping the room and a Hallelujah Chorus building to a crescendo. If it didn't actually happen it should have. *George had been touched by God.* I'm sure of it. The eyes were as round as marbles, the smile beatific. Fie, fie on you, Thomas Wolfe, you can go home again! The transformation was instantaneous. He was once more the Mr. Sulu of "The Naked Time," and once again Mr. Sulu was D'Artagnan of *The Three Musketeers. Swish, swish* went the blade as he tested its balance and struck a noble pose. I rejoiced for him and knew it was too special a moment to let pass. "Go, go my valiant friend," I whispered in his ear, "the enemy lies within." I hardly needed to point at the video store entrance. He knew what must be done.

I was on his heels as he crashed through the back door. Thrust-parry, parry-thrust. The weapon danced in his hand. He lunged, he leapt, he loop-d-looped. To be sure, there were some with gaping mouths, some with panic in their eyes—"the unbelievers," I call them. "AH HA!" he bellowed, and then once again, "AH HA!"

"There he be, mate." I pointed with the hook I had for a hand and felt the flutter of my parrot's wings close to my ear. I was looking at Jimmy Doohan but I was seeing Basil Rathbone.

D'Artagnan, with a talent I had not known he possessed, read my thoughts and was on the signing fiend in a blink. *Jab, jab, poke, poke* went the blunt-ended foil, finding purchase in Rathbone's ample middle.

And then suddenly the illusion was destroyed. Jimmy spoiled it all. "What the hell are you doing?" he snapped. George was a step behind me in abandoning the scenario. He ignored the mounting temper of his target and poked again. Jimmy boiled over like Vesuvius. "Stop it, you idiot," he shouted and snatched the business end of the weapon. A tug-of-war ensued. Pull-push, push-pull. Yes, it looked strange, but there was passion here and passion must not be denied even if it *were* unprecedented for movie heroes and their thin-mustached, black-goateed adversaries to engage in combat as ridiculous-looking as this.

It was about then that the fog lifted and reality crept in on little cat feet. George blinked a couple of times and discovered that he was half naked in a room full of people enduring a tension headache. His expression went from bewilderment, to sadness to embarrassment. It was far too demeaning an end for such a heroic fantasy.

The final indignity was that he lost the flip on the bus ride back and it was I who slept in Prince's chamber.

🪐

I've been to Star Trek conventions where the crowds were impressive and enthusiasm ran high. And then there were the others. One such took place in 1987. It could have been in Rochester, New York, or Kansas City, Missouri, or Sacramento, California. My best recollection, though, is Milwaukee, Wisconsin. I had the sense that the entire audience was made up of people who spent their lives chewing gum long after the flavor was gone.

The small gathering mandated a short autograph line and my "public" day came to a mercifully quick end. A long, dreary evening loomed before me. My host, perhaps a bit guiltily, invited me to attend a professional indoor soccer game that night. We were accompanied by two of his beefy friends who I assumed were simply along to enjoy the game.

The floor dimensions for the indoor game are considerably smaller than they are for an outdoor soccer field. This makes for a lot of action and prolific goal-scoring. That notwithstanding, the five-hundred-seat arena was only a quarter filled. The fact that the home team was at the bottom of the league standings might well have been responsible.

Before the game began my host whispered that he had a surprise in store for me. I was envisioning a pre-game march to the center of the field and the presentation of a gold key, or a Harley, or a keg of the "beer that made Milwaukee famous." Instead, the public address announcer began a series of commercials. They included coupons for dry cleaning at Baumgartner's, the reinstitution of "Ladies' Night" at Max's Roller Rink, and a special on "ice cream for the whole family" at Von Shrapnel's. The litany threatened to take longer than the game. After about the eighth promotion the p.a. guy said, "We are very pleased to have Walter Koenig from *Star Trek* here with us tonight. Let's give him a big round of applause!" At least ten percent of the audience spontaneously rose from their seats . . . and headed up the aisle to use the bathroom. To be perfectly fair there *were* at least a dozen others who raised their hands and waved . . . at the vendor toting the bottles of Schlitz. Immediately after the introduction the two beefy guys huddled around me. I realized then that they were there to protect me from the crush of the mob which, as it turned out, was far more concerned about its collective bladder and its collective gullet than it was about me. The lack of interest from the crowd would have been laughable had it not been so embarrassing. Okay, it *was* laughable.

All was not lost, however. There was a little black kid, about eight years old, sitting a few seats from me. I had a clear view of him and he was staring at me, brows knit, definitely struggling to put me into some familiar frame of reference. I could plainly see him mouth the words "Star Trek" over and over to himself. And then, as enlightenment began to dawn, he started repeating the two words out loud with the emphasis on "Star." It was beautiful to watch. The frown disappeared, he beamed with cogitative triumph. I was so pleased for him. He knew I was from a TV show and that the word "Star" was the important clue. He jumped up. I'm surprised he didn't audition with a little dance and a few bars from a song. He had gotten the connection: "Ed McMahon!" he proclaimed for all to hear. The lesson to be learned, I suppose, is that for some, "searching" is better than "trekking."

In the same year Julius Erving, the great Dr. J, retired from basketball. On his last trip around the league every NBA city organized a special "farewell" night for him. New York was no exception. In addition to the plethora of accolades and gifts, the host Knicks decided to commemorate Erving's final visit with a "doctors" theme for the proceedings. This meant that famous doctors, those who were real and those created by writers and played by actors, were also invited to be special guests.

Gulf & Western owned both Madison Square Garden, where the New York team played, and Paramount Pictures, where DeForest Kelley played. The celebrated actor was asked if he might be willing to attend the festivities as chief medical officer of the *Enterprise* and Star Trek's representative of the noble profession of healing.

The ceremony was conducted at half time and after Dr. J was acclaimed and feted, the roll call of the other "doctors" began. They included "Doc" from the Seven Dwarfs and the well-known Dr. Ruth, who dispensed knowledge on matters sexual to people who embraced the entire spectrum of libido dysfunction. She must have appeared very tiny to those sitting high up in the rafters. (Actually, since she was considerably less than five feet tall, she must have appeared very tiny to those standing next to her.)

The last guest came out of the tunnel and started toward the center of the court. The lanky frame and languid walk were recognizable around the world. "LADIES AND GENTLEMEN, DOCTOR 'BONES' McCOY!" The public address announcer was only halfway through the introduction when the capacity crowd erupted with a roar that was like a thousand tons of water crashing through a splintered dam. And it continued . . . and continued . . . and continued. The Garden holds nineteen thousand seven hundred and sixty-three people, and every single one was on his feet cheering and cheering. The ovation was deafening and full of love and it just wouldn't stop. DeForest was enormously moved, his legs trembled under him. He was having trouble keeping his eyes clear. When he has repeated the story since, he does it with a sense of wonder. I still don't think he understands the magnitude of the admiration with which the world holds him.

Admiration, that is, from all save one. As he reached center court there was a tiny person standing next to him. She wasn't much bigger than an eight-year-old. Her brow was knitted and she wore a heavy frown of confusion. "Who iz zis pairzon?" She left his side and toddled up the line of other celebrities. "Vhat haz he done?" The applause was into its fifth minute. "Vhy are zey screeching zo?" She craned her neck and looked up at Dr. J. He looked down at her and slowly withdrew his arm from behind his back. He held up his hand. The index finger clove to the middle finger as it separated from the ring finger and the pinky to form a "V". "Live Long And Prosper," said Julius Erving. The brow unfurrowed. Finally, a moment of enlightenment. "Ahhh," she said, "he iz from ze Peeze Corps!"

You know, if you look at it from a certain perspective—like standing on your head and peering through the end of a piece of twisted metal cable—DeForest's experience and my experience weren't *that* much different. After all, my eight-year-old and Dr. Ruth both experienced an uncannily inaccurate epiphany under similar circumstances and at the same time, when it happened, neither of them was taller than four-foot-five!

In addition to the experience with George Takei, the mad swordsman, video store appearances in general seem to be a particularly fertile source for unusual encounters.

In the mid-eighties I did the opening of a video store in Shreveport, Louisiana. It was a Sunday morning after church. The men were all dressed in their best brown suits, the women had on adorable flowered hats and spotless white heels. I was led to the entrance of the store and handed a large pair of scissors. I then discovered that hundreds of new dollar bills had been taped together to form a ribbon that wrapped around the building. If there had been any question in my mind about the crisp green nature of these proceedings it had now been dispelled.

And yet after the mayor's assistant gave a little speech welcoming me he then called on the little lady who ran the neighborhood Taco Bell to give the benediction. THE BENEDICTION? Whoa! Was this a business occasion or a religious experience? Evidently, it can be both. She blessed the store and all its videos in the name of Jesus Christ. Everyone bowed their heads while this very moving service was conducted. I only know this because I peeked. If they could have seen my smile I might well have been branded the devil's minion. As it was, when the Taco Bell lady finished a heavyset bodyguard type leaned uncomfortably close to me. For a brief moment I thought my sacrilege had been detected and that an energetic warning regarding the fires of hell was about to be whispered in my ear.

"Make sure when you use them scissors that you cut the tape and not any of them there dollar bills," was all the religious instruction I received that day.

In March 1986 George Takei and I helped open another video store in Chattanooga, Tennessee. This was a small business operation and the people involved were serious-minded and determined to make it a success.

They invited us to dinner that night in a private room at Michael's Cow Palace. We were accompanied by at least a dozen folks, husbands and wives, who were the staff and owners of the new store. It was one of those occasions where everyone was just a little bit more in awe of the visiting celebrities than they should have been. The conversation around the table was restrained, almost hushed. Funeral parlors are more boisterous. In fact, it reminded me of one because on top of everything else everyone seemed to be dressed in basic sepia. I think the only thing absent were veils and prayer books. If this was a celebration then the great Chicago fire of 1871 was a housewarming. It looked like it was going to be a very, very long evening.

Finally, one of our hosts rose to his feet and proposed a toast to George and me. It was a worthy effort full of praise and gratitude. He extolled our characters, emphasizing what fine upstanding citizens we were, and expressed his heartfelt appreciation for the long and difficult journey we had undertaken to grace their humble emporium. I half expected we would next be presented medals for neatness and courage. It was actually a very sweet gesture but one executed with such solemnity that it threatened to sink the evening beyond recovery.

George then leaped to his feet. My thought was that he meant to salvage the occasion with amusing banter. But no, he had been totally seduced by the gravity imparted to the proceedings and was determined to keep the mood alive (or dead, depending on your perspective). He raised his wine glass and looked out at the huddled masses striking a not unfamiliar pose. George, it must be said, has never met a superlative he didn't like, and so at considerable length he waxed rhapsodic, canonizing our hosts and glorifying the city of Chattanooga. There were several references to succulent cuisine, architectural grandeur, undulating verdant hillsides, and a final word, I think, about the inspiring stoicism of the little engine that could. (We were after all in, the home of the Chattanooga Choo-Choo.)

He spoke, as you can imagine, with an eloquence nonpareil, and everyone was quite moved. Unfortunately, the longer he talked the more it sounded like a eulogy, and at the end I saw more than one hand reach for a hanky. The only thing missing were the pallbearers.

At this point I felt obligated to speak up.

"There is no way that I can begin to approach my companion's mastery of the language. In fact, I am left almost speechless. So, the only thing left to say, and I think George will agree with me here, is that while we've been in Chattanooga we've both had a pretty *fucking* good time."

I am happy to report that everyone broke up and that the rest of the evening was considerably livelier.

People are always trying to provide me with security personnel at public gatherings. I keep saying it isn't necessary. I'm not a personality of the kind or magnitude that inspires fans to behave in an aggressive manner. No one has ever tried to tear off my clothing or snip away at my artificial locks. In May 1989 I was present at the opening of a Blockbuster in Birmingham, Alabama. A table inside the store was set up at which I was to sit and sign autographs. Two formidable-looking men in their mid-thirties who did not look like store employees were posted on either side of me. They were so close, in fact, as to make me feel claustrophobic. I asked them who they were and was informed that they were off-duty cops who had been hired to guard me. I felt this was patently ridiculous and told them as politely as I could that I wouldn't be needing their services. They moved a few inches away but were still well within what little space I had hoped to call my own. The autograph line was long and I tried to lose myself in the signing process but a low level of annoyance persisted. The fans remained quiet and polite. After about twenty minutes I became dimly aware that one of the hired guard had left my side. If I felt anything, it was probably some relief. I signed for another twenty or thirty people and then sensed the return of the absent officer. I looked up to see that he had been joined by yet another plainclothes fellow with a bulge under his jacket.

"Jeez, guys, it's *really* close in here. I'm flattered by the attention but I really don't need the protection. Can't you just . . . like, you know . . . spread out a bit."

The cop who appeared to be in charge was polite, even deferential, but at the same time resolute. They weren't moving. The two other guys stared straight ahead.

"The worst thing that's going to happen to me here is that somebody's going to ask me to say 'Where's da nuclear wessels?' You realize that, don't you?" My irritation was beginning to show.

And then a uniformed officer stepped out of the pack and moved to the leader's side. I was now surrounded by four guys with guns.

"This is nuts! *I don't need protection. Will you please go away!*" If only someone had blinked or twitched or scratched his groin, but they paid no attention to me at all. They were the Stepford Fuzz and I was the Invisible Man. Nobody has written a movie about such a combination for good reason. If you're working with emotionless automatons and, to boot, they can't see you, where the hell's the conflict? I slammed my pen down and uttered an expletive. The head bodyguard then left. So I offended him, so what? I mean, I was really ticked and he had it com—

And then I looked up and he was on his way back at nearly a gallop. Behind him, out in the street, I could see two police cars pull up. He was behind the table and had me under one arm before I could open my mouth. Just as quickly his buddy grabbed me under the other. My feet never touched the ground as I was carried out the back door to a waiting patrol car. To this point, not a word had been spoken. We were out of the parking lot with the siren wailing before the silence was broken.

"The autograph session is over," said the head guy.

As I was soon to learn, the growing security presence at my side was the result of an anonymous call placed to the local police station.

"Ahm goin' to come dah'wn theyah an' blow Mistah Chekoov back into outah space!" was the droll missive received by the operator. The forces of good started to gather around me shortly thereafter. When the would-be assassin called back and said he was a mile away and picking up speed they decided, my boorish behavior notwithstanding, that they would save my ass anyway.

I was never informed whether the creep was captured. I choose to believe that he was, that he was subsequently rehabilitated and now runs a pottery shop on a small island several miles off the Florida coast.

*

In about 1983 I did a Star Trek convention in West Virginia. During the course of the day I was approached by a young woman who introduced herself as a witch. She was heavily into the practice of black magic and invited me to help her sacrifice a chicken in her hotel room. I explained that I had outgrown that phase of my life but recommended to her the other guest at the convention. I thought it would make a good gag. He was an actor named Richard from another science fiction series.

When I saw him the next day he was haggard and unsteady. He looked, in fact, less like the practitioner of some occult rite and more like the subject. I learned that he had, indeed, accepted the woman's invitation only to discover a man's wardrobe in her closet. When queried, she admitted that the clothing was her fiancee's but that they had an "understanding" and he wouldn't be bothering them. Unfortunately, the fiancee was not apprised of this paragraph in the Witches' Manifesto, so when the room's occupants decided to abandon poultry strangulation for sexual abandonment there came a knocking on the door. When there was no response the knocking rose in volume. Quite soon there was more pounding going on outside the room than within. Since there was no exit other than the front door and the fiancee sounded in the mood for multiple homicides, Richard spent a rather fitful night beside the broom rider waiting for the door hinges to separate. He made a successful escape before dawn only because even would-be murderers must sleep.

✳

In the early eighties I did a convention in an abandoned meat locker in Texas. Hooks for animal carcasses still hung from the ceiling, and spatters of dried blood made cunning designs on the walls. They never got rid of the smell either.

☾

I was invited to a very special Christmas Star Trek convention in New York City in the winter of 1978. Registration was to be exclusive, limited to only five hundred people. I decided to take my son, who was then ten, with me. Nancy, the woman who organized the engagement, put us up at the Plaza Hotel, one of Manhattan's ritziest, with all expenses paid. We arrived a few days early so that we might take in some of the sights of the city. We attended Radio City Music Hall, went ice skating in Rockefeller Center, and visited my old stomping grounds in Inwood.

The day of the con we were limoed to a building in the Wall Street section very near the Twin Towers. We were ushered inside and discovered a three-story structure with steel staircases and a series of heavy metal doors on each landing that divided the space into different compartments. The building was clean, but there appeared to be no management personnel or maintenance staff around. I asked to what purpose the building was used and Nancy mentioned something about "physical therapy."

We climbed the three flights of stairs to a penthouse loft to meet the chosen five hundred. The room was smaller than I had expected. You couldn't comfortably seat more than sixty in this place. I know that because I counted heads and there were thirty-one people there, each lounging about in about twice the area they required. I looked around to see where they might be keeping the rest of the folks. There weren't any. This was it. The exclusive Christmas celebration was a disaster, and the people who were in attendance were mostly Nancy's friends, who had been imported to paper the house.

Of course, Nancy's credit card wasn't any good and the Plaza insisted that I pay the several hundred dollars' worth of bills that we had accrued.

What had gone wrong? I'll never know, but maybe New Yorkers knew better than I about their local landmarks. It turns out that the physical therapy building was really a massage parlor which, in this case, was a euphemism for brothel. Nancy the entrepreneur was really Nancy the Madame, who had given her girls a day off so that we could hold a Star Trek convention in a whorehouse.

★

In 1982 a convention was held in Houston Called "Ultimate Fantasy." Only Leonard among our cast did not attend. It was to be held at the Sheraton Rice Hotel and at the sixteen-thousand-seat Summit Arena, where the Houston Rockets play their basketball games. Such an overwhelming crowd was expected from all over the nation and beyond that the facility was rented for three performances. This was going to be a bigger celebration than even the one in New York City in the late seventies that had drawn thirty thousand people.

I had written a playlet for the occasion that involved Jimmy, George, Nichelle, Mark Lenard, Kirstie Alley, and myself. It had to do with Kirk being kidnapped and threatened with annihilation and the way each of our characters responded to the situation. Mark was the bad guy and would appear on monitors inside the arena while we performed on a facsimile *Enterprise* bridge erected on the floor at the center of the building. We rehearsed it at my house before we went to Texas.

Fans did, indeed, come in from around the country, but when they arrived they learned that the money paid in advance to the convention promoters for hotel rooms had not been used for that purpose. Large groups of people collecting in the lobby were being told they had no reservations. The hotel staff was as upset as the frustrated guests. They wanted to shut down the "Ultimate Fantasy" organization altogether, depriving them of both the previously rented space for panel discussions and contests and the room in which the dealers were to hawk their wares.

In the meantime, I was learning first-hand that all was not well at the sports arena. I was there supervising the setup for the script when I was told that the band contracted to play for the three performances and the people in charge of the laser light show had received no payment. Neither had any of us.

Additionally, Jerry, the guy in charge of this whole mess, had locked himself in his hotel room and wouldn't answer the phone.

Back at the Rice Hotel an extraordinary thing was happening. Fans and dealers alike were volunteering their credit cards to keep the convention afloat. I felt that we could do no less. Harve Bennett, who was with our entourage, called me for my input. Do we harm Star Trek more by backing out or by going on in less than ideal circumstances? I felt the former would be the greater error and he agreed. From then on, Harve took over everything going on behind the scenes in a Herculean effort to salvage the weekend, and I took over the show at the arena. Among other things, this meant convincing the musicians and laser folks not to abandon ship as well as some of our actors who, without their fees, didn't want to leave their rooms.

We did go forward. The production values were a little ragged but we got through all three shows during the two days. The dealers' room remained open at the hotel and the rest of the program there went pretty much as scheduled. Some events were cancelled but amidst the chaos that was to be expected. What was not expected was that little more than six hundred people showed up for an event which had been planned for forty thousand.

The point in recounting this episode is not the horrendous business management that Jerry was responsible for or that he bailed out when the going got tough but that there was more of a feeling of community between the fans, the dealers, and the performers than at any other time in our Star Trek history. It is when disaster strikes that one's true colors show. Everyone who pitched in to save the day came up looking golden.

The sad postscript here is that the convention produced its share of fallen heroes as well. Several people who generously offered their credit cards and even their mortgages in their zeal to help ended up losing their life savings.

And so foremost among all conventions I remember "Ultimate Fantasy." It was uplifting and poignant. It was fraught with conflict and even tragedy. It was altogether an astonishing experience. I guess only an actor would think of it as great theater.

FIFTEEN

"Back to the Future II"

As part of the contracts that most of us signed to do *Star Trek III* was a clause that gave Paramount an option on our services for a fourth Star Trek film. An option fixes the salaries for the next picture so that the studio doesn't have to go through the process of negotiations all over again. In the case of the supporting actors it included a modest raise which might have seemed reasonable at the time we agreed to it. *Star Trek III: The Search for Spock* went on to gross eighty-six million dollars domestically. This was actually about fourteen million dollars more than *The Wrath of Khan* had pulled in. In light of these figures, the option we signed didn't seem quite that reasonable after all but then, the option clause almost always favors the studio, and it most certainly did here.

George, Jimmy, and I were still represented by Steve at the time. The three of us entered into an agreement to hold out for a better deal. George and Jimmy were adamant that they wouldn't do the picture unless their fees were significantly higher. I explained at the beginning that I couldn't go to the wall on such an arrangement. We might have had a moral right to ask for more money but from a legal position they had us over a barrel and, frankly, I couldn't afford not to be in another Star Trek film.

The studio's response was to come back with a compromise offer that included about a fifteen percent raise over what we had initially accepted in the contract. I took it. George and Jimmy did not. Suddenly, I was the good guy in Harve Bennett's eyes and they were the bad ones. That was really a switch! It also made me feel a bit guilty that I had backed off from presenting a united front. The two of them were prepared to go down with the ship, or so they said, and I envied them their conviction. Only they didn't really know who they were up against. When they steadfastly refused to live by the terms they agreed upon, Paramount decided to play hardball. Both men were served hand-delivered notification that the studio intended to sue them for the cost of recasting their parts and rewriting the script for new actors. In addition, even if they were now ready to acquiesce, the offer of a raise beyond the option figure was to be withdrawn.

Steve, who had previously questioned my lack of fortitude, was now scrambling like mad to keep his other clients in the game. Jimmy started calling fans around the country to pressure Paramount while George, who had thought he had been working from a position of strength, now found himself on the defensive. George would later prove in other negotiations with the studio that he was no shrinking violet, it was just that in this case his position was untenable. In any event, they were both quite nervous, as it seemed possible Paramount would follow through on its threat.

I called both men and asked if they had any objection to my interceding on their behalf. They were my friends, after all, and, who knows, if I hadn't capitulated early on the three of us might have carried the day when negotiations first began. They gave me their blessing and I phoned Leonard Nimoy, who would be directing the film and, more importantly, I spoke to Harve Bennett.

I explained that both actors wanted to be in the movie but it was important that they not be whipped into submission. I was remembering my experience on *Star Trek III* when I had been denigrated by the producer and then given a take-it-or-leave-it offer. I said if they were treated with dignity they would both listen to a reasonable proposition. Harve said he understood and, in fact, within twenty-four hours they were both on board. George was grateful for my intervention. To this day I think Jimmy feels it was his agent, Steve, who was responsible for his change of fortune.

When Leonard learned the details of the negotiations he insisted that Nichelle, who had not thought to contest the original option figure, have her salary raised to match George's and mine. That was nice of Leonard and it's worth acknowledging here.

If people could tell from reading a script whether it was going to be a box office success there wouldn't be a seventy five percent failure rate for motion pictures. Certainly I claim no prescience in this area, but if ever I believed a movie was destined to be a hit it was after reading the script for *The Voyage Home*. It had humor, it had suspense, it was literate, and it did what Star Trek has always done best—it addressed an issue of conscience that was greater than the parameters of plot. And it did it in a provocative and entertaining way. It also had an adversary which, although not flesh and blood, was fascinating nonetheless. The Probe of *Star Trek IV* succeeded where V'ger did not because its intention was very clear from the beginning. That it was innocent of evil made it all the more intriguing. V'ger meant to destroy all carbon-based units, the Probe was simply trying to make contact with whales. There is a heightened sense of drama when death and destruction happens inadvertently. Great tragedy occurs when there is a great loss which is not the result of a deliberate action and which, therefore, might have been avoided.

Bill and Leonard were brilliant together. DeForest and Jimmy had some very choice moments and played off each other marvelously. Nichelle and I were not forgotten, and Chekov in particular had lines which were for the first time indigenous to character. The problem for the supporting cast has always been that our purpose was primarily to advance the plot. We were there as a tool of exposition, to help spell out what was going on. This time Chekov had a personality. He was written as a living, breathing human being. In the main, I have Nick Meyer to thank for that. He wrote the middle portion of the story when we travel back to San Francisco.

Among us, only Sulu got the short end. I never cease to marvel at how professionally George deals with adversity. If you don't know that about him you should. It's an extraordinary character quality. Actually, it needn't have been as bad as it was. Harve offered to write a scene for him if he could come up with a concept that was consistent with what was happening in the story. George bounced an idea off me about a little boy stopping us on the street and asking about the strange clothes we were wearing. It would give him a chance to tell the child about the future. "What if the youngster is your great-great-great-great-grandfather?" I suggested. He took it to Bennett, who wrote it up, and a child was hired in San Francisco to play the part when we arrived there.

Again, George's forbearance was amazing. The kid absolutely refused to cooperate. He was determined not to shoot the scene. It just goes to show that child monsters come in all races. He only relented when the decision to use his older brother in his place was made. By then, not only had the sun gone down but George's moment in it. the scene was never shot. Through it all I never saw Mr. Takei display temper. How does he do that?

There were scenes aboard the USS *Enterprise* aircraft carrier (actually, the USS *Ranger*) which focused predominantly on the Russian navigator. I would love to make you understand what that meant to me. Our film director was designing scenes with me as the principal player. The director of photography was composing shots with me as the featured performer. Lights were positioned to best catch my image, sound levels were adjusted to accommodate my voice levels. It was glorious, I was ecstatic, but if you think this was about getting to play at being a movie star you're dead wrong. What it was about was feeling important . . . to Star Trek. For the first and only time in all the years before the camera and for all the miles of exposed footage I felt like I was truly being called upon to contribute. For years and years when people told me they loved my character I knew what they were really saying was that they loved Star Trek. How much can you love a character who mostly says "Varp factor three, Keptin." I had just been along for the ride. For these few precious days in the San Diego port I *was* the ride. I was creating something that was uniquely Chekov's and mine and which served the mythos of Star Trek with pride. Am I making waaaay too much out of this and sounding like my sense of self-importance was out of control? Probably. But maybe if you understand now how I felt then you'll get a better picture of what happened to me and why I behaved the way I did during the making of the last of our films together.

Star Trek IV: The Voyage Home remains the highest domestic-grossing feature in the Star Trek series of eight movies. That despite the increase in ticket price in the twelve years since its release in 1986. It is the only film that has had box office sales of over one hundred million dollars in the United States and it is the only picture whose appeal can be legitimately said to have "crossed over" to the general public.

The reason why Star Trek films cannot exceed a specific length is because the theaters are mandated to squeeze in an extra screening per day. The overwhelming majority of our audience have traditionally been genre fans who go during the first three weeks of the picture's opening. There is a precipitous drop in attendance after that, so the thinking is to make the movie as available as possible early on by having an additional showing each day.

The Voyage Home, however, read the pulse of the American public as no Star Trek picture has before or since. It spoke to everyone whether they had already been fans or not, and so it remained on the box office charts far longer than any of the others in the series.

I felt that *Star Trek IV* would be so good that I suggested to Ralph Winters, the executive producer, that a curtain call at the end of the movie might be in order. A reprise of scenes featuring the cast, as I had seen done in other motion pictures, seemed the way to go. Now it's quite possible someone closer to the action also came up with this concept, but I like to think it was my idea. If it's not true, don't tell me.

✇

Before beginning work on *Star Trek V: The Final Frontier* I read an interview Bill Shatner had given about how he perceived the project. He said that he wanted to return to the concept of the three stars carrying the action as had been done in the series days. I, therefore, had no illusions as to what to expect and no reason for disappointment when I was called to work. In fact, *Star Trek V* turned out to be the most stress free project of the seven in which I performed. The only question I had going in was about the man, not the project. I had heard bad stories about Bill's conduct when he had directed on the *T.J. Hooker* television series and I was very, very apprehensive about how he would relate to Jimmy, George, Nichelle, and I. In fact, I told them that if he tried to bully any one of us I would walk. So imagine my surprise when Mr. Shatner turns out to be the Blue Fairy from *Pinnochio.* Such hugging, such smiling, such enthusiasm:

"Aye, aye, Keptin."

"Cut and print. Walt, Walt . . . that . . . was . . . gooood!" (Please supply halting delivery and proper inflection when reading out loud the preceding quote from Mr. Shatner.)

I only spent eight days on the film. Two of them were on location in Yosemite National Park. On one morning there George and I took the opportunity to jog some park trails. It was very pleasant.

It appears that it has been open season on William Shatner, the director, since *Star Trek V* was released. I'm not sure that's fair. It seemed to me that he had done his homework and was well prepared to direct the *The Final Frontier.* The problem was that *The Final*

Frontier was not the final frontier in scriptwriting. Not only wasn't it a pioneer effort, it didn't even cover old ground competently. In fact, I think there is a film course essay to be written comparing *Star Trek—The Motion Picture* with this fifth installment of the Star Trek saga. I'll only offer one example here: In both cases there was a lack of focus in the storytelling. Events that were supposed to goose the plot and give it propulsion became distractions that gave it lateral movement at the sacrifice of forward progression. In the first Star Trek movie there was a sidebar history between Captain Decker and the Deltan female, Llia, that detoured the story. In *The Final Frontier* there is an underdeveloped relationship between Spock and his halfbrother Sybok that runs out of steam long before the end. There is also a totally irrelevant sequence of scenes in which Sybok makes McCoy and Spock confront their greatest pain. What was that all about? In each film the denouement is blunted by asking the audience to shift its allegiances just before the story climaxes. V'ger isn't a bad guy after all, and it isn't Sybok that we must hiss but an alien life form on a planet hidden inside a black cloud. Last-minute revelations are legitimate only if they have been properly set up. If the "butler did it," then we had better damn well know from the beginning that there *is* a butler.

What I'm saying is that if Bill is to share responsibility for the failure of this Star Trek entry it should be for the story he conceived and not for his helmsmanship of the project.

In fairness, it should also be said that just as with *Star Trek—The Motion Picture* at the beginning, there was misjudgment in choosing the special effects company hired to enhance the production.

❖

Star Trek V: The Final Frontier grossed fifty-one million dollars domestically and 10.96 million dollars internationally. Both remain the low-water marks in the Star Trek feature film legacy. No one at Paramount was happy with these results. Is it any wonder then that when a sixth film was being contemplated Harve Bennett saw it as his opportunity to get out from under the long shadow of Gene Roddenberry and move the franchise in a new direction?

Let me set up the situation the fairest way I know how by arguing what I think Bennett's position might have been. The first film of which he had been in charge was *Star Trek: The Wrath of Khan*. That picture was a critical as well as popular success. Unquestionably, it was far superior to the one that preceded it that Roddenberry had produced. If it had been as colossal a mistake as had been Gene's effort, it might well have killed the possibility of any other sequels. A case can therefore be made for saying that Harve Bennett saved Star Trek. Additionally, worldwide box office sales for *Star Trek II* was 92 million, for *Star Trek III* almost 97 million, and for *Star Trek IV*, 132 million. Under the weight of those figures it is not illogical to consider that *Star Trek V* at just under 62 million was a one-time aberration unlikely to be repeated. And yet, while everyone else was achieving hero status in the genre audience's mind, Bennett was still being cast in the role of "The Great Bird's" (Roddenberry's) litter bearer. His public protests to the contrary, I know that must have been galling to him. He had been a very successful television producer and now he was an eminently successful producer of motion pictures. The Star Trek Creator, on the other hand, had made a very limited contribution to the success of the subsequent pictures and yet the franchise was still being called "Gene Roddenberry's Star Trek." Like all of us, Harve has an ego. He wanted the recognition that comes with creating a product in your own image. In this case, to do that meant reinventing Star Trek. To do that meant dumping the original cast and starting over. I think that was his motivation. It was certainly his objective. That's not to say I still don't think it was chicken shit of him to try to screw us over, but then we all have our vested interests.

While plans for the new movie were being discussed behind closed doors at Paramount I was invited to a lovely party that Majel Barrett, Gene Roddenberry's wife, had thrown for Gene. During a private moment Gene complained to me about Bennett's plans for *Star Trek VI*. I thought we were about to commiserate as allies but actually, his take was a bit different. He wasn't offended at all that they were going with a new cast, only that it should be he and not Harve that did the casting. "I know Star Trek better than anyone," he said. And of course it was true. Still, I can't imagine he expected me to offer words of sympathy. In any case, I couldn't have. At that point, my jaw was bouncing on the floor.

If you've ever been to even one convention I appeared at you've undoubtedly heard this story. I tell it now for the ten people who haven't because it provided one of the few moments of levity during this period of crisis. It involves George Takei, a bright and knowledgeable man with a less than fatal flaw: Because he is himself truthful he assumes everyone else will act accordingly and he is, therefore, susceptible to the big lie.

At this juncture, the rumors were flying back and forth about Harve Bennett's story idea. From what I could gather from my sources, the story was to be set in the past at the Starfleet Academy when Kirk and Spock were young cadets. Naturally, new actors would be called in to play their roles. No official announcement had been made yet and so we were hanging by the most slender of hopes that the situation might still change. George, Nichelle, DeForest, and I had had several telephone conversations regarding this situation.

During a period in which there was an information lull I placed a call to George on an unrelated matter. He wasn't in and I left word with his answering machine to call me back. He was out of the country at the time and when he did return my call ten days later I had by then forgotten the reason I had phoned him. However, I could tell by the tension in his voice that he thought I had some definitive news regarding the new movie and I felt honorbound not to disappoint him.

"Hello, Walter, I just got back into town. You're my first call. What have you heard?"

"Are you sitting down?"

"Yes."

"They've finally decided on the new movie, it's been in the papers—"

"Yes, yes?"

"They're going to do it in Claymation."

"Oh, my God! [pause] Well . . . are they going to use our voices?"

I'm not sure that George will ever forgive me for that preposterous story since I keep telling it over and over again.

There came a time when I had to decide whether I would accept silently what the fates had in store or go down fighting. Too often in the past we had felt victimized by studio behavior which we believed was capricious at best. My sense was that there was little I could do to change the tide of events but that I had, nevertheless, a moral responsibility to try. I typed the following letter to Frank Mancuso, then the chief executive officer at Paramount:

Jan. 31, 1990

Mr. Frank Mancuso
Paramount Pictures
5555 Melrose Ave.
Los Angeles, Ca.
90038

Dear Mr. Mancuso;

I'm sorry I was not available when you tried to return my call and that we've not been able to establish contact since.

Although I don't know any details I am fairly confident that a decision has been made regarding another Star Trek film. On the one chance in ten thousand that this isn't the case, however, I have put together a brief outline for a story that would be both epic in nature and poignant in the telling. It would address the "age" issue in a manner that has dignity but is, nonetheless, forthright and would wrap up the lives of the crew in a way that I think would be satisfying to the fans.

I know that there are ramifications and considerations beyond my ken having to do with "economic realities" in the making of <u>Star Trek VI</u>. I suppose that in the light of this lack of information it could be deemed presumptuous of me to forward a script idea to you that doesn't take into account what has transpired between the Studio, the banks, et al. On the other hand, I would always regret not having made the effort if I did not, at least, send this along to you.

I hope this submission is not construed as an attempt to go behind Harve Bennett's back. My philosophy is simply that if I'm going to be turned down I'd prefer that it be by the person who is the ultimate decision maker.

Warmest Regards,
Walter Koenig

P.S. I've had several screenplays optioned—though none made. They are available for examination.

With it was a step outline that I had written for the next Star Trek movie and which I had my fan club presidents, Tisha Kuntz and Carolyn Atkinson, put on their word processor for me. I don't suggest that this was as good a story as the one eventually written by Nick Meyer but I was hoping that, if nothing else, it might be a stop-gap measure to temporarily jam up the works and prevent Harve from going forward. I was prepared to write a considerably more elaborate screenplay based on the outline if I was given the least encouragement.

An interesting coincidence between my version and Nick's is that we both addressed the age issue again and, more specifically, that we both had former adversaries joining the Federation. Please see the appendix for my outline for *Star Trek VI* entitled "In Flanders Field." Also please note that I had Scotty suffer the fate of most of the crew in my version because this was written before he had appeared on *Star Trek: The Next Generation.*

Just for the record, let me repeat that I thought Nick's script was excellent and better than anything I could have devised.

I never did make personal contact with Mr. Mancuso, but independent of my submission the Star feet Academy story was running into problems. Although Bennett had Sid Ganis, President of the Motion Picture Division, ready to jettison the old crew, he didn't have the CEO. Mancuso felt that one more picture with the original cast to celebrate the twenty-fifth anniversary of the series was in order.

Bennett decided to "take all his winnings and play it on one turn of pitch and toss." "If you don't do my story I walk" is what he said in effect. And just like in the Kipling poem he lost. Ganis left the studio shortly thereafter.

Nick Meyer's screenplay had everything required to make it into a gratifying motion picture experience. It had that great triple play combination—mystery, intrigue, and suspense. It had complications which all resolved themselves appropriately. It exposed the gray area between right and wrong and forced us to make choices that were intellectual as well as visceral. It presented bad guys with whom we could relate even if we didn't like them. The principal side story, the relationship between Spock and Lieutenant Valeris, was constructed to organically play into the story's ending, and there was enough action written into the script to make it a satisfying sensory experience.

Nick has been quoted as saying that his pictures should be able to stand on their own as self-contained pieces independent of any history attached to them. *The Undiscovered Country* really does that, and even as that is its strength it is also its one weakness. While the story has epic qualities it does not take into account the epic history of twenty-five years of Star Trek. This was to be our last Star Trek picture together. It was not only the final story, it was the wrap-up of all the characters' lives. I believe time should have been taken to say farewell to each of the seven crew members (most particularly Captain Kirk) after their long record of service in ways appropriate to each of them. There is a nod in this direction at the end but it is too little and it comes too late. This is the one story component that isn't addressed as conscientiously as it might have been in Meyer's screenplay and it is what prompted me, in part, to write the following letter to Ralph Winters, our producer on this film:

January 1, 1991

Ralph Winters
Star Trek VI
Paramount Pictures Corporation
5555 Melrose Avenue
Los Angeles, CA 90038

Dear Ralph,

It was a pleasure speaking with you over the holidays.

On the assumption that we get past the present difficulties regarding the option extension and that *Star Trek VI* will be made, I offer the following additional comments to those I've already made concerning the film's story line:

At the center of the screenplay as it now stands, is a driving force that is philosophical and intellectual. The crew must overcome its prejudices and learn to accept the Klingons. We do this, ultimately, through new found insight and an awakening sense of compassion. Aside from the fact that it is a false premise to assume we are racist, the transformation is accomplished without palpable external instigation. We arrive at a new level of understanding through self-determination alone. It is like a football player carrying the ball the length of the field without opposition. It's a touchdown all right, but without the satisfying drama of broken field running, dodging some tacklers, leaping over others and bowling over the rest. A hundred yard run is far more heroic if the protagonist staggers across the goal line bloodied, drained, and just barely still on his feet. The second scenario ball carrier is the myth maker; the one who has faced enormous odds, faced epic conflict and still triumphed.

It is the stuff of legends, then, I believe we must have if this picture is going to double the box office of *Star Trek V* and gross a hundred million dollars. It *can* be done. I truly believe it can be done, but right now we are staring at an equation that is only half complete.

The potential here is for a conflict as classic in its own right as that of the Campulets and Montagues. Not Romeo and Juliet, of course, but of the families of those tragic figures who must somehow get past the agony of loss and achieve a peace and understanding that defies the blood that has for centuries boiled in their veins and been spilled on the streets of Verona.

There is only one course of action that will make this story monumental in scope and create a theatrical event worthy of a series-ending, historically significant grand finale to twenty-five years of extraterrestrial tales. It requires the employment of a theatrical device that is so shocking and emotional that it will claim the attention of *Star Trek* and non-*Star Trek* audiences alike. It is the place where no one has gone before, but the only place we can logically go, where the mythos dictates we *must* go:

The death of Captain Kirk. He must be assassinated by the dissident Klingon forces, just as the Klingon leader met a similar fate — as did Romeo and Juliet, so that their warring families could finally know peace.

People who don't know *Star Trek* will come to *this* motion picture. They will come out of curiosity (morbid and otherwise), and the people who love *Star Trek* will come to this movie; a goodly number, perhaps, with anger and protest, but invariably they will come and stay and be transported by a story that is ultimately about love and tolerance and the ennobling of the human spirit. Yes, our leader has died and our initial reaction as his crew is violent and vengeful, but in the end we transcend the base instincts of our kind and move toward the higher plane of forgiveness and tolerance.

This is the legacy we leave for the next generation of space adventurers. The only one I can think of that is equal to *Star Trek*'s imposing heritage. (I won't even address the significance of such a story as a Christmas release.)

I know that Gene Roddenberry is opposed to killing off any of the crew, but I believe that if he is approached along the lines that Kirk's death brings dignity to us all and is truly a promise of a better universe to come, he might concede the merit of this culmination to the *Star Trek* saga.

Kirk's demise is also the perfect conduit for soul-searching individual expression by each of the crew members that is currently absent in the writing. I mentioned to you before, I think, that the speeches by the crew are by and large interchangeable, and that we come away with no new understanding as to who these people are, what they feel, believe, aspire to. Two and a half decades of living with these characters and in the final episode we are no more enlightened about them than we ever were. A tragedy of the proportions I've described would certainly afford us the opportunity for dialogue from Uhura, Sulu, Scotty, Chekov, etc., that could be introspective and profoundly personal.

I have the utmost respect for Nick Meyer. I personally know no writer more capable of exacting the last ounce of value in a screenplay, and I think he should be given license to use every story element that could be made available to him to make it happen. *Star Trek II* and *Star Trek IV* were both pictures in which his skill was boldly evident and in whose success he rightly shares. *Star Trek VI* could well be his crowning achievement of the series.

Thanks, Ralph, for creating an atmosphere that makes this letter possible.

Best,
Walter Koenig

An addendum thought is that if the killing of Kirk is untenable, then the death of one of the rest of us—although not as theatrically dynamic—could also work along the same lines. In which case, for the record, I volunteer Chekov.

As it turned out, my letter to the contrary, many people feel that Nick Meyer's work for *Star Trek VI* was his crowning achievement on the Star Trek series. Hey, what do I know?

Ralph Winters had been executive producer on three of our films. When Harve left he became producer. Unlike the situation in television, the producer on a motion picture set generally wields more power than the executive producer. It was almost impossible not to like Ralph. He was bright, congenial, and respectful of everyone's input. He told me that he thought my letter had merit and that he would send it along to Nick. I wasn't necessarily expecting to hear from Meyer, I was only waiting to see if he would implement any of the suggestions I made. I saw nothing in the subsequent script drafts to ease my concerns. At this time, Nick was having his own problems. A very heated argument with Gene Roddenberry led him to actually quit the project as the director. Fortunately, this was resolved quickly, but what with the atmosphere being somewhat charged I chose not to pursue my letter with a follow-up call to him. Maybe if I had it would have resolved a lot of the problems I had on this picture.

I have made some reference early on to my state of mind on this shoot, and now I feel compelled to examine it. Frankly, it is so odious to me that I shall try to make my remarks as brief as possible. If in their brevity they lose some impact, trust me, my behavior sucked.

Going into this picture I felt very much the way I had when I played the chicken delivery boy in the *Goodby Raggedy Ann* television movie. I was seized by a sense of impotence. Chekov was written as an incidental character and I felt anonymous playing him. I was experiencing a crisis of identity that manifested itself not as panic but anger. And I found a way to be angry with almost everyone I worked with.

Leonard was off-camera in a setup in which Nichelle and I were trying to read a Klingon-English dictionary. Perhaps we played the scene a little broadly, but not to the degree that Leonard was pantomiming as he mimicked me behind the camera. I was instantly reminded of the time on the television series in 1968 when he had cautioned me about mugging. Then it was advice. Now it was ridicule. I was seething and had trouble finding my way back to a civil relationship with him during the rest of the shoot.

We were doing a scene on the bridge that wasn't dramatically significant and I was speaking in a quiet voice. The sound boom picked up my speech but Jimmy, standing a few feet away, could not. Somehow he equated my soft tones with the behavior of a "movie star" and accused me of behaving like one. The comment was silly but didn't deserve the anger it engendered in me. My stomach churned on that one for days.

Nichelle tried to get me out of my funk by making light of it and I rejected her teasing. How did she know that I wasn't mourning a death in the family? Give me some space, please! I gave her a lot of space for sometime thereafter.

Nick ordered me to stay out of a newly "dressed" set that he wanted to be a surprise and I demanded an apology for the tone of voice he used. My own voice was so constricted by emotion I could barely get the words out.

Shatner took exception to my leaving early one day to attend my daughter's high school graduation and I wanted to kill him for his protest. But then, there was actually nothing new about that.

I was no better at home. Judy, with her own life and her own

career, had always found time to be in my corner, but I would not be
placated. Her forbearance was admirable.

In each case my behavior was off the scale. We were in the process
of making a terrific film and it was only fury that I could feel. The fact
is, I don't know if anyone on the set knew to what depths I had sunk
because I kept most of it inside. And all the while I was going through
it I was most angry at myself because I could not pull out of it. On the
last day we set up for the cast shots. The photographer positioned me
in the back row. As far as I was concerned it was just one more igno-
minious gesture. I told them to take the pictures without me and started to walk off. They ended up making an adjustment and that made me
feel even more stupid.

There is one moment I remember on *The Undiscovered Country*
for other than its effect on my volatile state of mind. I was sitting in my
chair on the soundstage and Shatner was sitting in his a couple of feet
away. Nimoy came over and sat next to Bill on the other side but still
close enough for me to hear their conversation. Leonard's opening
remarks were in frustration about a contentious family experience over
the previous weekend. As have we all, I have heard this kind of conversation hundreds of times during my lifetime. The thing is, I had
never heard Mr. Nimoy talk like this. He was complaining, one guy to
another, and it really should have been the most natural thing in the
world. Then why did it seem so incredibly out of character to me?
What began to crystallize was the realization that I did not know
Leonard Nimoy at all. I actually had less of a sense about him than I
did about Bill Shatner. That we had such an unformed relationship
which spanned so many years could only be the result of conscious
effort—on his part, not mine. There's nothing in the rule book that says
we have to be friends. What I didn't know before and what his conversation with Bill showed me was that the personal detachment he
maintained was not a result of natural reclusiveness but was an active
and discretionary choice. That isn't to say that he was in any way
antagonistic or even antisocial. In fact, he had gone to bat for the supporting actors on several occasions. If it wasn't for Leonard's stand on
Filmation's animated *Star Trek* TV series, George and Nichelle would-
n't have been included in the cast. I've already mentioned that he stood
up for Nichelle in the contract negotiations on *Star Trek IV*. I asked
him to write the foreword to my novel *Buck Alice* and he did so will-
ingly. When several of us decided not to do the thirtieth anniversary
convention in Huntsville, Alabama, Leonard intervened on our behalf

with Paramount and effected a change in our contracts. I'm sure there were a dozen other examples of selfless behavior on his part when it came to our interests, but I daresay that Jimmy, George, and Nichelle found him no more approachable than I did. The only explanation I am left with is that, like Bill, he bought into the idea that his star status tempered how close a bond he could form with those not of the same professional rank. If that conclusion is accurate then the least generous explanation for his otherwise generous actions on our behalf is that it came from a sense of noblesse oblige: "the obligations of the high born to display honorable conduct." It's not a very flattering analysis and most likely shows a lack of gratitude on my part. Chalk it up to the fact that I have always had respect for him, and miss not having been considered an equal and a friend. It was particularly tough because, despite the occasional breakdown in maturity, I have generally thought of myself as someone worth knowing.

You know, I keep thinking about Patrick Stewart and Jonathan Frakes and the rest of the cast of *The Next Generation*. From all the reports I have heard such distinctions between the regulars did not exist for them. If there is anything I envy these folks it's their commitment to a feeling of camaraderie. They are all to be applauded.

Lest I be remiss, let me add that, along with Bill and Leonard, DeForest Kelley was also one of Star Trek's shining lights. The highest compliment I can pay him is that you would never know it to talk to him. There wasn't anybody that De didn't treat with courtesy, warmth, and respect. De Kelley has been everyone's good guy for the thirty-plus years that Star Trek has been around. I'm only sorry that you can't all have had the opportunity to know him the way we have.

SIXTEEN

"Thunderhead—Son of Flicka"

IN 1986 *STAR TREK: THE NEXT GENERATION* WAS ANNOUNCED BY Paramount Studios as a new Star Trek television series to be produced by Gene Roddenberry.

Dorothy Fontana came aboard in December of that year as an associate producer. She went on to write the pilot film, "Encounter at Farpoint, Parts I and II" (with rewrites by Gene Roddenberry) and stayed on till the expiration of her contract in November of the following year. David Gerrold, the writer of the enormously popular original series episode, "The Trouble With Tribbles" joined the company as a staff writer at about the same time Dorothy came aboard.

I received a call from David in the early spring of 1987. He told me that both Dorothy and he were interested in having me write for the new series. In fact, Dorothy had seen a play I directed called *Twelve Angry Men* by Reginald Rose and wanted to submit me as a director once production on the TV series began. Gene Roddenberry had been approached, I was told, and seemed receptive to my involvement.

I was tickled by the enthusiasm of these people whose work I respected. I was sent the "writer's bible" for the series and learned from it the do's and don'ts of the *Next Generation* concept. In time I came up with a couple of ideas. I pitched one to Dorothy and one to David and each felt they had enough merit to pass on to Gene. He turned them both down but again indicated his enthusiasm for my participation.

Again I came up with two ideas. Dorothy suggested that I take them directly to Bob Lewin, a writer-producer on the series. I did and he was extremely supportive. It was only a matter of deciding which one we would do this year and which the following season, he said. He just needed to go through the formality of informing Gene, but it was for all intents and purposes a done deal. He would let me know in seventy-two hours. I was quite excited. When I didn't hear anything I called and he said he would get back to me but, rest assured, Roddenberry was still high on using me. Another week rolled by and Bob phoned to say it would be best if I pitched my ideas directly to Gene Roddenberry and that we should do it over lunch.

Gene was hobbled and in obvious pain: the series of small strokes he had endured had taken their toll. Nevertheless, his disposition remained sunny. He was to be admired for that. He told me he was happy to see me and we sat down to a congenial lunch in the Paramount commissary.

My first story had to do with Data beaming down in the middle of a battlefield. He is in the line of fire and is rendered inoperative. The warring factions are primitive and represent two extremes of religious devotion. On the one side are the fire-and-brimstone worshipers of a wrathful God; on the other, the blood-and-sacrifice devotees of the Devil. The fight ceases momentarily as both sides examine the mysterious being who has appeared from thin air. Because Data is Data he is able to regenerate and is soon "alive" again. The God fearers believe that his revival is a miracle of resurrection and that he is there for them. The Devil followers are convinced he is an incarnation of the evil spirit to whom they pay homage and has come to join their forces. A new battle ensues, with each sect trying to capture the living icon for their own side. The point being made is that fanaticism on either end of the religious spectrum can be equally as destructive and that both sides are, consequently, indistinguishable from one another.

When I was through, Gene expressed what he said was his only concern: How do we explain why Data beamed down? It took me a moment to absorb the question and then I began rattling off a list of reasons that seemed fairly accessible. Excavation, answering a distress call, geological disturbance, Data's personal quest . . . I finished and waited for a response. Gene reached for a glass of water, took a swallow, and then asked me to tell him the other story I had. I looked to Bob for help but he was staring straight ahead. I had no place to go but forward.

In the second story a message is received that is directed to the crew of the *Enterprise*. When Riker and company arrive at the world from which it emanates their presence is rejected by the race living there. These people live for several hundred years and, like the Navajo, their culture has no concept of time, past, present, or future. They had called for the crew of the *Enterprise* but it was the team from the original *Enterprise* they were signaling. Once before, Kirk et al. had saved their civilization from genocide by solving a highly abstruse riddle conceived by a ubiquitous force of astral beings. This same superordinate species has come back and is now putting these people to the test again. Unfortunately, the planet dwellers, cynical and suspicious, think these new space adventurers are imposters and will not accept any help from them.

Because they will not give Jean-Luc Picard and his group any information that might help them answer the riddle and because the captain will not abandon them to their own extinction, a plan is devised to pluck some of the original *Enterprise* crew out of the past. When they arrive, however, it is not the full complement. This is important because the solution to the problem last time depended on everyone involved making a contribution. The riddle could only be solved by the symbiotic relationship of all those involved in the mission. They were like puzzle pieces; the personal input of each person was needed to fit with all the others so that a bigger picture formed and the riddle could be solved.

The presence of the old crew reassures the planet's inhabitants, and the basic information needed to work on the riddle is coaxed from them. The three or four of the old group cannot arrive at the solution by themselves, however. Picard hits on the idea that his people must also be part of the equation in order to achieve success. And so what happens is a joint effort by two crews which, in reality, exist several hundred years apart. This sharing process, not the solution they are seeking, is the real answer to the riddle. These astral entities have returned because the planet's population had again lost sight of its sense of community, had turned self-serving and was on the path to self-destruction. The whole adventure of the two crews working together was designed by the omnipotent force as an example to the people of this world that only through cooperation could they survive.

Gene said he liked the story but that it would be too expensive to hire on all those original cast members. I said you probably could get away with using just one member from the original series and the rest from the *Next Generation* folks. Gene reached for his water glass again and the discussion suddenly did a right turn into a critique of day-old chocolate cake. The story conference was over. I never tried to pitch to "Next Generation" again while Gene was still involved.

I ran into Bob Lewin several years later. It was interesting that neither of us had to bring up the subject of our last meeting together. It was on both our minds simultaneously. More curious still was that neither he nor I said a word. He just looked at me with a very sheepish grin, shrugged, and shook his head. I could have asked him what happened back then but I didn't want to be told that it simply wasn't in the cards, that, for whatever reason, Roddenberry was never going to let me write for his show. On the other hand, it could have simply been that Gene thought my ideas sucked.

Gene Roddenberry died in 1991 at the age of seventy, long enough to see the twenty-fifth anniversary of his creation. The funeral was held at Forest Lawn Cemetery. There were several speakers, but the only one who I remember clearly was Patrick Stewart. He spoke with eloquence and humor. It was altogether a very moving tribute. It occurred to me for the first time that Gene probably belonged to the cast, crew, and staff of the *Next Generation* series as much as he did to us. That had never sunk in before. I said earlier that I am uncomfortable deifying Gene Roddenberry. In truth, I am uncomfortable deifying anybody. I don't think it's in my nature. What I can grant to Gene, which few others in the entertainment business can claim, is the impact his work has had on so many lives. I'm not talking about fans. I wouldn't know how to quantify something that ephemeral. I'm talking about the lives of actors, writers, producers, designers, executives, and manufacturers. Gene Roddenberry is that proverbial pebble in the road. Every career that has bumped up against Star Trek has had its course changed in some way. Obviously, the degree to which this has occurred varies greatly, but unlike so many others who have spent fifteen minutes with fame, it cannot be said of Mr. Roddenberry that he made no difference.

We stepped out of the chapel into the bright sun. Overhead, three Air Force jets roared past in the Missing Man formation. I gulped hard. It was a moment I will not forget.

I saw a first draft of the *Star Trek Generations* script early in 1994. In addition to the *Next Generation* cast, all seven of us from the original show were represented. This did not, however, fill my heart with joy. I had two speeches in the story, neither of which was more than a couple of lines long. I discarded out of hand the possibility that I'd want to be involved in this movie.

A few weeks went by and my sources provided me with another draft of the script. This one had reduced our cast participation to the big three: Bill, Leonard, and DeForest. Bill's role was of course substantial, but Leonard's part was actually smaller than De's. I would have been surprised if either man had agreed to join up. A small curiosity of this version is that it was Chekov's daughter who was the new navigator aboard the *Enterprise,* not Sulu's. Then they write a third draft and poor Pavel has a family wiped out of existence.

When in fact both Leonard and De did demur. *Generations* producer Rick Berman called Jimmy Doohan and myself to replace them. I guess this is called working one's way down the food chain. I asked to see a script of this new draft before committing myself. (My sources had not yet provided me one.) Almost no effort had been made to change the dialogue from the preceding version, so Chekov was just saying words that had been previously assigned to McCoy. Although a fee to be in the film had not yet been negotiated, I assumed it would be substantial. I considered that point for about five seconds and then decided to reject the offer anyway. *Star Trek VI* had not been the swan song I had hoped it would be and I was bitterly disappointed by that. I saw no purpose in further sullying the dignity of Mr. Chekov by letting him participate in such a nominal fashion. I called Rick Berman and explained why I was turning down the opportunity. He was surprised and asked if I would meet with his writers and himself.

The meeting was pleasant and I was asked how I saw the Russian's role improving. My thought was that there could be additional banter between Kirk and Chekov that would humanize the navigator and, most importantly, a more detailed moment between Scotty and Chekov when we believe that Kirk has died. Neither suggestion required an overhaul of the story. We were just talking about a few words here and a few there. Everyone was amenable and when the revised draft arrived my modest input had found its way into the script. But now I felt that Chekov breathed. He was a real human being! I signed aboard.

It would have been fun to have had some interaction with the Next Gen cast. Still, as I indicated earlier, working on this project for ten days was generally a pleasant experience. I particularly appreciated the work of the director, David Carson. He was one of the few Star Trek directors who did not simply assume that the actors were on top of things and leave them to their own devices. That he was British and therefore, courteous and understated probably made the actors more responsive to his suggestions. That he had a keen understanding of what he wanted from each scene was without question. I always felt confident that his ideas were sound.

Evidently Bill Shatner felt the same way. I braced myself the first time Carson offered an alternative approach to a scene Bill had been rehearsing. There was nothing wrong with Shatner's approach to the material and, in fact, it was effective. David's ideas, however, took the interpretation in another direction. Shatner had no problem with trying it a different way and brought to his lines the same dedication he had done previously. It didn't require great insight on my part to see what was happening. He admitted to me that for the first time he didn't feel like the star of the production. Not carrying all that baggage did wonders for his sense of proportion. He was much more a regular guy than I had seen him be before.

In the absence of Leonard and De he also turned to me for the small talk around the set. I kidded him a lot. Particularly in his efforts to establish some kind of rapport with Jimmy Doohan. Jimmy was always professional but remained distant. Jimmy has spoken a thousand times about his differences with Bill Shatner. He wasn't about to have a change of heart now.

Now I'm going to relate a story with a one-word punchline. The reader might well wonder why I have included such an apparently innocuous incident here. Innocuous to you, maybe. To me it was historic. We were setting up the scene just after I introduce Sulu's daughter to Captain Kirk. We are both standing on the bridge, the Captain above and slightly behind Chekov, as we watch the young woman move away. The camera is facing us. "I vas neverr dot young," says the wistful Russian. We rehearsed it a couple of times looking out past the camera, as was natural. Then Bill quietly suggested that, instead, I turn to him while saying the line. It doesn't take Ansel Adams to figure out that if I do that my back is to the lens and there is only one face in the shot. "No," I said. I can't ever remember saying "no" to Mr. Shatner before. That it took twenty seven-years and was such a big deal to me probably says more about my character flaws than his.

I have far more conflicted feelings about what happened in the small moment I had asked the writers to include when Scotty and Chekov talk about losing their captain. As an acting teacher, I have always encouraged my students to investigate who they are and draw from their own experience to bring emotional honesty to their roles. I have assumed that when I have performed competently I have done just that. There never was an issue of conscience involved for me. Any experience, no matter how personal, was fair game if it would enrich the work. And yet, when I finally completed this scene I wondered if I had not simply prostituted a great sorrow and in so doing violated a spirit of morality.

The first time or two we rehearsed the moment, what I had projected was a feeling of shock that after all these years our captain was dead. Being numbed by it was an acceptable interpretation and the director made no objection. When we actually began shooting I found myself suddenly overwhelmed by a sense of sadness. My brother, Norman, had died three months before and I now saw him on the bridge with me. Nothing spooky here, just his image in my mind's eye but very clear to me. He was smiling and saying, "Hi, paisan." No, we aren't remotely Italian, it was just a favorite endearing expression he used with me. The smile was a killer. The words were very hard to hear. I started my lines in the scene and I began to cry. We did the scene over seven times and each time he was there with me and each time the tears flowed. That had never happened to me before as an actor, never. I didn't question it at the time. I just let it happen. On the eighth take David Carson said, "We know your pain now, this time see if you can hold it back a little." And on that take I just bottled it up inside. It was even harder to play the scene that way but it probably was the better choice.

After viewing dailies the next day, Carson said the work was "A+". The scene never made it to the final edit. It may have been just as well. As I said before, I'm not sure it's conscionable to exploit personal tragedy, even for an artistic goal. I shall be more circumspect how I instruct my students in the future.

SEVENTEEN

"The End of a Day"

When I was seven years old and very attached to my mother I became preoccupied with the fear that something was going to happen to her. I promised myself that if she lived until I was forty-three I'd be able to handle her passing. Why forty-three? Who knows? It probably felt sufficiently ancient to me that I would have by then grown up. My mother died in January 1980. I was in my forty-third year at the time. She was to her last breath a loving, supportive friend and my biggest fan. There's no question that life dealt her the short end of the stick. There's not much I could have changed except maybe inviting her to the occasional parties we held. Shame on me for being embarrassed by her out-of-date clothes and her out-of-date manner.

★

I had my heart attack in July 1993. Four months later my sister, Vera, passed away. Two months after that I lost my brother, Norm. Vera was thirteen years older than me and we had never spent a lot of time together. She made the choice of not letting heroic measures be used to save her. She had spent far too much time in hospitals during her life to allow the indignity of chronic illness assail her further.

✱

My brother's death was also a long time coming. He had had a non-malignant tumor cut from his brain several times during the last ten years. Each time he resumed his medical practice and each time it grew back. After the last surgery he exacted a promise from his family not to cut him open again. This time the tumor returned malignant. It grew through his eye. He spent the last two years in a convalescent home, never in pain, but slowly losing the battle to live. Norman Koenig died in January 1994. He was my friend, he was my champion, and he was my most severe critic. He was a very complicated person. He was as cynical as my father, very defensive, very strong-willed, intimidating, and, at the same time, a wonderful doctor, a caring father, and a loyal pal. He was my brother and I'll never have another. I knew him longer than anyone else in my life. I sometimes marvel that I have been able to go on without him at my side.

✦

I first met Mark Lenard at a Star Trek convention. It might have been in Boston, it might have been in Baltimore. It was not on a Star Trek set because we didn't work in the same shows on the same day during the series. He first appeared as the Romulan Commander in the first-season episode "Balance of Terror," written by Paul Schneider. He also played a Klingon in *Star Trek—The Motion Picture*. He is, of course, best known as Sarek, Spock's father, and first appeared in that role in the second-season episode "Journey To Babel" written by D. C. (Dorothy) Fontana.

Sometime in the late seventies we ran into each other again at the Actors' Studio's West Coast branch. We were there as observers but ended up doing a play together. It was a Harold Pinter work called *The Collector*. In the piece, his character comes to see mine with an accusation about sleeping with his wife. Like much of Pinter's writing there are several interpretations available regarding the various relationships in the story, and one is left to wonder who has actually slept with whom.

Mark and I were of very different temperaments, but we seemed to get along well. Generally, he was more mellow than I was, but he was not without a contentious side. When the skies were dark and the wind was blowing in the wrong direction he could be almost as big a pain in the ass as I was. We fought but never stayed angry at each other. We enjoyed working together, and it eventually led to our taking a one-act play entitled *Actors* by Conrad Bromberg on the road to be performed at conventions. What we did have in common was a love for the theater and a desire to present to our genre audiences something more than just the same Star Trek anecdotes.

Actors was quite successful and we took a turn at mounting another short work called *Box and Cox* by Sullivan of Gilbert and Sullivan fame. We hoped it would work as a companion piece to the first play. We did it in Los Angeles a couple of times and my wife Judy played the landlady, the third character in this one-act farce. We all got lots of laughs but we decided the set was too elaborate to stage *Box and Cox* in convention ballrooms as we had done with *Actors*.

In time I began to feel I was getting too old to play the Young Actor in *Actors* and reluctantly we stopped performing it.

In 1990 Mark approached me with a full-length play called *The Boys in Autumn* by Bernard Sabath. It was about Huck Finn and Tom Sawyer meeting again forty years later. He would play Huck, I would play Tom. The parts were marvelous and the writing evocative. I went about securing the rights and putting together a staff to produce it in Los Angeles. I hired Alan Hunt to direct the work. I had known Alan from the many times we had found ourselves in casting offices together back in the sixties. He went on to be a regular on the television series *Voyage to the Bottom of the Sea*. Alan had developed an excellent reputation as a director and was the perfect choice to maintain order when either Mark or I started grating on the other's nerves.

I was looking for people to help finance the show and held a backers' audition. Gene Roddenberry came and indicated that he enjoyed the reading very much. Two friends of long standing, Richard and Esther Shapiro, the creators of the immensely successful *Dynasty* television series, made a substantial contribution. I was very proud of their confidence in us. To my surprise a couple who had not shown up at the backers' audition and who hadn't even been solicited also offered a donation. J. Michael Straczynski and his wife Kathryn Drennan wrote out a check because they believed in live theater and because they appreciated the work Mark Lenard and I had done in the past. To be sure, I had met Joe Straczynski before on several occasions, but we weren't soul-bearing buddies. Besides, how can you hug someone who is, quite literally, a foot taller than you? I was absolutely floored by the gift but as I was to learn in the years that followed Joe would land me prostrate (that's a good thing) on more than one other occasion. Mark's work in the play was received with uniform approbation. He really shone in the part. All of his talent came to bear. The critics were a bit more divided about my contribution. The most important review, however, was from the late Ray Loynd in the *Los Angeles Times* on August 4, 1990, and that was a rave. I quote it here partly because the guy liked me and partly as a tribute to my departed friend.

> [T]he production is flawless, with vivid and even sublime performances by Mark Lenard as Huck and Walter Koenig as Tom . . . These aging men might not be so interesting if we weren't captives of Twain going in, but Lenard and Koenig live so thoroughly in the long shadow of Huck and Tom, and Allan Hunt's direction is so pristine, that the production overwhelms the predictable sentiment in Bernard Sabath's play.

Bernard Sabath, the playwright, flew in from Florida to see the show opening night. He told us he loved it and although he had seen it performed with George C. Scott in New York and with Burt Lancaster and Kirk Douglas in San Francisco this was his favorite production. At the end of our six-week run we were playing to standing room only.

After that we took it on the road and during the next five years we performed it at conventions in places like Denver and Chicago, at Northwestern State University in Louisiana, and at theaters in Lancaster and Poway, California and in Hershey and Wilkes-Barre, Pennsylvania. Our last run was for two weeks in February 1995 at the Forum Theater in Thousand Oaks, California. Mark, who divided his time between homes in New York and California, was supposed to come west in February of '96 to rehearse the show again for a performance in May at a convention in Cardiff, Wales.

We both thought of *The Boys In Autumn* as not only a satisfying aesthetic turn but as an annuity. There was no limit to the age the characters might be and so we believed we would continue to play them well into our old age. We didn't count on the decision being taken out of our hands.

Mark didn't come west after all. I canceled our engagement in Wales. I tried phoning him on several occasions, but it was his wife Ann who returned my calls. I knew he wasn't well but apparently he did not wish the extent of his infirmity to be revealed. I did not know that he spent almost the entire year of 1996 in a hospital battling cancer, infection, and pneumonia. He died in December. I hadn't talked to him in over twelve months. I lost a superb performing partner. The Star Trek world lost a man of grace, dignity, and charm.

❖

In 1992 I participated in a "career day" program at the 52nd Street School in Los Angeles. This was an inner-city grade school with a student body comprised almost exclusively of minority students. My sense was that the harsh realities of life made it difficult for them to relate to fanciful stories about spaceships and adventures on far-off planets. In any case, they didn't know much about *Star Trek* and even less about me. They seemed most interested in knowing what movie stars I knew. My little talk about making it in show business seemed about as relevant as a lecture on the bacchanal to an order of monks.

During the lunch break the guest speakers repaired to the library for sandwiches. Again, almost all those in attendance were Americans of African, Asian, or Hispanic heritage. I found myself talking to a young black man whose last name was Evers. He was an attentive listener and I began telling him about an incident that I had been involved in nearly thirty years before. The trigger for the conversation was that his last name happened to be the same as that of the principal character in my story. I began by explaining that I had been rather devastated by what had occurred at the time and had never been able to shake off the effect it had on me.

The American Civil Liberties Union was holding a series of meetings at a Beverly Hills high school during this period of the sixties. The topic under discussion was how to make the motion picture craft unions more accessible to minority applicants. The month before Marlon Brando had been in attendance. There was a buzz in the room that he might return for this meeting as well. More important than that was the fact that Charles Evers, brother of NCAA field secretary and slain civil rights activist Medgar Evers, was the guest speaker. The aura surrounding both these men caused the room to be packed with what appeared to be an audience equally divided between blacks and whites.

Brando didn't show up but it didn't matter. The audience greeted Charles Evers' introduction with rousing applause. He spoke eloquently about the need to carry on his brother's work and to better integrate a film industry which had only given lip service to the concept of equal opportunity.

After his summation he invited questions. I raised my hand. I didn't know it at that moment but I might as well have raised a noose. My concern was in force-feeding minority personnel into skill positions without the proper training. I was trying to make the point that without the tools they were bound to fail, causing a racist backlash effect. As with all bigotry, the claim would then be made that "these" people were not capable of succeeding and deserved their low station in life. Had I been allowed to finish I would have explained that what was needed was an apprenticeship program that could properly train the applicants so that they could enter the game on a level playing field.

I never got close to getting all of that out. The *entire* group of approximately six hundred people, whites and blacks alike, rose to their feet as one, pointed their fingers at me, and started screaming. In the years that followed I have often thought of that scene in *The Invasion of the Body Snatchers* (the 1978 version) where the pod people denounced the humans among them by similar pointing and screeching. I could have been wearing white robes with the emblem of the Grand Wizard of the Klu Klux Klan so vehemently denounced was I by the crowd. If anything, the Caucasians in the mob were more disposed to violence than their black brothers. Ina Balin, a white actress and reasonably successful at the time, stood closest to me. Her face was so contorted with anger that I began to suspect that what I was being subjected to had less to do with moral outrage than catharsis. She wasn't alone. There was a knee-jerk reaction going on that was *meant* to be threatening. Six hundred people needed someone to vent their fury on, to prove by a display of hate how committed they were to achieving love and equality among the races. Sure it was ironic and hypocritical, but you know something? I do understand it. In order to back the unpopular movement of racial fairness against the force of prejudice with its three-hundred-year old history you have to weigh in with a passion that accepts no middle ground. You are either for us or against us. Don't talk to us about rationality, don't talk to us about waiting any longer. We want it now!

Well, I'm great in a theoretical argument but being personally subjected to so much malice is quite another thing. I was very, very shook up. Not so much for concern over my physical well-being but because I was being so incredibly misunderstood. When calm was restored and everyone returned to his seat Charles Evers likened me to Bull Connor. He was the Birmingham, Alabama sheriff who went out to face down the equal rights marchers with a bullwhip and attack dogs. *Bull Connor, for Christ's sake!*

When the meeting broke up I went over to Mr. Evers and tried to explain what I had been trying to say. He turned his back on me. A very well-dressed African American got in my face and went on about how he had risen in the ranks of one of the movie studios while several times interjecting, "Is it all right with you, *boss*?!"

I staggered out of the room feeling that I was ten years old again and nobody wanted me on their stickball team.

The young man to whom I had told my tale listened without interruption. I was grateful for that. I had wanted to tell this story for a long time and particularly to a black person. If I wasn't going to find exoneration at least I could unburden myself.

For a long moment he said nothing. Then he chuckled.

"Old Uncle Charlie, he sometimes gets carried away, doesn't he?"

It took me nearly thirty years but I finally got someone to understand. Sometimes closure comes with death and sometimes it comes with a smile on the face of a young black man who is Medgar Evers' son.

EIGHTEEN

"Untitled"
(A Work in Progress)

IN CONJUNCTION WITH THE RELEASE OF *THE VOYAGE HOME*, *TIME* magazine did a cover story (with Leonard on the cover) about the movie and those involved. In the article I was quoted as saying that I'd be available to work in a low-budget film in a well-written script that had a good part for me. Tex Ragsdale, the writer of a screenplay called *Moontrap*, contacted me through my agent. I read the script, met the director-producer, Robert Dyke, and in short order a deal was worked out.

The film was shot in a converted warehouse outside of Detroit in the dead of winter in the year of the coming of the second great glacial age of 1988. Not since I lived in Iowa had I experienced the phenomenon of nose hair freezing over. How cold was it? When I tell you I couldn't feel my penis (and God knows I tried) you begin to understand the tragedy of the Fahrenheit free fall in which I found myself.

My physical discomfort aside, the six weeks I spent working on this picture was some of the very best time I have had in show business. It was important to me that *Moontrap* was a union film. I do believe that everyone has the right to a fair wage and decent working conditions. The practice of featherbedding does exist, however, and can weigh heavily on the budget of bigger productions. On *Moontrap* everyone pitched in and helped each other. Costumers moved flats when asked, grips helped serve lunch, and I'm sure personnel from various departments offered to apply body makeup to the leading lady.

Just to keep the record straight, the failure of many well-made movies to turn a profit and, thus, discourage the production of more well-made movies lies at the feet of *all* those involved who inflate costs: executives and their huge salaries, movie stars and their astronomical fees, and cost overruns that frequently camouflage skimming by individuals within the production. In fact, the craft unions are probably held more accountable for budget extravagance than they deserve. Too frequently they are disproportionately blamed for excesses and used as the reason to make a picture non-union to save money. Non-union films are a growing and very disturbing trend and remain the principal excuse for runaway production. It used to be that runaway productions meant making movies in other countries. Now it can just as easily mean shooting motion pictures in other states with right-to-work laws that obviate the need to hire union personnel.

But I digress. It was a very happy and friendly atmosphere in which *Moontrap* was made. I was particularly pleased that my wife Judy Levitt was in the film, playing the role of an astronaut. Beyond that delight was also the fact that I got along with everybody. Bruce Campbell played my buddy. Originally, the public knew Bruce through all the *Evil Dead* films, then through his own television series, and more recently in a series of important roles in major motion pictures. Leigh Lombardi was the "moon girl" and my character's love interest. She's a talented actress who has worked in many film projects.

There was one moment between us in the story that had to be dealt with, and I must say that I've spent the last nine years congratulating myself for my actions—may I even say "my valor"—under circumstances which, without fear of contradiction, may well have been the most severely testing that any man has faced during the period of the last several hundred years.

The scene called for Leigh to remove her top during an intimate moment between us, and being a very modest young woman she felt uncomfortable with the idea. The set was cleared for the shoot with only the director, the cinematographer, and myself present. To further reduce her self-consciousness, I then made a promise in blood to look only into her eyes during the course of the filming. Don't talk to me about Pork Chop Hill, Dunkirk, or for that matter, the Battle of the Bulge. This was heroism, this was nerves of steel. Would that every man could display such resolve, such fortitude, and wouldn't it be a better America if they could? I kept my promise.

I have avoided saying it until now, but I feel compelled to mention that I did have the lead role. That was a first on celluloid for me and not very hard to take at all. The neatest thing was that I proved to myself what I long suspected. I may be a sore loser but I'm a good winner. My conduct was beyond reproach. No one had any complaints about me. It's nice to know that if you're going to bitch about other actors' behavior when they are in a position of empowerment that you can do it with a clear conscience.

The company in charge of distributing the movie got cold feet at the last moment and instead of a theatrical release it went straight to video. That notwithstanding and with relatively little publicity *Moontrap* sold fifty thousand copies. A rather prodigious number for such a small picture. Robert Dyke did a terrific job and deserves all the praise he has received. Bob and his wife Mary Petryshyn are to this day close friends of Judy and me.

It was two o'clock in the morning in late July of 1993. I was in a hotel room at a Star Trek convention in Chicago. In classic denial, I attributed the pain in my chest to indigestion. I kept telling myself that if my brother were there he'd tell me it was nothing else and to think otherwise was to border on the hysterical. That wasn't fair to my brother, but he was a man of considerable cynicism and I used it as a convenient ploy to ignore the discomfort. When I began to experience pain in my jaw and broke out into a full body sweat I decided that hysteria was the better part of valor. By now an hour and a half had passed. This particular hotel had an emergency number. I have been in hundreds of hotels and never remember seeing that particular feature on the telephone menu before. Within a few minutes a hotel staff person was at my door. Within a few more minutes paramedics had arrived. They used a portable monitor but couldn't find anything untoward. I was relieved. Thanks for coming, I was about to say. They lifted me onto a stretcher anyway (thanks guys, for not listening to me) and transported me by ambulance to Resurrection Hospital. I'm not sure whether I was supposed to take comfort in the hospital's name or not.

In the emergency room they kept asking me how severe the pain was on a scale of one to ten. I knew that this wasn't the greatest pain I had ever experienced so I figured "eight" seemed reasonable. After about an hour a doctor showed up and told me I had suffered a heart attack. I don't know at what point they started me on a morphine drip but my response seemed a bit dislocated. I felt some shock but hardly any fear. I had been a runner since my late thirties, I had never been more than five or six pounds overweight, my red meat consumption was down to about one portion a month, and I neither smoked nor drank. Why would this be happening to me? Surely someone has made a mistake. That's what kept running through my mind for the first several hours. What I wasn't taking into account was a likely genetic disposition (my father having had his first heart attack at the age of fifty-three) and the high level of stress at which I had functioned my entire life.

Judy was at my side during the entire period I was in the hospital. I was very lucky to have her there. We all know that old story about how your life is supposed to flash before your eyes when you are at death's door. In my case it was the "shoe dropping" syndrome played out on a loop. The first bit of news was reported with a big smile by one of the attending doctors: I had only one blocked artery, and an angioplasty, a procedure in which they insert a tube into the artery through your leg to clean the plaque out and expand the opening, could be performed to solve the problem. Angioplasty is a relatively minor procedure and not nearly as invasive as what you see on the *ER* and *Chicago Hope* television programs. "Congratulations!" I was told.

The second time he returned a smile was still discernible but this time I couldn't see teeth. It turns out, he told me, that there was more than one blockage, but angioplasty was still a possible option.

It was another doctor the next time, and I had the distinct feeling that the execution of his smile actually required the burning of some triple-digit calories. I had seventy to ninety-five per cent blockage in four arteries and would require open heart surgery, he explained. The good news was that it could wait until I returned to L.A.

His next visit was a few hours later. His smile had flatlined like the heart monitor graph of one recently expired. He told me that it was five impaired arteries. It now appeared that my condition was no longer stable and that cracking me open had acquired priority status.

Whatever consolation I needed beyond my morphine drip Judy provided. She also made the decision that I be transferred to St. Frances, another area hospital with state-of-the-art operating facilities. By now my daughter Danielle has arrived from the West Coast. I love her dearly and was overjoyed to see her. At least as overjoyed as I can be beyond being overjoyed by my morphine drip.

My son Andrew was flying in from Vancouver. My main concern was that he arrive before surgery began. At that point, I had very little fear about death. I just wanted to be sure that If I didn't make it I'd at least have said a proper goodbye to the three most important people in my life. One could say that I was very brave, or that like V'ger I had achieved a new level of philosophical enlightenment. On the other hand, it could just have been my morphine drip.

My stay in the hospital was eight days. During that time I received several hundred letters and phone inquiries from Star Trek fans. For some reason, I was particularly touched by those folks who said they were burning candles for me. Being at best an agnostic, peoples' prayers were a bonus I didn't think I qualified for. I found it reassuring.

I also received one hundred and three phone calls from friends. One hundred and two of them were very supportive. I know the precise number because aside from watching *The Bill Cosby Show* reruns and Chicago Cubs baseball games there was nothing else to do during the long daylight hours. Something screwy had happened with my vision and there were blank spots on the page when I tried to read. This passed after a week. Among the calls were those from Star Trek cast members. It was very nice to hear from them all.

One of the first people I phoned when I learned of my condition was J. Michael Straczynski. In addition to being a benefactor on our production of *The Boys in Autumn* he was also a novelist, had worked as chief story editor on the new *Twilight Zone* TV anthology and had done time on the *Murder She Wrote* television series as a writer-producer. He was also the creator and co-executive producer of a new science fiction series called *Babylon 5*. He had written a part for me in an episode that was to shoot in September. There was no way my doctors would let me go to work by then and I had to tell him I wouldn't be available. He had already floored me once back in 1990 and if I hadn't already been on my back he would have done it again. He said he would postpone shooting my show until I had recovered. I cannot tell you what a lift that gave me. There are a few people who have put themselves on the line for me during my career: Joe D'Agosta with the *Mr. Novak* series and with *Star Trek*, Ken Geist on the casting of *The Deputy*, Harlan Ellison pressuring Twentieth Century-Fox to use me on *The Star Lost* Canadian TV series, and now Joe Straczynski.

As it turned out, the *Babylon 5* company ran out of shows to do before I was well and they had to recast and shoot the episode I was supposed to be in. Damned if it didn't turn out better for me that way! While I was recovering, Joe wrote a new script and included a new character for me to play. His name was Alfred Bester, a telepath and member of an elite if somewhat insidious force known as Psi Corps. Joe named the character after the science fiction writer of the same name known for his brilliant novels *The Demolished Man* and *The Stars My Destination*. I know there was skepticism in science fiction fandom when Bester first appeared. For thirty years I had been identified with the role of Chekov in Star Trek. Was anyone going to buy me playing an individual who could conceivably be thought of as a diametric opposite? I'd say it was a gutsy move to cast me that way if Joe had had to wrestle with the question. Frankly, I don't think it entered his mind. Joe marches to his own drummer. He knew my work and believed I could do justice to his writing. It's the highest compliment I could be paid. Bester has had sufficient impact to be written into seven more episodes in the last four years. Maybe *that's* the highest compliment I could be paid.

One final note about Joe Straczynski. Of the forty-four episodes shot in seasons three and four he has written forty-four. For those of you conversant with the enervating schedules of television production you know what an absolutely astonishing effort this has been. For those of you who don't—trust me. That the work has also been consistently superior, among the very best done on the tube, makes the achievement all the more remarkable. At some point someone in the Television Academy of Arts and Sciences is going to realize what he has accomplished, the brilliance of his craft and the historical significance of his output, and he will be honored accordingly.

During the course of this book I have complained on several occasions that Chekov was more sketched than written. I have also whined about a shortfall in the status of those not assigned star billing in the Star Trek universe. How extraordinary that at this rather late date in my life fate has stepped out of a phone booth. Alfred Bester has been a multidimensional, challenging role, and I could not ask for a better group of people to work with than those with whom I've come in contact at *Babylon 5*. A terrific role and a great staff, cast, and crew. Wow!

I shall go to my grave bonded to the world and people of Star Trek, and that means everyone. Our blood and our sweat and our tears have been too much mixed for it to be otherwise. Thirty years has been too long for it to be otherwise. And still, how nice to learn that after all this time there still remain new adventures for me on this planet and, with that in mind, new ways to yet view the universe.

★

In December 1996 I was back in my Star Trek uniform. George Takei, Bill Shatner, and I had been hired to perform as our characters in a CD-ROM game called "Starfleet Academy." An attractive group of young people carried the story, but we were on hand to lend support. As on the *Generations* movie Bill and I did some shmoozing. In fact, at one point we broke into one of those convulsing giggles that generally strike fourth graders in a classroom and make it impossible for them to stop laughing. And this was happening while the camera was rolling. As I've said previously I'm a sucker for a sense of humor and this bit of childishness on our parts made me feel closer to him than I ever had before. The feeling was heightened even farther when we began a discussion about the new Next Generation movie, *Star Trek: First Contact.* It was breaking box office records for its opening week and he indicated that the news depressed him. I asked him why and he replied "Because we're not a part of it." I hope Bill doesn't feel that I have betrayed a confidence in revealing this moment of truth because I see it in a most complimentary light. For years the sense I had gotten from him was that Star Trek was just a stopover in a very busy career. I wasn't even sure if he remembered my name when we began working on *Star Trek—The Motion Picture.* He would leave our project and go on to a television series called *Barbary Coast,* or another one called *T.J. Hooker.* All through the seventies and eighties he would guest star on different television programs. While we waited with bated breath to hear if there would be a second or a third Star Trek movie he was doing starring turns in TV Movies of the Week and feature films. He was frequently quoted as saying that he didn't comprehend Star Trek's fascination, and he did a skit on *Saturday Night Live* in which he told a group of fans to "get a life." I felt that even as he was the most celebrated of our Star Trek group he was the one most detached from it.

But somewhere along the line it snuck up on him. It seduced him, it became a more important part of his life than he had cared to admit. One wonders how he could have resisted so long. Second only to a collection of musicians: Presley, The Beatles, and Michael Jackson, Captain Kirk is known the world over. How could Bill Shatner's psyche *not* be thoroughly wrapped up with that of his alter ego? I only ever thought about the fact that he had the most to *gain* from Star Trek's success. It had never occurred to me that he also had the most to *lose* when it passed us by. "It depresses me because we are not a part of it," he said. It was the most vulnerable moment I have ever seen him have and I was touched by it.

I have made a very conscious decision in the writing of this book to exclude my family life from its pages. Judy, an extremely intelligent and gifted performer, has been my loving companion for thirty-three years. Andrew and Danielle are both extraordinarily talented, but even more important they are good people. I take enormous pride in who they are. This despite the fact that I was something less than an ideal role model. Too much insecurity, too much stress, too much gloom and doom in the way I handled my life. I feel particularly blessed that they keep giving me new chances to get it right. But I have kept them all out of this chronicle because they are my private life and, as such, it is the one area of my existence that must remain inviolate.

The first play I did in Los Angeles was the *Girls of Summer* by N. Richard Nash. While performing in it I met an actor named Lee Delano. He has gone on to play hundreds of characters on television and the movies. Star Trek fans know him as Kalo from the original series episode "A Piece of the Action" by David Harmon and Gene Coon. He's also had the distinction of going on tour for years with Sid Caesar and Imogene Coca, doing comedy sketches from the classic *Your Show of Shows* fifties television series.

Lee's greatest character, however, was probably Morty Banks. Morty was someone he invented to be his personal manager. Morty would call up casting directors and producers and, sounding very important with a forceful New York accent, would extol the virtues of his "client." "I'm tellin' yah, this guy Lee Delano is incredible. He's a terrific talent and he's gonna be big, very big!" More often then not it got him interviews. Occasionally it got him parts. Naturally, no one ever got to meet Morty himself.

Every actor needs a Morty Banks. If not to make phone calls at least as that part of him who's always in his corner, who never lets him down, who always believes he's a credit to his craft and that he will eventually be successful. If he doesn't have a Morty inside him, life in general, and the ups and downs of this business in particular, can be a killer. I've spent six decades trying to keep my Morty afloat. So far so good.

The following two letters were written within a week of each other in October 1989. They're really the whole story on a page and a half. It's what life has been about for sixty years . . . .

October 6, 1989

Dear Mr. Koenig,

I am a longtime Star Trek fan from Massachusetts & I recently read your novel "Buck Alice and the Actor-Robot" and just saw the movie "Moontrap" that you did (on video). What happened? Me and a half a dozen other ST fans who watched "Moontrap" with me thought it was cheap, laughable, and embarrassingly poorly-acted. You'd be better-off if you'd never done it.

As for your so-called novel., it was also so-called trash; it sounded like you were either heavily on drugs or else losing your mind (or both) when you wrote it.

We hope that in the future you'll stick purely with "Chekov" because although he's only a marginal character at best, he is still better than any of your solo endeavers put together. The only thing is, Chekov's appeal used to be his youthful looks, but even those have now faded, leaving a more-than-middle-aged man who is becoming pathetic in not knowing when to give-up. Please spare the public any more of these embarrassing "solo endeavers" of your's.

Sincerely,

Laurie

P.S. Speaking for the Boston Star Trek community, we used to believe all the hype in the fanzines + your personal interviews that you'd been "typecast" as Chekov. Now we know the real reason why you couldn't get any other acting jobs.

12 October 1989

To: Mr. Walter Koenig   From: Dr. Robert R. Hoffman
    c/o Creation   Adelphi University

Dear Mr. Koenig:

My wife and I attended the recent convention in New York, at which you gave a recitation of a story from H. P. Lovecraft.

We wanted to write you this note to say how much we enjoyed it. The story is, or course, a classic of psychological horror, given its multiple interpretations. Furthermore, your performance was an enthralling reminder of how much effort and practice it takes to be a good actor and performer.

Unlike Lovecraft, we are at a loss for words, and words that can be found are inadequate to express our sentiments.

Thank you for coming to the New York Cons, and for performing for us. Thank you, of course, for all the joy and stimulation that you and all of the Star Trek family have brought into the world. Much of our motivation for becoming scientists came from the visions presented by Star Trek.

Best of luck with your future endeavors.

Fans forever,

Robert R. Hoffman, Ph.D.	Robin Akerstrom-Hoffman, M.A.,
Associate Professor of	Human Factors Psychologist
Experimental Psychology	

I wouldn't trade a minute of it. Well, maybe a minute.

Coming Attractions

I TAPPED THE LAST PERIOD ON THE LAST SENTENCE OF THIS BOOK ON June 25, 1997. Two days later Joe Straczynski called to say that *Babylon 5* had been picked up for a fifth season. Three days after that I was off to Great Britain. I spent the first week there on a personal appearance tour that took me to Glasgow, Edinburgh, Belfast, and London. I was unprepared for the strong turnout at each venue. I was a bit more surprised to discover that I was currently being featured in at least four English magazines, two of which had my picture on the cover. I don't have a press agent promoting me so that added to my sense of wonder.

The second week in the U.K. saw me travelling with Judy to Blackpool, England for a *Babylon 5* convention put on by Wolf 359, a fan-based convention group. Every single member of the cast was there, including several actors who had recurring roles like myself. Members of the staff including executive producer Joe Straczynski and producer John Copeland were also in attendance. So were over three thousand fans.

On opening night the actors and other personalities were introduced one by one. With computer graphics a "jump gate" had been designed and projected on to a huge screen overhanging the stage. In turn, each person came from behind the screen as if coming through the jump gate and appeared on the stage. The applause was deafening.

Someone decided, however, that I should make my appearance from the back of the auditorium rather than from behind the stage. The Psi Corps Fan Club in England had made me a uniform similar to the one I had worn on the series. There were also about thirty members of the club similarly dressed flanking me as the announcer introduced me as "the villain you love to hate." I began my walk down the aisle toward the front of the room. Three thousand people rose in their seats and cheered wildly as I marched past them. A spotlight picked me out and flashbulbs were going off like Fourth of July fireworks. The audience reaction was as sustained as it was because I had such a long way to come. I hadn't taken three steps before I began to feel that I wasn't Walter Koenig at all. The fans weren't cheering me. They were cheering the evil Alfred Bester. I was halfway to my destination when it occurred to me that the long-rumored telepath wars that were yet to happen in the *Babylon 5* chronicles had actually already been fought and "we" had won! These weren't fans of the show, they were fellow telepaths, *my* people. I was overcome by this extraordinary sense of power. I was Caesar, Napoleon, and several unmentionable dictators of more recent vintage. I, Alfred Bester, had come to this meeting hall to receive the acclamation of the mob, proclaim my triumph, and accept my appointment as leader-for-life of EarthForce. All this in the fifteen seconds it took me to reach the stage. What an amazing experience it was! I've never had one quite like that before.

The five days of the con were terrific. This was the first opportunity I had to mix with all the *Babylon 5* folks over a sustained period of time. Bruce Boxleitner (Sheridan), Jerry Doyle (Garibaldi), Mira Furlan (Delenn), Peter Jurasik (Londo), Andreas Katsulas (G'Kar), Richard Biggs (Franklin), Bill Mumy (Lennier), and all the others. They really did like each other! This really was family!

The closing day of the con was Monday, July 14. None of the attendees had left. The auditorium was as packed at it had been on opening night. We came out for final bows. Everyone was cheered madly. The loudest applause was for *Babylon 5*'s creator, Joe Straczynski. Just as it had been with Gene Roddenberry he was the star of stars. I found myself flashing back to the 1970s. I had not felt this kind of excitement, this kind of energy, this kind of extraordinary fan support since the New York City Star Trek conventions of that era. I had experienced it then, but I had never expected to be part of it again.

It felt eerie. It felt as if time had somehow doubled back on itself. And since that isn't possible what I was feeling made me giddy, almost euphoric. Twenty years ago I had been the "youngster" among the Star Trek group, swept up in an amazing demonstration of love. Now, among this contingent of actors and staff, I was the "grand old man." Maybe it should have depressed me, but I felt the opposite reaction. It was as if life was saying to me I wasn't done yet. It wasn't all behind me. There were still exciting mountains to climb.

The future was happening all over again.

Appendices

Notes to Harv Bennett on *Star Trek II*

11/2/81

Harv Bennett
Paramount Pictures
5451 Marathon
L.A., 90036

Dear Harv,

Many thanks for shooting the script out to me. I thoroughly enjoyed reading it. It is a tightly structured high adventure and I'm sure it will be enthusiastically endorsed by Trekkies and general audiences alike. In fact, had you not solicited my response (to do a "Trekkie run") I would feel perfectly comfortable in ending this note with the above critique. Understand, therefore, that that which follows, with a couple of notable exceptions, is mainly nit-picking and should be viewed in that context.

P. 2, Sc. 1 : Uhura's final speech: "Give your <u>spatial</u> coordinates." <u>Spatial</u> is implied and, therefore, unnecessary.
P. 3, Sc. 1 : Sulu's final speech: "Klingon <u>Neutrality</u> zone." Sounds awkward. Should be "neutral," I believe.
P. 4, Sc. 3 : Computer Voice first speech: "Klingon <u>neutrality</u> zone." As in P.3, Sc. 1.
P. 5, Sc. 3 : Crew members in chairs have arm rests that convert to seat belts in S.T. T.M.P. They would not fall out of chairs.

P. 7, Sc. 4 : Kirk's last speech: "Carry on Mister." If it is correct military address in the twentieth century to call female officers "Mister" I submit that, in the light of E.R.A., Women's Lib. et. al., that form of identification will have changed by the time of our story. I think the heightened consciousness of the science fiction genre fan would find such an apellation disagreeable.

P. 13, Sc. 10 : David's second speech: "Well, don't have kittens." Sounds too contemporary and also a trifle effeminate.

P. 13, Sc. 10 : In general, this scene could better serve if it made us feel some sympathy for David. All we see throughout our story is an angry young man. I think we'll like him better in his final confrontation with Kirk if we glimpse a more sympathetic side here.

P. 14, Sc. 11 : Kirk's last speech: "Twenty-two, eighty-three" We've always taken pains to not speak in specific dates. Might be better to say "One hundred and fifty years old" or use a star date.

P. 15, Sc. 11 : If Romulan Ale is an "instant drunk" there should be some reference to same. Otherwise it may look as if the actors don't know how to play intoxication with subtlety. Other solution would be to have the ale bubbling like an erupting volcano. That would get over the idea that it's powerful stuff.

P. 17, Sc. 11 : Kirk's last speech: "Don't mince words." Topical ideomatic expression that sounds too contemporary.

P. 17, Sc. 14 : The following is totally self-serving but I believe can be justified by helping tie the picture to the golden age of the series. During that time Chekov was frequently heard to allude to his Russian background as the creators of this or the inventors of that. Admittedly, the jokes were sophomoric but not unappealing as a preponderance of my mail attested to. My suggestion, therefore, (and this is the only time I do this during the course of this tome) is to have Chekov - upon materializing on Ceti Alpha V. - say, in a throw away, "This place, I tink it was inwented by a liddle old lady from Siberia."

P. 19, Sc. 19, 20 : What do you do with the baby after this? Does it go on the Reliant and subsequently get destroyed? Kirk's speech at the end of the story indicates there are survivors on Ceti Alpha V but Joachim's speech on P. 33, Sc. 45 suggests that all Khan's followers are on board the Reliant. Needs to be clarified, I believe.

P. 19, Sc. 21 : "Lethal looking odd swords." Although their appearance here helps I'm still troubled by their use in Khan's duel with Kirk. The way they are established here might be too subtle. Should you be wedded to a sword duel (I will amplify on that later), Perhaps Khan should be wearing one at his side when he first confronts Terrell and Chekov.

P. 21, Sc. 25 : Khan's last speech: Rather than have him use Chekov to launch into the exposition—"Do you mean he (i.e. Chekov) never told you the tale?"—which I believe is too obvious a way to set up the retelling—have Khan holding a garment or an artifact that belonged to Lt. McGiver (they've just come from burying her) and do a soliloquy to that as if remembering, reflecting, with some pain what has transpired over the last fourteen years that has led to McGiver's death and to this moment. It becomes, then, a private personal moment that gives us insight into Khan rather than the pervading feeling now of a device to explain back story.

P. 28, Sc. 34 : Preston's last speech: could anyone, even a fourteen-year-old in jest, get away with calling a Star Fleet Admiral "Blind as a Tiberian Bat"? I don't think so.

P. 38, Sc. 52 : "Saavik reaches out and touches a button." Is turbo lift button-controlled or voice-controlled?

P. 42, Sc. 56 : Kirk's second speech. I'm not sure how to change it, but it's both-ersome to have Kirk suddenly take command again. It is so similar to what happened in S.T. T.M.P. that it begins to resemble a convenient ploy. Perhaps the way to circumvent the feeling is to kid it, to have a dry interjection from Bones of "Here we go again!"

P. 53, Sc. 75 : "Crew sent flying." Arm rest safety belts.

P. 53, Sc. 80 : Scotty's speech: "Get back there, you yellow dogs!" Not in char-acter, I don't believe.

P. 54, Sc. 84 : Kirk's last speech: " . . aux power." I don't ever recall using the abbreviation for auxiliary.

P. 55, Sc. 84 : Spock's first speech: "We can't run for it on aux power." Better, I think to have him say, "We can't retreat on auxiliary power."

P. 62, Sc. 102 : Scotty: "Nineteen in hospital." I can't recall hearing sick bay referred to as "hospital" before.

P. 63, Sc. 106 : The death of Preston is tricky - that's never happened on Star Trek before. You are adding a sense of reality that goes beyond anything so far tried. It is possible you could estrange your audience by doing that. It is such a disonant brutal note in what is, after all, a family fantasy adventure. Pragmatically, it is also possible that it would reduce the effect of Spock's death later on. If following a child or animal act on stage is an anathema for a per-former, then following a child death with an adult one may also be anti-cli-matic.

P. 64, Sc. 106 : Bones' last speech. If you keep in Preston's death then I feel you need a more moving speech from the doctor. He is far too human to be so per-functory. In which case, he'd go onto "I'm still in the dark" to keep from break-ing down.

P. 68, Sc. 115 : Rats on a space station? A bit too obvious a metaphor unless it is a white laboratory rat established earlier.

P. 69, Sc. 118 : Kirk hasn't seen Chekov this whole story. Shouldn't his first exclamation be that, ergo, "Chekov!"?

P. 78, Sc. 126 : David's first speech, "That was disgusting." A bit unrelenting, I feel. It's going to be awfully hard to like this boy unless we see that sensitive side of him earlier.

P. 84, Sc. 140 : Do we, perhaps, need an explanation why the Ceti eel crawls out of Chekov's ear?

P. 88, Sc. 149 : (The following is definitely one man's opinion) I'm still not con-vinced that the use of swords evolves organically in the story. Among other things, it seem a transparent steal from Star Wars, Excalibur, etc. (That in itself isn't bad, I suppose, but if we come up short, the comparisons will not be flattering.) Furthermore, swords were not used in the 20th Century that Khan eludes to several times. It seems anachronistic somehow. My gut feeling, and I reiterate that this is one man's opinion, is that the fight should be without weapons, mano-a-mano, and, at that, the most extraordinarily choreographed and physically punishing battle yet recorded on film. the wonderful character element that has been included regarding Kirk's age becomes a part of this war. Kirk isn't as young as he was, and our concern for his safety doubles because of this. His herculean effort, therefore, has us rooting all the harder. I think, hand to hand, the fight becomes more real and more devastating. Not backflips and flying drop kicks but crunching, crushing blows to the body and the face. "Rocky" in a rocky cavern. Kirk is fighting to regain his youth. His defeat is painful because we know how conscious he is of growing old but it does not induce despair because we know that he's up against a superior adversary—not even a youthful Kirk could have fought better. There is glory in the effort. No matter what Kirk might think of himself, he remains heroic to us.

P. 94, Sc. 162 : I just think it would be a blockbuster moment if at the bottom of the page Saavik just looked at Spock incredulously and it was Spock, in his imperterbable way, who had the line "I lied."

P. 96, Sc. 165 : Spock: "What's sauce for the goose . . " Not a Spockian expression. He would dress it up, I'm sure.

P. 109, Sc.17 : Has the radiation room already been explained, or have I missed something? I think you've got to establish the reactor room earlier, more directly. We've got to know what is does, the danger being inside it, etc.

P. 112, Sc. 231 : Bones Voice: "Jim, you better get down here." I think you need something more or something less from the doctor. Perhaps an inability to articulate at all—to set up Kirk's long run down the stairway to the engine room.

P. 117, Sc. 241 : (You're going to hate me for this one.) Amazing Grace is gorgeous and would certainly evoke the right feeling, but unless it is traditionally played in military funerals and I don't know it, how does one justify a five hundred-year-old black spiritual coming out of Scottish bagpipes honoring a dead Vulcan in the twenty-fourth century? Couldn't a new, beautifully mournful and touching composition be created for this moment?

P. 117, Sc. 244 : Kirk: "Set the course......and we'll pick up survivors." As referred to before: P. 33, Sc. 45—Joachim's second speech implies all of Khan's followers are aboard.

P. 121, Sc. 247 : Kirk: "He died so it might be born." Is it only me or does this line call up a strong religious association with the birth of Christianity? I'm not sure we want to suggest that Spock is the Second Coming or the Second Going.

P. 122, Sc. 249 : Should you not choose to do the Spock Memory Retrospective as Scene 240, you might consider doing it under end credit roll.

　　The only other objection Trekkies might conceivably have is to the omission of an ascerbic exchange between McCoy and Spock somewhere within the bowels of the story. Not only would it be a welcome moment of recognition for the audience, but it would have a dynamic impact in the scene where McCoy watches Spock die. Think of the doctor's torment and its effect on the viewer if McCoy has to watch the painful death of the man he had been earlier harranguing. You've done such a neat job with the Kirk-Spock and Kirk-McCoy relationships it's really too bad we don't have a bit more of the McCoy-Spock banter as well.

That is pretty much all I have to say except that I think you'd better start getting use to being a feature film producer. I suspect there will be a great many offers after Star Trek II arrives on the local neighborhood screen.

Best,
Walter Koenig

"Star Trek VI: In Flanders Fields"

(A Step Outline)
by
Walter Koenig

Registration #426498 WGAw

Romulan society is being destroyed. Their strongest and ablest have been mysteriously dying. Some kind of pestilence? No one can identify it, but it has shredded the fabric of the culture. Fear transcends all, and neighbor has turned against neighbor. The domino theory is in place; corruption in high places, looting in the streets, anarchy prevails. Civil war is imminent. Something never before conceivable happens: the Romulan government turns to the United Federation of Planets for assistance. They wish to join and receive the benefits of its help in stabilizing their society.

The Klingons are furious. This would strengthen the Federation even more, give it yet another ally against the Klingon empire. When they cannot coerce the Romulans from signing a pact with the Federation, they invade them. The Romulans call on the Federation to beat back the invading force.

For the first time in centuries, there is a full-scale war. The entire Federation fleet is put on standby. As part of battle readiness, fitness reports are conducted on crews of all ships that might have to engage the enemy.

Most of the *Enterprise* bridge personnel register marginal scores. Age has at last taken its toll. Starfleet is sympathetic, but the ravages of time can be ignored no longer. They are relieved of active duty and reassigned to Earthbound service. They are present, however, when the *Enterprise* is handed over to its new crew of commissioned officers: trim, attractive and *young*. (The next crew of the *Enterprise* for succeeding films?) Only Spock, a superior physical and mental being even at his advanced age, is ordered to remain aboard ship.

The old crew on Earth. Angst...the sense of loss...soul searching. Chekov goes to see an old girlfriend, but he's been out of her life too long. She has left him behind. Sulu, determined to prove to himself that his reflexes are still as keen as in *The Naked Time,* enters a foils competition and loses quickly to a younger, more adept *woman.* Scotty drinks and spins stories about the good old days — happier dwelling in the past than contemplating the future. Uhura is lost trying to apply the new technology of Communications in her headquarters-based job. McCoy retires to his farm and more and more talks to the animals...and to himself. Kirk asks for a leave of absence and disappears.

The word is given. The battle in space begins — Klingons against

Federation forces. Not one ship pitted against another, but a war of monumental proportions. A raging, visually colossal Armageddon, the likes of which have never before been seen. The new crew of the *Enterprise,* with Spock alongside, fights with particular valor. Heroically, they come to the aid of sister ships, beat back the enemy and help turn the tide of battle. At last, victory!

The *Enterprise* and its new officers survive. Already, the word has been passed through Starfleet that they fought brilliantly and that commendations for all aboard will be forthcoming. They are returning to Starbase as heroes, and then the *Enterprise* and all her personnel *disappear.* Not a trace of them anywhere. It isn't the Klingons — they are broken, dispirited and in retreat.

With the fleet disabled, limping home, there are no able, fresh teams to search for the *Enterprise.* The last resort: Kirk, McCoy, and company. It won't be a war maneuver, just a search mission. All are eager to go; deep inside each person is the secret, cherished belief that he or she — given one more chance — can achieve vindication, can turn back the clock, can prove that each is still the vital, immortal creature of his or her youth. That is, all are eager to go except Kirk, who cannot be found. McCoy, reprieved from senility, takes a sworn oath to find him and does at last...in the desert. Kirk, now a bitter, self-pitying recluse, refuses the call. McCoy is by turns sensitive, bullying, eloquent. Kirk recants at last, because Spock is aboard the missing *Enterprise.*

The ship they are given is a scout vessel—a vintage model, pulled from mothballs.

The search begins and the crew proves its mettle. The *Enterprise* is located orbiting an uncharted planet. Orders are to seek and discover and return with information. The temptation is great, but Kirk will obey these orders. Even if the ship is being held captive, he will not confront the enemy. But then they become aware that each crew member is being scanned by an energy probe, and before they can react, their tiny vessel is jolted by a blast across its bow. Sulu is hurt by the fire, but the rest of the group survives unharmed. Unmistakably, it is a warning — leave or be destroyed. The injury to Sulu and the threat to them all are more than Kirk can bear; he polls his team. As one, they agree to seize the gauntlet. They pretend to leave, doubleback and from the dark side of the planet beam down. Sulu, wounded but protesting, is commanded to stay behind. McCoy is instructed to remain with the injured helmsman.

On the planet, Kirk and party discover what has happened to the new *Enterprise* crew. They are being held captive by a species that farms humanoid forms as a source of energy. It is their youth and vitality that is being drained by creatures (not yet seen) to replenish their own waning life forces — a breed desperate to remain alive. (It is this race that also destroyed Romulan civilization.) *Ironically, they didn't bother capturing Kirk and the others because they were too old.* Despite their efforts, the aliens are now only a few in number. The new *Enterprise* officers, locked away in a dungeon, are close to death. There is, for the old crew, only one logical plan — a rescue attempt or death in the trying.

Sulu escapes McCoy's care and, still in pain, beams down to help his comrades.

The final battle. One by one, Sulu, Uhura, Chekov, and Scotty fall on the field of battle but not without taking the creatures with them—who are seen for the first time in this last scene. Not stunt guys in suits, not blue-skinned furries with horns, but truly repulsive sewer-dwelling worms of slime and putrefaction. These are not sterile-looking Klingons in body armor, but rather the things that the monsters in *ALIENS* evolved *from*. Kirk, mortally injured, starts toward the dungeon. He never makes it. He gasps his last breath and dies in the mud.

McCoy beams down and slowly walks among his dead comrades on the field of battle. There is a moment as he steps among each of the fallen, that he flashes back to a previous adventure (from either the series or the films) and remembers Uhura singing; Sulu, the mad duelist; Chekov boasting about Russian "inwentions," Scotty pleading for more time to fix the engines, and Kirk, in command of his ship, demonstrating the authority and strength that made him so great a captain. Once again, at least in McCoy's mind's eye, the officers of the *Enterprise* are young and vital—their lives, their future ahead of them. But harsh reality intrudes; the field of dead becomes an unbearable burden. He turns away, desperately trying to hold himself together.

McCoy arrives at the dungeon and frees its captives. They can barely walk, so frail and haggard have they become. McCoy catches a staggering Spock in his arms and half-carries him outside. Spock stops in his tracks, stunned by what he sees. He tries to gather himself together—at all costs, he must remain the stoic Vulcan. He pulls himself away from McCoy's assisting hand and tries to walk past. The enormity of the tragedy and his own weakened condition are too much. He stumbles and falls to his knees. McCoy comes up behind him and stands there...waiting. Slowly, Spock raises his arm and McCoy reaches out for it, to help him rise to his feet. In this loneliest, most desolate of moments, Spock has permitted himself the one expression of friendship that he has never before admitted to: his need of Leonard McCoy. Spock leans against the doctor for support, and the two men—adversaries in a thousand arguments over the years—walk off together.

Filmography

Babylon 5 (1998, "Cat and Mouse")	Alfred Bester	TV
Babylon 5 (1997, "Rising Star")	Alfred Bester	TV
Drawing Down the Moon (1997)	Joe Merchant	Film
Star Trek: Starfleet Academy (1997)	Pavel Chekov	C.D. ROM
Viva Variety (1997)	Himself	TV
Babylon 5 (1997, "The Face of the Enemy")	Alfred Bester	TV
Babylon 5 (1997, "Moments of Transition")	Alfred Bester	TV
Babylon 5 (1997), "Epiphanies")	Alfred Bester	TV
Space Cadets (1997)	Himself	TV
Blonde Justice (1996)	*details unavailable*	Film
Maximum Surge (1996)	Drexel	C.D. ROM
Almost Perfect	Himself	TV
Babylon 5 (1996, "Ship of Tears")	Alfred Bester	TV
Babylon 5 (1996, "Dust to Dust")	Alfred Bester	TV
Babylon 5 (1996, "A Race Through Dark Places")	Alfred Bester	TV
Babylon 5 (1996, "Mind War")	Alfred Bester	TV
Star Trek: Generations (1994)	Pavel Chekov	Film
Star Trek VI: The Undiscovered Country (1991)	Pavel Chekov	Film
The Real Ghostbusters (1990, "Russian About") (cartoon)	Vladimir Maximov	TV
Star Trek V: The Final Frontier (1989)	Pavel Chekov	Film
Moontrap (1989)	Jason Grant	Film
Star Trek IV: The Voyage Home (1986)	Pavel Chekov	Film
Star Trek III: The Search for Spock (1984)	Pavel Chekov	Film
Antony and Cleopatra (1983)	Pompey	TV movie
Star Trek: The Wrath of Khan (1982)	Pavel Chekov	Film
Bring Them Back Alive (1982, The Reel Wolrd of Frank Buck)	Toder	TV

Star Trek: The Motion Picture (1979)	Pavel Chekov	Film
Columbo (1976, "Fade in to Murder")	Sgt. Johnson	TV
The Men from Shiloh (1974, "Crooked Corner")	details unavailable	TV
Deadly Honeymoon (1973)	Deputy Sheriff	Film
The Starlost (1973)	Oro	TV
The Questor Tapes (1973)	Admin. Assistant	TV movie
Ironside (1972, "The Summer Soldier")	Leo	TV
Goodbye, Raggedy Ann (1971)	Jerry	TV movie
Medical Center (1969, "Between Dark and Daylight")	Harry Seller	TV
Star Trek (1968 and 1969 series regular)	Pavel Chekov	TV
Mannix (1967)	details unavailable	TV
Jericho (1966, "Both Ends Against the Riddle")	Paul	TV
I Spy (1965, "Sparrowhawk")	Bobby Seville	TV
Gidgel (1965, "Foreign Policy")	Gunnan	TV
Mr. Novak (1965, "The Firebrand")	Paul Ryder	TV
Ben Casey (1965, "A Rambling Discourse on Egyptian Water Clocks")	Tom Davis	TV
Mr. Novak (1964, "With a Hammer in His Hand, Lord, Lord!")	Jim Carsey	TV
Alfred Hitchcock Presents (1964, "Memo from Purgatory")	Tiger	TV
The Lieutenant (1963, "Mother Enemy")	details unavailable	TV
Mr. Novak (1963, "The Boy Without a Country")	Alexsei	TV
The Untouchables (1962)	details unavailable	TV
Great Adventure	details unavailable	TV
Combat! (1962, "The Prisoner")	sentry	TV
The Norman Vincent Peale Story (1962)	details unavailable	film
Strange Loves (1961)	Robert	film
General Hospital (1961, pilot episode)	details unavailable	TV
Day in Court (1960-1963)	various characters	TV

Information compiled by Carolyn Hotchkiss, Tisha Kuntz, Jane Melander, Tim Neely, Teegar Taylor.

Bibliography

Asherman, Allan. *The Star Trek Compendium.*

Dillard, J.M. *Star Trek: Where No One Has Gone Before.*

Okuda, Michael, and Okuda, Denise. *Star Trek Chronology: The History of the Future.*

Okuda, Michael, Okuda, Denise, and Mirek, Debbie. *The Star Trek Encyclopedia: A Reference Guide to the Future.*

Solow, Herbert F., and Justman, Robert H. *Inside Star Trek: The Real Story.*

Whitfield, Stephen E., and Roddenberry, Gene. *The Making of Star Trek.*

Index